# The Official Joomla!™ Book

# The Official Joomla!™ Book

Jennifer Marriott
Elin Waring

✦✦Addison-Wesley

Upper Saddle River, NJ • Boston • Indianapolis • San Francisco
New York • Toronto • Montreal • London • Munich • Paris • Madrid
Capetown • Sydney • Tokyo • Singapore • Mexico City

Many of the designations used by manufacturers and sellers to distinguish their products are claimed as trademarks. Where those designations appear in this book, and the publisher was aware of a trademark claim, the designations have been printed with initial capital letters or in all capitals.

The author and publisher have taken care in the preparation of this book, but make no expressed or implied warranty of any kind and assume no responsibility for errors or omissions. No liability is assumed for incidental or consequential damages in connection with or arising out of the use of the information or programs contained herein.

The publisher offers excellent discounts on this book when ordered in quantity for bulk purchases or special sales, which may include electronic versions and/or custom covers and content particular to your business, training goals, marketing focus, and branding interests. For more information, please contact:

U.S. Corporate and Government Sales
(800) 382-3419
corpsales@pearsontechgroup.com

For sales outside the United States please contact:

International Sales
international@pearson.com

Visit us on the Web: informit.com/aw

*Library of Congress Cataloging-in-Publication Data*

Marriott, Jennifer, 1969–
  The official Joomla! book / Jennifer Marriott, Elin Waring.
       p.    cm.
  Includes index.
  ISBN-13: 978-0-321-70421-4 (pbk. : alk. paper)
  ISBN-10: 0-321-70421-5
1. Joomla! (Computer file) 2. Web sites—Authoring programs. 3. Web site development. I. Waring, Elin J. II. Title.
  TK5105.8885.J86M37 2011
  006.7'8—dc22

                                        2010041150

Pearson Education, Inc.
Rights and Contracts Department
501 Boylston Street, Suite 900
Boston, MA 02116
Fax: (617) 671-3447

ISBN-13:  978-0-321-70421-4
ISBN-10:     0-321-70421-5
Text printed in the United States on recycled paper at RR Donnelley in Crawfordsville, Indiana.
First printing, December 2010

*To my husband, Pete*

*—Jennifer*


*To Tom, Bobby, and Linnea*

*—Elin*

# Contents at a Glance

# Contents

# Foreword

Joomla! is steeped in a rich and sometimes controversial history. During its tumultuous start in August of 2005, no one could have imagined how far this little project would stretch in terms of reach, nor could anyone have imagined how much it would grow in terms of depth of participation and resources available to the community. I still vividly remember the day I published the now famous "Open Letter to the Community" that you find in Chapter 1 of this book. Those were uncertain times for the 19 founders and hundred or so members of the forum team to leave comfortable surroundings and start over with nothing but courage and raw determination.

Today, I am writing this foreword having just attended a 200-person-strong local conference in San Jose, California, and my compatriot across the table is off to Italy to address 700 at a similar event. These are but two of dozens of such events held all around the world each year, on every continent (except Antarctica of course, but maybe one day), to celebrate as a community this amazing thing called Joomla! The right words are hard to find, but one is certainly appropriate: Wow!

Joomla!'s mission is "to provide a flexible platform for digital publishing and collaboration." To that end, and at the time of this writing, we have 64 official languages; hundreds of professional service providers; over six-thousand (that we know about) Joomla! extensions; thousands of template designs to choose from; and tens of millions of Web sites deployed all around the world. Joomla! is arguably the easiest software program of its type—both to use and to master. It has been designed both for the most basic user and for the master artisan who wants to take a site beyond the normal limits of the core download. Joomla! carries a legacy of a user interface with pleasing eye-candy and a wide choice of the most beautiful templates available for any site-building system in the world. Particularly close to my heart is our passion for continuing to improve the way in which we deliver Joomla! to more and more people in their own languages.

All together by name and all together by nature, Joomla! (meaning "all together" in Swahili) sought from the very beginning to ensure it would be free for the entire community at its founding and into the future. It was set up deliberately to ensure that no one person could ever "own" Joomla!, a detail that gives Open Source Matters—the Joomla! nonprofit—the freedom to provide stewardship in the best interests of the project rather than a parent company's bottom line. Combined with the two main project leadership teams for software production and community management, Joomla! as a whole has one of the most progressive and mature leadership structures of any open source project.

Five years after its founding—and on the heels of both Microsoft and eBay becoming collaborators and contributors to the Joomla! core source code—we begin another phase in our life journey as a project: the inception of Joomla! Press and the first (with extreme emphasis on "first") official Joomla! book. Joomla! is about allowing ordinary people to do extraordinary things, and that is exactly what the authors of this book do for its readers. So, without further ado, I present this book for your pleasure. It begins with how we began and takes you on a journey through which you can be empowered to reach the world.

—Andrew Eddie
Member of the Joomla! Production Leadership Team
October 2010

## Joomla! Press Mission Statement

The mission of Joomla! Press is to enhance the Joomla! experience by providing useful, well-written, and engaging publications for all segments of the Joomla! Community from beginning users to framework developers. Titles in Joomla! Press are authored by leading experts and contributors in the community.

# Preface

When planning what should be in a book about Joomla!, we thought hard about the process we go through when building Web sites and when helping others build sites. We decided that this book should be about building a Web site using Joomla! rather than how to use Joomla! to build a Web site. Even though you can make a Web site using Joomla! in a few hours (or less), most likely it won't be a great site, and it won't allow you take advantage of the power of Joomla! The focus should always be on how you envision your site, the goals of the site, and the audiences you want to reach rather than on the technology used to create it.

Fortunately, with its combination of power and ease of use, Joomla! lets you keep your focus on the big picture of your site and the small details of your content and not on mastering a complicated set of processes. This is why we start with a thorough discussion of things to think about *before* you start building your site.

We've also built a set of very simple sample sites that will give you a good idea of the initial process of thinking about and then building sites for various purposes. We hope that you'll follow along with the construction of those sites so that you understand the process that site developers use. If you do these tasks first, you will be ready to build your own site with confidence and a good plan.

In addition, we try to help you have a basic understanding of how Joomla! really works "under the hood" so that when you are ready to take advantage of the power that comes with its extensibility, you will have the knowledge to do that in the right way. We think that, like us, you will want to steadily increase the sophistication of your site and your knowledge and understanding of Joomla! So, we've written this book with the idea of giving you a strong foundation for the future of your site and other sites you may build in the future. Free and open source software is empowering, but you need to have solid knowledge of the fundamentals to take advantage of it.

We're passionate about Joomla!, and we hope that you will be, too. That's why we take time in this book to introduce you to the Joomla! project and the Joomla! community. We hope that you'll want to become an active participant in the Joomla! world. And we hope that you enjoy building your site so much that you end up building other sites for the friends, family members, organizations, or causes you care about.

# Acknowledgments

This book benefited greatly from the help of many people, named and unnamed. We thank them for their assistance.

We especially thank all the contributors to the Joomla! project who have worked so hard together to produce and support this amazing software. All of the people we interview in Chapter 12 have taught and inspired us day in and day out, many since the day the Joomla! was born, and we are lucky enough to consider them friends, too. Thanks to Andrew Eddie, Chris Davenport, Brad Baker, Wendy Robinson, Louis Landry, Ian MacLennan, Sam Moffatt, Mark Dexter, Ryan Ozimek, Vic Drover, and Gary Brooks. There are dozens of others whose knowledge we have built on including Anthony Ferrara, Michelle Bisson, Toni Marie Swats, James Vasile, Rob Schley, Dave Huelsmann, Lorenzo Garcia, Jean-Marie Simonet, Angie Radke, Andrea Tarr, Alan Langford, Leslie Hawthorn, and others.

We also thank all those participants in the Joomla! forums who answered our questions and asked us their own questions and contributors to the Joomla! documentation wiki, both of which taught us how to use Joomla! in more depth. The Joomla! Bug Squad has been a continuous source of inspiration.

Then there are the people who really made this book possible. Pete and Tom, Linnea and Robert, our families, and the Odd Sheep who were so supportive and put up with a lot while we were writing. Also, to our numerous friends who were given a sudden introduction to Joomla! and who gave of their time to read chapters and give encouragement and suggestions, thank you.

A very special thank you to Terrence H. Pocock for bringing home a Teletype, which inspired a lifetime love of technology in his youngest daughter. And to Joan and Fred Waring for showing their daughter a counter sorter.

Thank you to Gabrielle Heller, who read the whole manuscript, and of course Debra Williams Cauley at Addison-Wesley, who was a tireless advocate for Joomla! Press and kept us on track.

# About the Authors

**Jennifer Marriott** owns and operates a Web development company, Marpo Multimedia, that specializes in Joomla!-powered Web sites. Her company is located in northeastern Oklahoma, and although separated by distance, Jennifer stays close to her Canadian roots.

Jennifer joined the Joomla! community during the beginning days in 2005 and began volunteering as a forum moderator shortly after. Over the years she has taken on various roles in the community in addition to moderator, such as Joomla! Bug Squad member, Joomla! Google Summer of Code coadministrator and mentor, and Trademark and Licensing Team Leader. Although Jennifer has stepped down from her official roles in the Joomla! project, she remains an active community member.

In addition to her work in all things technology related, Jennifer is a professional musician. She has two CDs released, and in 2010 she went back into the studio to record her third release.

**Elin Waring** is a longtime Joomla! user and former president of Open Source Matters, the nonprofit organization that provides legal, financial, and organizational support to the Joomla! project. In that role, she led a number of initiatives ranging from writing the translation policy to obtaining a trademark for the Joomla! brand. She has made more than 6,000 posts on the Joomla! forums and wrote most of the Frequently Asked Questions for Joomla! 1.0. She is an active member of the Joomla! Bug Squad and participates in many Joomla! events.

Elin is a professor of sociology at Lehman College, City University of New York, where she teaches research methods. She has published a number of books, including *White Collar Crime and Criminal Careers* (Cambridge University Press, 2001), *Crimes of the Middle Classes: White Collar Offenders in the Federal Courts* (Yale University Press, 1991), and *Russian Mafia in America: Immigration, Culture, and Crime* (Northeastern, 2001) as well as scholarly articles in the areas of white collar crime, organized crime, and social organization.

# All About Joomla!

In this chapter, there is a little bit of history, a little bit of future, and a lot about where the Joomla! project is right now, including how it is organized and how to navigate through the Joomlasphere. Over the years since the project started in 2005, there has been tremendous growth both with the code base and with the community that supports, works with, and contributes to the code. As with a number of open source projects, Joomla! is more than just about code; it is about the people and culture that surrounds it.

Joomla! is used by people all over the world to create millions of Web sites. It powers sites ranging from personal blogs to large corporate infrastructures and Web brands. It is easy to use and administer for novice Webmasters and flexible enough to be used for complex Web solutions.

## A Brief History of Joomla!

On August 17, 2005, Andrew Eddie, the lead developer of the Mambo open source project, wrote this letter to the community:

> Much has been said about the Mambo Open Source project and the establishment of the Mambo Foundation to benefit the future of Mambo.
>
> We, the core development teams, unanimously believe:
>
> * An open source project is about people producing free and open software and contributing to something as a team for the benefit of others.
>
> * Open source projects reflect the spirit of collaboration and fun while garnering community feedback and providing good governance that allows for business to confidently invest in its development.
>
> * Open source projects are open to the participation of anybody who can contribute value and is willing to work with the community.
>
> We, the development team, have serious concerns about the Mambo Foundation and its relationship to the community. We believe the future of Mambo should be controlled by the

demands of its users and the abilities of its developers. The Mambo Foundation is designed
to grant that control to Miro, a design that makes cooperation between the Foundation and
the community impossible.

* The Mambo Foundation was formed without regard to the concerns of the core
  development teams. We, the community, have no voice in its government or the
  future direction of Mambo. The Mambo Steering Committee made up of development team and Miro representatives authorized incorporation of the Foundation and
  should form the first Board. Miro CEO Peter Lamont has taken it upon himself to
  incorporate the Foundation and appoint the Board without consulting the two
  development team representatives, Andrew Eddie and Brian Teeman.

* Although Mr. Lamont through the MSC promised to transfer the Mambo copyright
  to the Foundation, Miro now refuses to do so.

What we will do: We will continue to develop and improve a version of this award-winning
software project currently released under the GNU General Public License. We wish Miro
and the Mambo Foundation well and regret that we are not able to work with them.

We have retained the Software Freedom Law Center to advise us in this matter and will
release more information about our short-term plan in the near future.

For more information please visit Open Source Matters

17 August 2005, The Mambo Development Team :

Andrew Eddie

Emir Sakic, Andy Miller, Rey Gigataras, Mitch Pirtle, Tim Broeker, Alex Kempkens, Arno
Zijlstra, Jean-Marie Simonet, Levis Bisson, Andy Stewart, Peter Russell, Brad Baker, Brian
Teeman, Michelle Bisson, Trijnie Wanders, Shayne Bartlett, Nick Annies, Johan Janssens

---

Andrew Eddie
<><
Mambo Core Developer February 2003–August 2005

The same letter was posted to the new forums located at OpenSourceMatters.org.
With that letter, one of the largest open source project forks began.

Within 24 hours, approximately 600 community supporters had joined the forum at
OpenSourceMatters.org, and a call went out to the community to suggest a name for
the new project. While this was going on, the forked code base was going through a
transformation, making it ready for rebranding and structure under the new name, as
well as a few bug fixes. Hundreds of names were suggested for the new project. The
Core Team at the time enlisted the help of a marketing and branding consultancy to
assist them in making this important decision. Two key factors were heavily considered
while determining the new name of the project. The first was the importance of the
name being uniquely new and unused, and it needed to signify what the project was all
about in terms of its community philosophy. On September 1, 2005, the chosen name

was announced as Joomla!, which was derived by using the English spelling of the Swahili word *jumla*, meaning "all together."

The next request to the new Joomla! community on September 7, 2005, was a contest to create a logo with the new name for the project. Approximately 500 community members submitted logos for consideration, and on September 14, a poll was announced with the top five logo designs selected by the Core Team.

On September 16, Joomla! 1.0 was released to the community, and the Developer Forge was announced at *http://developer.joomla.org*. On September 18, the Joomla! Demo site was announced as operational, and on September 19, at the end of the voting period for the logo contest, the community had cast a total of 2,761 votes, with 31 percent of the votes going to the entry "Joomla 01" designed by Alan Urquhart, community member, photographer, and graphic designer. Figure 1.1 shows a copy of his winning entry.

Joomla! 1.0 was followed quickly by 1.0.1, which contained some small bug fixes and completed some of the rebranding process. On October 2, 2005, 1.0.2 was released with the rebranding effort complete.

In 47 days, with the help of approximately 7,100 community forum users, a dedicated Core Team, and a wide user base, the Joomla! open source project began its official journey to being one of the most widely used content management systems in the world.

On October 6, it was announced that the Joomla! project won "Best Linux/Open Source Project" for 2005 and that Brian Teeman, a founding member of the project, had won "UK Individual Contribution to Open/Source" for 2005, both at the Linux & Open Source Awards in London, England.

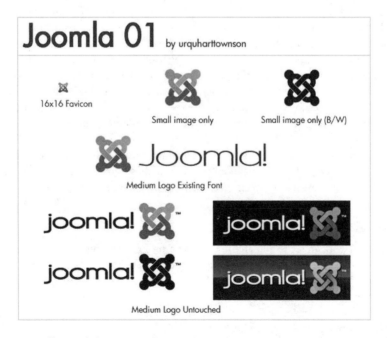

Figure 1.1  Alan Urquhart's winning logo contest submission

# Joomla! the Content Management System

A content management system is software that allows you to create and manage Web pages easily by separating the creation of your content from the mechanics required to present it on the Web.

In a site, the content is stored in a database. The look and feel are created by a template. The Joomla! software brings together the template and the content to create Web pages.

To expand on that specifically in relationship to Joomla!, it is a content management system that is Web-based and that allows content and data to be collaboratively shared and created. Joomla! allows people with or without technical knowledge of coding to be able to have dynamic Web sites that they can easily manage.

One way we like to describe Joomla! to people who are new to content management systems is to compare it to a standard office. The whole of Joomla! is the room. The filing cabinet in the office is the Article Manager, where you have sections (drawers of the filing cabinet), categories (file folders), and your articles and content items (pieces of paper, images, videos, sound, and other data inside the file folders). You can extend or add things to your office such as a phone (Joomla! extension: live chat extension), fax machine or scanner (Joomla! extension: form submission), and computer (Joomla! extension: content editor) to make your workflow easier. The great thing is Joomla! keeps all of it organized for you. (Extensions are described more fully later in this chapter in the "Joomla! Extension Directory" section.)

Another powerful way that Joomla! allows you to manage your site is through the User Manager. The User Manager allows you to control how your users interact with your site through the use of simple user groups, which is similar to being able to lock your door to your office or filing cabinets. This allows you to give permissions on specific levels to those viewing or browsing your Web site and a different set of permissions to those who are contributing content to your Web site or managing your Web site with you. The Media Manager helps you manage your media files such as images, videos, or documents by allowing you to create folders to organize them, and it integrates with the built-in Content Editor, which makes it easier to insert them into your content items. It is very similar to how your computer helps you store and find your files to use them effectively.

Joomla! right out of the box has the functionality that most people need to have a basic, easy-to-manage, informational Web site. It also allows for a very high level of extendability to create very complex Web sites and information systems.

# Joomla! the Framework

Software frameworks refer to the architecture of a program. Frameworks are efficient because they allow for code to be reused as part of the design.

Understanding the Joomla! framework isn't necessary for most users of the CMS, but it is the integral foundation that makes the CMS work so well. The framework is the base set of software libraries and design patterns that the CMS runs on, and it is the part of Joomla! that makes it easily extendable.

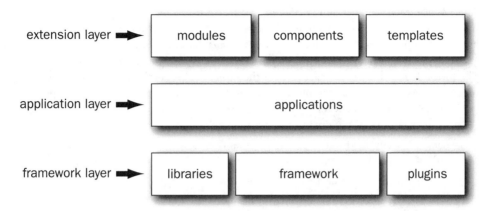

Figure 1.2  Diagram of how the three layers (the framework, the CMS application, and the extensions) work together

Joomla! 1.5 introduced the Joomla! framework as the first step to separating the framework elements of the program from the CMS application. This was done to allow for the framework to support multiple applications, not just the CMS. Figure 1.2 illustrates how the framework supports the CMS application and how the CMS application is extended with extensions.

Framework, libraries, and plugins make up the foundational layer. Libraries are reusable "collections" of code that perform a specific function and that can be reused by different independent applications and the framework. Libraries allow data to be used and shared in a modular way. Plugins are used to extend the functionality in the framework.

Applications are programs that run using the functionality of the framework. The Joomla! CMS is an application that runs on the Joomla! framework. The separation of the application layer from the framework layer allows developers to create other applications to run on the framework's functionality.

Modules, components, and templates are items that extend applications. Modules, for example, are a way to present data, components are a way to organize and store data, and templates are a way to visually organize data presentation.

# The Joomlasphere

The Joomla! project is a very broad and diverse community made up of users and developers of all levels of experience. To support the community, the project offers a number of resources to help people use Joomla!, extend it, and develop on it. The first stop in the Joomlasphere is the Joomla! forum.

## The Joomla! Forum

Internet forums or message boards are used for online discussions between groups of people both small and large. As of the writing of this book, the Joomla! forum (*http://forum.joomla.org*) has almost 350,000 registered users, 440,000 topics of discussion, and close to 2 million posts, making the Joomla! forum one of the largest forums on the Internet. The popularity of the Joomla! forum means that lots of people have asked questions and received answers on how to get started, install, use, and extend Joomla! The forum is also one of the places where the project helps keep the user base informed with announcements, including information on the current status of the various aspects of the project, and it also allows the project to get feedback from users.

Most Internet forums are organized with the same basic hierarchical structure.

- *Forum:* Usually the front page that gives an overview of the organizational structure of the forum, showing what boards are available to read and post in.
  - *Board:* A general subject category.
    - *Topic:* A specific topic of discussion. Topics are started by someone making a new post to ask a question or start a topic of discussion.
      - *Posts:* Individual communications from one user.

The forum is divided into a number of main boards that help direct users to the proper place to find an answer, ask a question, or start a topic of discussion. Some of the main boards have subboards that divide the subject matter into smaller themes.

The first step is to register your account on the forum. Near the top of the forum is a Register link. Once you click it, you are shown terms and conditions for using the forum and the software that runs the forum. If you agree to the terms, you can continue with the registration process. After you have agreed to the terms, you are taken to the registration screen where you will type in the username that you want to use, your e-mail address (which needs to be a valid e-mail address), and a password. You can also set your language preference and your time zone. There is a spam prevention captcha, which consists of a word recognition puzzle at the bottom that you must solve, and then you can submit. After you submit the registration form, a verification e-mail will be sent to the e-mail address that you specified. The e-mail sent to you, after submission, will ask you to verify your e-mail address by clicking a link that directs you back to the forum. If you do not perform this step of verification, your forum account will not be activated. If you do not receive the e-mail fairly quickly, check your spam e-mail box to see whether it was redirected there. If you still have not received a verification e-mail, you can visit the forums again and click Login; from that screen, you will be able to have the forum resend the activation e-mail.

The first board is the Joomla! Announcements forum, which is used for the project to announce important events such as a new release (version of Joomla!), security bulletins, and other information important to the community at large. Subscribing to a board allows you to get e-mails when new announcement posts are made. To subscribe to the Announcements board, you need to be inside the board itself. You do this by clicking the Announcements board title on the front page of the forum. Once you are inside the Announcements forum, you will find the Subscribe forum link just under the title Announcements. It is highly recommended that everyone in the community subscribe to this forum.

If you have come to the forum to solve a problem you are having, using the search function can save you a lot of time. The search box is located in the upper-right corner of the screen. This search box searches all the Joomla.org sites for words or phrases matching your search query. Most common issues and questions have already been asked and answered a number of times on the forums. When searching the forum, it is important to try to use search terms that are relevant to your issue but not so broad as to return results that are too general in nature. For example, if you are having an issue installing Joomla! because it won't let you continue to the next screen, you could use the search query *installation will not continue.* This will lead to a search results page that combines all the results from all the sites. At the top of the results screen, you can filter the results according to the site the results came from. If you click the Forum link, it will show only results from the forum. You can then browse the results and determine whether one of the results can help solve your problem. If the results are not satisfactory, you can try searching again using different terms or proceed to posting your situation on the forum to get the assistance of the community.

### Tip

If you are getting a specific error message, try including the specific message, or portions of it, in your search query.

To submit a new post to the forum, it is best to look at the different boards available and find the one that applies the most to the issue or problem you are having. This will help you get assistance more quickly a lot of times, because a lot of community members tend to watch specific boards where they think they have the most experience and where they can do the most to help others. Using our example search query regarding installation, the best fit to get assistance would be the Installation board. When you enter that board, you can scan the available topics to see whether there is already a discussion that applies to your situation; also, at the top of most boards are "sticky" posts that are always situated at the top of the board. These sticky posts usually contain the answers to most commonly asked questions, resources for more help, and posts that are important to that particular board.

### How to Ask Questions That Get Answers

To create a new topic on a board, click the NEW TOPIC button. The screen will refresh, and you will see a text editor where you can fill in the details of what you want to post.

- You can choose an icon. This is usually for fun or to show with a green check mark that a problem has been solved. It is important if you have received an answer that solves your problem to go back to your first post and edit it by marking it with the green check mark icon. This tells people that it is answered but also allows people looking for help to know a helpful answer is available in the topic.

- Make your subject title as descriptive as possible while still fairly short. Using "Help me" as a title or "URGENT" does not describe your issue, and most people will skim past posts with titles like that. Also, do not use ALL CAPITAL LETTERS. Using all caps won't get you help more quickly and tends to be looked upon as an Internet social faux pas because it conveys SHOUTING. Having a descriptive title not only helps those wanting to help you but also helps those who are seeking answers.

Using our example of installation, a good descriptive title could be "Installation won't continue past the fourth screen."

- In the message body of your post, try to be as descriptive as possible regarding your issue. If you have gotten an error message, try to copy the exact error message you have received into your post. Try to describe what you see on the screen and what steps you were doing when the issue occurred. Sometimes it is helpful to post a link to your site (such as with template questions). Having a link to a site allows people to see exactly what is going on so they can help troubleshoot your issue.

- At the bottom of the screen, you will see the ability to upload a file, which can very helpful if you can't provide a link to your site. Screenshots can be helpful to show what is happening if you cannot share the link to your site or your site is not available for public viewing.

- When you are satisfied with the content of your post, click Submit.

After you have submitted your post, please be patient. Sometimes a community member will answer immediately, and other times it may be a few hours or even a day or two. If your question is not answered within a day or two, you may have to make another post to your topic to give more information. Always be polite and considerate of others, and remember to say thank you if someone gives you assistance.

The Joomla! forum is also the best place for people new to Joomla! to contribute to the project by answering questions of other users. No matter where you are situated in your Joomla! experience or your level of skills, there will always be someone else who has a question that you can answer. One of the very best ways to improve your knowledge of Joomla! is to explain what you know to others.

### Tip

At the top of the forum there is a link that asks you to read the forum rules. These rules outline the community's code of conduct and make all the resources on the Joomla.org sites collaborative and friendly to everyone. The rules are pretty straightforward and common sense and are based on basic principles of being a good global citizen.

## Joomla! Community

The Joomla! community (*http://community.joomla.org*) is comprised of everyone and anyone who uses, creates with, develops for, manages, or is a fan of Joomla! (and everyone in between too). The community front page gives a snapshot of almost everything that is current, showing the latest blogs from both project leadership and community members, helpful tips, quick links to download or demo Joomla!, upcoming events, and information about Joomla! User Groups. The Joomla! Community Magazine provides articles on a monthly basis related to Joomla! targeted toward users and developers. Also linked in with the community site is the Joomla! People Portal site (*http://people.joomla.org*), which is a social networking public space.

### Joomla! User Groups

Joomla! User Groups (JUGs) are geographical organizations created by users and are located all over the world. These are groups of Joomla! users meeting in person to discuss, develop, promote, and help each other with using Joomla! They are a great way to meet new people, and a lot of JUGs find interesting ways to contribute to Joomla! through events and activities. As of the writing of this book, there are more than 100 JUGs.

Starting a JUG is as simple as finding other people in your geographical area who are interested in Joomla!, having a primary and secondary contact person, and registering your group. Registering your group gives your group access to resources and materials that will help your group be successful in running events and organizing activities.

### Joomla! Days

Joomla! Days are a variety of events that are organized by JUGs and other groups in the Joomla! community and are supported by the Joomla! project. They typically take the form of a one-day conference, with speakers and demonstrations.

### Joomla! Developer Conferences and Summits

Joomla! Developer Conferences are similar to Joomla! Days but are targeted toward people of moderate to high coding skill who develop for, develop with, or extend Joomla! The conference schedule usually includes talks by the lead developers of the project on the current status of the code base, the road map for future development, and how to utilize the framework and application layers to extend Joomla!'s capabilities. It is also a chance for developers to get together and assist each other and their own individual projects and create a good sense of community within the greater community. There is also the opportunity to speak to developers of other open source projects who interact with Joomla!

### Joomla! World Conferences

Joomla! World Conferences are large international events that span several days, organized by local teams working within the Joomla! project. The first one will take place in 2011.

Other community events are held regularly throughout the year such as bug-squashing (finding and patching bugs in the code), documentation camps, and user guide creation.

## Joomla! Demo Site

The Joomla! Demo site (*http://demo.joomla.org*) provides people with a way to try Joomla! The site gives you a 30-day account with your own individual Joomla! installation. You can explore the use of Joomla! and even build a fully functioning Web site. At the end of the 30 days, you can either continue with paid hosting or export your site to a different location.

## Joomla! Extension Directory

The Joomla! Extension Directory (JED) is a centralized information portal (*http://extensions.joomla.org*) on GNU GPL extensions that have been created for Joomla! Extensions help expand the functionality of the Joomla! CMS and the framework, and most likely if you have a need for some functionality that isn't in out-of-the-box standard Joomla!, there has been an extension created for it. The other service that the JED provides is a platform to support the vibrant commercial and noncommercial GNU GPL developer community because its contribution to the Joomla! community is imperatively important to the growth and use of Joomla!

### What Is a Component, Module, and Plugin?

- Components are mini-applications that integrate with the framework or CMS. They have their own specific functionality, their own database structures, and their own presentational aspects. Examples of components are a Web forms application suite, a photo gallery or document download system, or the Web Links component found in the default Joomla! installation.

- Modules are presentational elements. They take information that already exists and present them in visual "packages" that you can place in your template in a flexible manner. Modules also help extend components by allowing the data from a component to also be presented visually. Examples of modules include a latest photo from the photo gallery or a slide show of the photos. The default Joomla! install has a latest news module that extends the Content component to show a list of the latest articles added to a site.

- Plugins are small portions of code that work behind the scenes to assist how something behaves. As a page in a site is loading, plugins will scan the page and, based upon what is being sent to the browser, act according to the instructions that it has been designed for or programmed to do. Example plugins might insert the code from your analytics supplier such as from Google or Woopra, they might place a border or shadow around an item automatically, or they might be the editor that you use for editing your content. Joomla! has a number of default plugins such as the e-mail cloak that stops e-mail addresses presented on your site from being read by spambots.

The directory itself is set up so that individual extensions are grouped by the functionality they provide. A listing will generally contain information about an extension, what it does, and whether it is a module, plugin, or component. It will also list the developer's name or company name, include the date it was added to the directory, and include the last date that the extension's listing was updated by the developer along with links to download. Some developers include links to a demos, support options, or documentation.

The JED also allows users of extensions to rate and review them. An extension can be rated on a scale of 0 to 5, with 0 being unrated or low and 5 being excellent. Reviews are all read and approved by the JED team of editors before publishing. The analysis of reviews before publishing allow the JED editors to assure that the review follows the rules and guidelines that are published in the FAQ located on the JED site.

As of the writing of this book, more than 6,000 extensions are available on the JED site, with new extensions added every day.

> **Tip**
>
> Extensions are a great way to bring your Web site to life with added functionality that improves your users' experience. One thing to note is that if you install an extension and find that you don't want to use it or it doesn't supply the functionality that you need, you need to remember to uninstall it completely. Having outdated and unused extensions installed on your Web site can be a security risk. Also, it is good to keep a list of the extensions along with the version number of the extensions you are using on your site. It will allow you to be more easily informed if an extension needs updating. It is good practice to sign up for any update notifications that a developer may send out to the users of their extensions and also periodically check the developer's site for update or information. The vulnerable extension list (VEL) is a list of extensions that may have security issues that is updated as often as possible by the VEL team. A link to that list is shown at the top of the Announcements forum, and the list itself is located on the Official Documentation wiki (*http://docs.joomla.org*).

## Joomla! Resources Directory

The Joomla! Resources Directory (JRD) is a recent initiative of the project to help users connect with professional providers of services that relate to Joomla! (*http://resources.joomla.org*). It is also a platform that helps professionals in the Joomlasphere promote their services, which fosters a greater community of contributors to the project. There are categories of service listings ranging from consultancies and freelancers to tutorials and training.

### Sometimes You May Want to Call in a Professional

Many people hate to do it, but sometimes a professional is needed to either advise or assist someone in getting a job or a task done, whether it is a decision made at the beginning of a project or during the process before the project is done. There are times when we all overlook the benefits of hiring a professional, whether it's because we think we can do something for ourselves, because we believe we can learn our way through an issue, or because the funding to hire a professional just isn't available.

The good news is that Joomla! professionals come at all price levels and different areas of expertise, giving good value to their customers. Here are some examples of when to call in a professional.

- *If your site has been compromised or attacked because of a security vulnerability:* It is best to get the advice and services of professionals, even if it is only to check on the steps you did yourself to clean up and restore your site. If your site and database are not checked properly to make sure that all the compromised files and data have been removed, you are at risk of having the same issue happen again.

- *If you are under a deadline to launch a site:* Sometimes we can all underestimate how long something is going to take. If you have a business and have prepared advertisements for the launch of your site and business, it may save you a lot of time and headache to have a professional help you meet your goal.

- *If you have an existing site but are unsure how to maintain it and keep it updated:* In that case, lots of Joomla! professionals offer training on both a one-on-one basis and in group classes. One class with a professional can make the difference between frustration and success.

- *If want a site and you just want it done, preferably sooner rather than later:* You just want to be able to log in and create or edit your content and get on with running your business or organization. Contracting a professional to create your site from start to finish is a good choice.

That being said, there is no absolute reason to hire a professional, because you always have the forum, documentation wiki, and a multitude of sites that offer documentation on various aspects of Joomla! such as Joomlatutorials.com or other sites that are similarly created by the community at large.

## Joomla! Bug Squad

The Joomla! Bug Squad was created in late 2007 as a subgroup of the Development Working Group to take over maintaining releases of the code base once in stable release and to take the lead in the testing and polishing work in the final stages of preparing a new software release. Software releases usually follow a specific schedule set by the development team; usually the release schedule is as follows.

- *Pre-alpha:* This is the stage where functionality and design are fleshed out and is a period where new features are discussed and implementation starts. It is typically where bits and pieces of the software to come are brought together in the planning stages. These are usually development releases that are being analyzed and modified by the developers of the specific software itself.

- *Alpha:* This release is unstable and not suitable for live or production sites. An alpha release is usually the first release to a wider network of developers and experienced testers of a new major version of software. Alpha releases are used for testing, acceptance, and stabilization of the basic functionality that has been implemented. There can be any number of alpha versions released until the code base is determined to be stable enough to release as a beta release.

- *Beta:* This release is unstable and not suitable for live or production sites. Beta versions of software are usually feature complete, meaning that no major changes in features or functionality will be implemented during the remainder of the release cycle. Beta releases are major versions of software that have passed the alpha stage of testing and are usually released to a much wider group of testers to test; it is also the time when the general users of the software can begin to submit bugs or issues where the software is not working as expected or broken. The beta stage is one of the most important testing stages to give feedback to developers and is where the software is "polished" in terms of stability and usability. There can be any number of beta versions released until the code base is determined to be stable.

- *Release candidate (RC):* These releases are ones that are potential stable releases that are receiving wider real-world testing by early users. These releases are feature complete and have passed security review. They may be used on live sites, although in general only experienced users and early adopters would do so. A release candidate may be redesignated as a stable release, but there may also be several release candidates.

- *Stable:* This release is stable and suitable for use on live and production sites. When software is deemed to be stable, it performs as expected and should have no remaining major bugs. At this point, the software moves into maintenance mode.

- *Maintenance:* These releases are stable and suitable for use on live and production sites. Maintenance releases continue to stabilize the code base and address any bugs that are reported on the tracker, as well as any reported security issues. The Joomla! Bug Squad is responsible for maintaining Joomla! releases that are in maintenance mode.

Alpha versions are usually when a software release is given its numerical versioning number. An example version number and naming convention such as used by the Joomla! project would be *1.6.0 Alpha 1.* This naming convention follows the format of *Major.Minor.Maintenance* and in the case before a stable release indicates whether the release is alpha or beta, as well as their respective versions of alpha or beta. A major release number indicates software-wide changes to the code base and can be incompatible with previous releases. Minor releases indicate that some changes to functionality may have occurred but that a high level of backward compatibility exists with other versions that fall in the same major release number. Maintenance releases indicate very little to no functionality changes but instead are incremental releases to address any bugs or security issues. Joomla! 1.5 at the beginning of 2010 was at version number 1.5.15, meaning there had been 15 maintenance releases since 1.5 was officially released at the beginning of 2008.

## Joomla! Internationalization, Localization, and Translations

Internationalization in software terms is the ability for software to support multiple languages. Localization is the software mechanism that allows for internationalization. Translations are the pieces of text that are translated into various languages.

Since the Joomla! project began in 2005, internationalization, translation, and localization have been important factors in its worldwide positive reception and usage. Joomla 1.5 showed a marked improvement in the internationalization of the code base, including support for all major character sets and right-to-left presentations, as well as efforts to continue to improve internationalization, which is an ongoing process. The Joomla! project as well as a number of independent developers continue to improve the ease of creating multilingual sites. The International Zone on the Joomla! forum contains 44 international boards, and the number of international JUGs has been steadily increasing, both of which provide quality support to the international Joomla! community.

Translation Teams are responsible for creating installable language packs that contain the translated language strings in the core code base as well as translating sample data and help screens. The wider translation community also offers translations to many extensions. Joomla! 1.5 has been translated into approximately 60 languages, and the Joomla! project is supported by a group of 60 accredited Translation Teams.

A number of translation components are available to extend Joomla! JoomFish has been the most popular and longest available extension, and in recent years a number of other translation components such as Nooku and plugins such as Gtranslate have further solidified Joomla! as the leading CMS for international applications.

Translation components such as JoomFish allow visitors to your site to switch to a language of their choice if you offer it. Although translation components do not actually translate your articles, they allow you to efficiently organize multiple copies of your content that you have had translated, and they also help you keep a consistent structure and presentation for every language you offer. Most translation plugins that are available utilize online translation services, such as Google Translate, giving visitors the ability to translate your content "on the fly" as they surf.

## Joomla! Wants You: How to Be a Contributor

Joomla! is an open source project supported by the community. The project is run on volunteer people-power, and it depends on an ever-growing contributor base as it continues to grow.

As was mentioned earlier, contributing to the forum is very easy to do, by asking and answering questions. The forum gets approximately 1,400 new topics every day. Each one of those topics is typically a question from a community member needing assistance or information. Your helpful response can make a real and marked difference to the experience of those you help. Most of the time when someone shows a real interest in helping others on the forum, they are asked whether they would like to become a moderator to help keep the forum a friendly, collaborative, and pleasant place for the community. The Moderator Team is a great team to be part of, and there is always a need for new members. On a personal note we can attest that helping someone solve a problem they have presented on the forum is a very enriching and rewarding experience.

The Documentation Team is always looking for people to assist with adding helpful articles to the Official Documentation wiki (*http://docs.joomla.org*) or updating articles as things change. There is information on the wiki regarding how to register and start adding documentation content. Documentation consists of any and all helpful tips, tricks, and walk-throughs that specifically deal with how to install, manage, develop for, and generally work with Joomla! the framework and Joomla! the CMS.

The JBS is always looking for both technical and nontechnical people to help in the efforts to keep the maintenance releases stable, bug-free, and secure. There is truth to the open source philosophy that more eyes are better. Testing Joomla! releases on as many different combinations of server setups and operating systems is an integral part of every release cycle. It is also a good way for developers to introduce themselves to the Development Team and learn how to work with the code base.

JUGs help promote Joomla! and also bring users together to experience collaboration on a face-to-face basis. They perform a significant role in the community and community building.

The Translation and Internationalization Teams are always looking for new members to introduce new translations and help in the internationalization process.

The various editorial teams that manage the range of resources for the community (such as the VEL, Joomla! Connect, Joomla! Extensions Directory, Joomla! Resources Directory, Site Showcase, and Magazine) actively look for and encourage people to contribute and join. The community site (*http://community.joomla.org*) supports community blogging and commenting, which is another great way to take part in discussions relating to the project.

The options for contributing to the project are really quite limitless. We have mentioned only a few of the more prominent ways of contributing, and as the project continues to grow, more opportunities and new avenues for contributions will grow as well. Over the years we have participated in all of these, and we can't stress enough how much we benefited from this, whether by improving our knowledge or skills or by meeting other community members.

As always, if you find a bug, please post it on the tracker. Joomla! really appreciates those contributions too.

## Project Leadership

There are four teams each with specific responsibilities that form the overall leadership and governance of the Joomla! project.

- *Leadership Team:* This team consists of the combined members of the Production Leadership and Community Leadership Teams. Their focus of responsibility is the general guidance and management of the development project and the community.
  - *Production Leadership Team (PLT):* The PLT is responsible for managing all aspects of the project that go into the release of the framework and CMS. This also includes documentation, internationalization, translation, and other software-related contributory efforts such as core code development, patches, Joomla! Labs, Joomla! Bug Squad, localization, internationalization, security, and outreach to students.
  - *Community Leadership Team (CLT):* The CLT is responsible for managing and maintaining the structures and resources that facilitate and foster the community aspects of the project such as the Joomla! forum, social networks, communications support, Joomla! Connect, Joomla! Extensions Directory, Joomla!

Community Portal, Joomla! Community Showcase, Joomla! User Groups, Joomla! Demo site, JoomlaCode, and the Joomla! Resource Directory.

- *Community Oversight Committee (CoC):* The CoC is responsible for appointing members to the Open Source Matters board of directors. They can also remove people from the board of directors. The CoC members are leadership members who were on the now-restructured Core Team. (The Core Team was restructured in 2009 to help organize the responsibilities of leadership into the PLT, CLT, and CoC.)

- *Open Source Matters Inc.:* Open Source Matters Inc. is the nonprofit corporation that was formed in September 2005 by the original founding members of the Joomla! project. It was created to oversee the legal and financial needs of the project, as well as any other organizational aspects of the project that fall outside the other leadership teams.

Each leadership team leads Working Groups (WGs) that contain a number of separate teams that have specific responsibilities to the project such as the JED, JRD, Moderator Teams within the Community Working Group, Trademark and Licensing Team, Events Team within Open Source Matters, and Joomla! Bug Squad and User Documentation Team within the Production Working Group, to name but a few.

## Conclusion

What started with a brave and united purpose by a small group of dedicated people has grown up to be the Joomla! project as it is today (Figure 1.3). Joomla! 1.0 had millions of downloads before it was retired from service officially as of July 2009. Joomla! 1.5 had already taken center stage by that time, and the development of Joomla! 1.6 was no longer a distant point on the horizon, with the alpha release having been made in the preceding month of June 2009.

Joomla! 1.5 as of early 2010 has had more than 19 million downloads, and tens of millions of Web sites are powered with Joomla! Adding to that a global community of hundreds of thousands of members, it has been an amazing journey to this point, and the future is certain to continue the tradition as we turn our gaze to the horizon and Joomla! 2.0.

Figure 1.3  Joomla!...because open source matters

# 2

# What Now and Where Do I Begin: Before You Install Joomla!

A lot more than installing and configuring Joomla! goes into creating an online presence, and over our years of contributing to Joomla!, there are a number of questions and subjects that have come up repeatedly that aren't Joomla! specific but are more about the basics of where to begin or how to correct a mistake that may have been made before Joomla! was even installed. This chapter aims to answer those common questions and address some of the issues that may be quite confusing for those very new to running their own Web site. Experienced users may also be inspired to take a look at their Web strategy to see whether it needs an improvement or update.

## Identifying Your Purpose

One of the most important groundwork items you can do before you get started creating your Web site is to identify the purpose. Why do you need a Web site, what do you want it to say to people, and do you want people to take action based on what you are communicating to them? Answering these questions can be tedious and frustrating, and sometimes the answers can be irritatingly elusive. The good news is that this step will help you avoid stuffing your Web site with items and functionality you don't need, making it easier to maintain and retain focus. Joomla! on this point is an excellent choice as a framework to base your Web site on, because of the flexibility it offers. At any time you can reevaluate your needs and extend Joomla! to meet any functionalities you may want to offer your Web site visitors in the future.

Here are questions to ask yourself and then answer as specifically as possible.

- Why do I need a Web site?
- What do I want to offer to visitors of my site?
- What information do I want from them?
- What actions am I expecting visitors to take while on my Web site?

- What actions am I expecting visitors to take after they leave my Web site?
- What kind of communication path do I want to use?
  - A one-way communication directed outward from me to visitors?
  - A two-way communication between myself and visitors?
  - A collaborative communication environment where visitors communicate not only to me through my Web site but also with each other?

As you refine your answers to these questions, you can begin to list the functionality you will need for your Web site. This step is vitally important to help you choose appropriate extensions for your site that work well together. It can also help you avoid using too many extensions or having unused extensions installed on your site.

> **Tip**
> One of the main ways people expose their sites to security vulnerabilities is to keep unused and/or out-of-date extensions installed on their Web sites. If you aren't using an extension, uninstall it, and check to make sure that all files and folders for the extension have been removed. Keep your extensions up to date. This is the time to pick your extensions wisely. Make sure extensions you have picked have an active developer or development team. Other helpful things to look for that make an extension stand out are a user forum, available documentation, and responsive communication availability with the developer or development team.

# Domain Names: Registering Your Domain Name

Choosing the domain name of your Web site can be a difficult and trying process, and to people new to the concept, it can be confusing. Domain names work similarly to how our telephone system works. Just as telephone numbers are universal and unique, so are domain names. As with telephone numbers, the Internet runs on a number system called the Internet Protocol address, or IP address. The Domain Name System translates these hard-to-remember numbers into an easy-to-remember string of letters (for example, 000.000.000.000 to *mysite.com*). This number system determines how one computer knows how to find another computer.

The worldwide body in charge of keeping the universal Domain Name System stable and operable is Internet Corporation For Assigned Names and Numbers (ICANN), a nonprofit organizational and consensus development body. The top-level domains (TLDs) that we are all mostly familiar with are *.com*, *.net*, *.org*, *.gov*, *.edu*, and *.mil*. Also, there are the two-letter ISO country codes that can be used such as *.us*, *.ca*, and *.uk*. These TLDs were intended to act like the country codes and area codes of our telephone system, helping us identify where a site is geographically located. As the Web has exponentially expanded, some of these country codes are now being used for specific purposes, such as *.tv* (country code for the islands of Tuvalu) being used to imply television.

One of the places to search to see whether a domain name is available for use is to go to Internic.net and do a whois (pronounced "who-is") search. Whois means exactly that—you will be searching to see whether a domain name is already in use and who is using it. Also at the Internic.net site, you can find information regarding registrars. Registrar companies are where you go to register your use of a domain name. Prices vary widely from company to company, as can the related services each company offers. One of the main points to keep in mind is to make sure you are using an accredited registrar and that when you register the domain name you want to use, you are registering it yourself, in your own name; if you are going through a third party such as a hosting company or development or Web design firm, make sure they are registering the domain in your name. The Internic.net site also has a lot of information and FAQs on how to resolve issues regarding domain names and their registration.

> ### Tip
> The importance of your domain being registered in your own name cannot be stressed enough. You are creating your Web presence, a lasting memorable experience for your users and your online reputation. Many people have fallen into the trap of fly-by-night, disreputable companies that offer domain name registration, only to have the company disappear, holding your domain name in limbo because it is registered in that company's name, and therefore they retain control of the domain. Also, a common trap is that a domain name you register with a company may be available to you for your use for only as long as you retain other extended services from that company. If you decide you want to get those services somewhere else, they can retain all rights and ownership to the domain name they registered for you. Remember to always read the fine print, and don't be afraid to ask questions.

Pick a domain name that is relevant to your Web site, be it your company name or something catchy that people can relate to you and/or your Web site. Remember that people are going to be typing in your domain name, so make it as simple as possible, and if you can avoid complicated or cryptic acronyms and extremely long domain names, you really should. Also, your domain name can help people find you in search engines, so the more relevant to your Web site and your target audience, the better. Watch out for domain names in existence that may be similar to yours or misspelled that may direct people away from your site and to someone else's site. Think about *.com*, *.net*, and *.org* and the country ISO code for your country when registering, because those are the most popular TLDs that people know and use. When you do a whois search, you will be able to see whether someone has one or all of these registered with your preferred domain name. Consider any conflicts that may occur if you don't own all the main references. You may want to purchase all that are available to protect your brand. All of these tips are good things to consider when the time comes to pick a domain name.

# Trademarks, Licensing, Copyright, and Legalities

Let's start this section with this statement: We are not lawyers (or in popular online acronym speak, IANAL). That being said, remember if you have true and compelling legal questions that can be a showstopper for your Web site or business, you need to have the advice of a competent attorney who is familiar with your specific situation. You can find lots of information on the Internet that deals with general legal information, great resources, and best practices, but the law is serious and can have very serious consequences if ignored, misunderstood, or otherwise handled inappropriately. This section will give you a general overview of some of the legalities you may want to keep in mind as you embark on creating your Web site with Joomla!

## Trademarks

A trademark is a distinctive sign used by an individual, business organization, or other legal entity to uniquely identify their products or services to consumers.

Think of your favorite product. What comes to mind? They have a memorable logo or slogan that instantly identifies that product to you. Trademarks are the unique way a "thing" or "entity" is associated with some sort of relational cue, be it visual, audible, or some other sensory perception. It is what makes a product memorable and is probably the largest part of "branding."

Trademarks help businesses protect their uniqueness, and although a trademark can be acquired through legitimate use, such as a business name or logo that you have used for years, the best way to protect your trademark is to register it. The processes and legalities regarding trademarks vary from country to country; it is always best to seek the advice of a legal professional in your geographical area.

Registering your trademark provides a number of legal benefits in defending it.

- It allows you to protect and defend your trademark more effectively in a court of law.

- Depending on the country, public notification is given of your ownership of your trademark.

- It aids in facilitating the registration of your trademark in other countries, which is especially important if you are planning on doing business internationally and want an internationally known brand.

- It also helps others that are researching trademarks to not infringe on you because they can find your information easily.

That last point can be important to consider when you are brainstorming your branding. It never hurts to search the trademark registries to make sure you will not be infringing on someone else's trademark. Nothing is more disappointing than coming up with an entire concept, only to realize you cannot use it or there are restrictions on the use of all or some part of your branding. Your search is not a substitute for a professional search, but it will catch obvious duplicate names.

If you want to utilize someone else's trademarks in your Web site, be it a name, logo, or slogan, because you are affiliated with, work with, or otherwise have a relationship with another entity, remember to look up any restrictions or permissions you may have to follow to utilize that other entity's marks. A little preparatory work in this area can go a long way to avoiding heartache in the future.

## Copyright

The definition of copyright according to the Library of Congress is as follows:

> Copyright is a form of protection grounded in the U.S. Constitution and granted by law for original works of authorship fixed in a tangible medium of expression. Copyright covers both published and unpublished works...Copyright, a form of intellectual property law, protects original works of authorship including literary, dramatic, musical, and artistic works, such as poetry, novels, movies, songs, computer software, and architecture. Copyright does not protect facts, ideas, systems, or methods of operation, although it may protect the way these things are expressed.

You can learn more about the U.S. copyright system at the Library of Congress Web site (*www.copyright.gov*).

Copyright gives the author or creator of original creative works the exclusive right to use, adapt, distribute, and publish their works and control who else can use adapt, distribute, or publish their works for a period of time. The time lengths differ greatly from country to country, but in general the basic point is to give protection to a creator to use their work as they want, protecting that work from being copied or to have derivatives of their work made by others. Most countries follow the Berne Copyright Convention. Copyright typically exists from the moment the work is created in a tangible fixed medium or form. Some examples of copyrighted works are songs, lyrics, written stories or articles, an image or picture, and code.

A lot of common misconceptions and myths revolve around online media and the extreme availability of everything.

- *Myth: If something is online, it is public domain:* This is not true. Public domain is a specific term used to typically denote works that are "public property." How a work is determined to be public domain depends on the specific circumstances of the work in question and from which country the work originates.

- *Myth: If something is online, it can be used under "fair use":* This is not true, and more information on "fair use" can be found at numerous resources both online and offline. "Fair use" is a legal mountain all on its own and rather out of scope for the purposes of this book.

- *Myth: If I find something online, I can alter it or adapt it by [enter some arbitrary amount or percentage here], and it becomes my unique work:* This is not true and gets a lot of people in a ton of trouble. Specific circumstances do exist that can allow someone to alter, adapt, or use a work, but legally it is a complex and complicated issue.

All of these myths have created a number of problems for people not only since the beginning of the Internet but since the beginning of the time when people could put a creative work into a tangible medium. Most problems were caused not because a person wanted to "steal" someone else's work (that's not to say that intentional theft doesn't happen) but because they innocently believed the hype of these myths. The best way to protect yourself is to create your own works to suit your needs or hire someone with the skill set to create the works you need.

When in doubt, if you come across some form of a work belonging to someone else (meaning you didn't create it) that you want to use, track down the copyright owner, and ask whether they permit others to reproduce, distribute, or adapt their work. This applies to offline, online, or anywhere you may find works by others.

Copyright usually encompasses a work as a whole, not necessarily the pieces or parts that may have gone into the work individually, and in some instances those individual pieces may have their own copyright that may belong to totally separate copyright holders.

This brings us to the next section. Trademark owners can license the use of their trademark, and copyright holders can license the rights of their creative work to others.

### Tip

When a work is created as a "for-hire" work, the right to sell or license the copyrighted work is transferred automatically in advance to the contractor or employer unless other contractual provisions have been made between the two parties.

## Licensing

Licensing refers to permissions that are associated with the use of a work. Licenses are granted by a party ("licensor") to another party ("licensee") as an agreement between those parties. A short definition of a license is "an authorization (by the licensor) to use the licensed material or work (by the licensee)."

As was mentioned earlier, Joomla! is licensed GNU/GPL version 2 or later (the "or later" is used to offer the most flexibility in terms of compatibility with subsequent versions of the GNU/GPL). GNU/GPL is a free software license. A lot of people get confused regarding the use of the word *free* in regard to software. In the case of this license, free refers to the freedom associated with liberty and not the freedom in terms of price or cost. The basic philosophies of the GNU/GPL are based on four main freedoms:

- The freedom to run the program, for any purpose
- The freedom to study how the program works and change it to make it do what you want
- The freedom to redistribute copies so you can help your neighbor
- The freedom to improve the program and release your improvements (and modified versions in general) to the public so that the whole community benefits

These freedoms are integral to the GNU/GPL. The greatest precondition to meeting the four freedoms as described earlier is for the source code of the software to be accessible, which is also termed as *open source*.

Because Joomla! is licensed GNU/GPL v2 or later, it benefits from all the advantages that the freedoms transfer. It allows anyone from anywhere to see, run, modify, and share the code with others. Every day as people contribute to the code, Joomla! becomes more functional, stable, and secure.

# The Basics of Branding

Branding is a distinguishing unique name and/or symbol intended to identify a product or producer.

You may already have a brand developed for your services, product, organization, or business. As you venture into the realm of the Web to promote yourself, it may be a good time to evaluate your branding, including whether it is working for you and whether you are effectively using your branding to increase your visibility and market share.

Branding is key to success and failure. We all can instantly bring to mind companies and products that have excellent branding. Sometimes the psychological effects that branding can produce will make us choose one product over another similar product without question of changing because of the symbolic trust we have that our expectations will be met and our needs will be satisfied. Brand loyalty is one of the biggest commodities of any successful business or product.

Creating a strong brand identity can be a daunting task that takes creativity, ingenuity, and attention to detail. Coming up with a branding strategy could include the name of your business, a logo or identifying mark, color branding, or the use of a slogan or saying. All of these things are brand elements individually, and when used in combination, they help develop your overall brand identity. There are some well-known tricks and tips that you can use to effectively create a brand.

- Your name can be the biggest part of your branding identity. Choose it wisely. Avoid using a name that is already trademarked or registered (especially if in a similar business).

- Remember that your logo will be used across many mediums—most likely print, Web, merchandise, and advertising—so make sure the quality of the look translates well to each one.

- Simplicity increases visual recognition, meaning your logo should be clean, simple, bold, and memorable.

- It is always best to go with an original design—make sure your logo doesn't look similar to other logos. It should be either electronically or hand drawn and not comprised from clip art or stock image sources.

- If you have a slogan, it should be simple and easy to understand. Making people think is a good thing, but they shouldn't have to try too hard to figure out what you mean.

- Your slogan should communicate what your product, business, or organization stands for in a meaningful manner.

- All of these individual elements should be able to stand on their own as well as stand as a collective.

> **Tip**
>
> A new trend in branding is "no-brand" branding. This sort of marketing strategy relies on word-of-mouth or the most simple kinds of advertising, as well as the consumer experience and expectation. It tends to hold the function and design of the actual product over the package that the product is contained within and typically represents a "back to basics" approach to product, delivery, and consumer communications. IKEA is a popular example of this sort of branding.

## Memorable Logos and Why You Need One

We are all familiar with the "swish," or the specific lettering that defines a product for us. They are those logos that seemingly without effort can immediately conjure up a good memory of using the associated product. They evoke emotional responses and help us "feel" what the product means to us.

There are basically two categories of logos—those that use an image or icon as their primary visual mark and those that use their name as their logo. The latter has just chosen the combined letters to be their "icon." If you have a unique, memorable, or interesting name (preferably one word), that may be the best way to go in terms of creating your logo. Creative use of typography as a logo has been behind some of the most beloved brands in history. Those that use their name also may have a bit of a leg up on recognition because the name is their icon, so they almost get to double dip into the subconscious of consumers, giving them name retention and also the visual recognition element.

Iconic type logos have two subtypes. There are logos that utilize an illustrative image as their icon, such as a messenger service using an envelope, and those that use an abstract symbol or image, such as the infamous swish of a well-known athletic brand. This latter choice is risky and usually takes funding and a professional team of marketers and advertising companies to present and solidify an abstract image as your "identity" to your potential consumers, as well as encouraging brand loyalty with those potential consumers who are converted into actual consumers of your product.

Here's some practical advice.

- Don't use a swish.
- Make sure the typefaces you use are easily readable, and don't use more than two different typefaces if possible.
- Don't use special effects such as gradients, shadows, or glows. They usually don't translate to print well, especially if used in black-and-white printing.
- Test your logo in plain black-and-white.
- Try not to use too many colors. The general rule is to use no more than three, tops.

Again, keep it simple, vibrant, and representative of the image you want to project and have associated with your business.

## All About Color and Color Schemes

One mistake that is commonly made in Web design is poor use of color. Color works on our subconscious and conscious minds to create associations that imply meaning. For example, the color green can signify growth, and red can imply power. When you think of the colors you want to use for your logo design or Web site, it can be helpful to think about words you would use to describe your purpose or product. Once you have that list of words, try assigning a color to each word. This exercise should produce an idea of what your dominant color could be. The next step would be to pick a shade of that dominant color that appeals to you. That first color can become the starting point of your "color scheme."

The color wheel is a common tool used in the creative process for visual mediums. One of the first types of the color wheel originated from Sir Isaac Newton and his experiments utilizing prisms and light refraction, which were published in 1672. The basic color wheel consists of 12 colors (as shown in Figure 2.1) that are each classified in one of three categories: primary, secondary, and tertiary.

- *Primary colors:* Red, yellow, and blue
- *Secondary colors:* Orange (red and yellow), green (yellow and blue), and purple (blue and red)
- *Tertiary colors:* Yellow-orange, red-orange, red-purple, blue-purple, blue-green, and yellow-green

There are a few different ways to go about filling in the rest of the colors for your color scheme, but what is vitally important is creating a harmonious effect that is pleasing to the eye. Color harmonies can be created using a number of techniques.

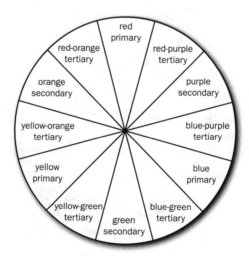

Figure 2.1  Basic color wheel

Figure 2.2  Monochromatic grayscale color scheme

- *Monochromatic:* One specific color used as the dominant color and then varying shades from light to dark of that specific color (as shown in Figure 2.2).
- *Analogous:* One specific color as the dominant and the colors that reside on either side of it on the color wheel or the two colors either to the right or to the left of the dominant color. Here's an example: red, red-orange, and red-purple (as shown in Figure 2.3).
- *Complementary:* One specific color as the dominant and the exact opposite of that color on the color wheel. Here's an example: red and green (as shown in Figure 2.4).
- *Split-complementary:* One specific color as the dominant and the two colors that reside on either side of the complementary color. Here's an example: green, red-purple, and red–orange (as shown in Figure 2.5).
- *Triad:* One specific color as the dominant and the two colors that are evenly distributed on either side (on a 12-color color wheel, they are 4 colors apart). Here's an example: green, purple, and orange (as shown in Figure 2.6).

All of the color wheel images noted in the previous list can be found in color on *The Official Joomla! Book* Web site (*http://officialjoomlabook.com*).

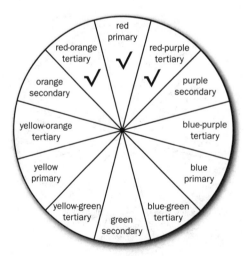

Figure 2.3  Analogous color scheme

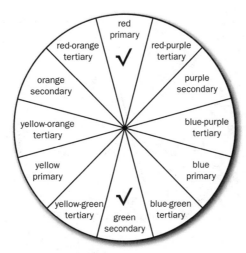

Figure 2.4  Complementary color scheme

Figure 2.5  Split-complementary color scheme

In visual design, it is important to not overload the viewer's eyes, because doing so can distract your audience from your message. The basic rule is to start with one dominant color and then use the other colors in your scheme as accents.

There are a number of books such as David Carter's *The Big Book of Color in Design* (Collins), online resources such as ColourLovers.com and kuler.adobe.com, and programs such as ColorSchemer that can help you design the perfect color scheme for your project.

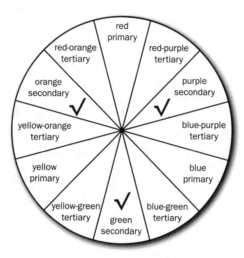

Figure 2.6  Triad color scheme

Don't be afraid to be as bold or as understated as you want to be. This is your site and your creation. Have fun with it.

# Identifying Your Target Audience: The Who, What, Where, and Why

There are close to 2 billion users with access to the Internet and trillions of Web pages out there. You have to find a way to narrow it all down to your target audience. The Web is a big place, and the point isn't to be just another forgotten page out there in cyberspace but a reliable source for people interested in your product, ideas, organization, or business to reference, purchase from, or otherwise engage with you. You may think your audience is "everyone," but the reality is, it isn't everyone. If your site is about restoring antique cars, then your broadest audience is going to be people who are interested in cars. People interested in flower arrangements would most likely visit sites about flowers.

## Knowing Your Visitors

If you identify your audience, it will point you to what functionalities to consider for your Web site. A local restaurant most likely does not need a forum, but it may want to use a contact form to get feedback from their customers or a forms solution to handle online ordering and delivery tracking. A national or international organization will have specific communication needs and may need a forum to handle the interaction between their target audience of members and supporters. A musician will need streaming media, something that ties in their social networking accounts, as well as a robust calendar, because their target audience would be their fans and the new fans they are hoping to attract. When starting out, it is usually best to very closely define your audience and excel at giving that well-defined group the best experience possible. As your site grows, you can then expand your target audience appropriately.

> **Tip**
>
> We have all come across sites that have it—the forum with no posts and no users, blog post after blog post with comments enabled but no comments, or menu items that go nowhere or, even worse, to an under-construction page. Nothing says unprofessional or wastes people's valuable clicks more than these items. The rule of "less is more" really does apply just as equally to Web sites as it does to everything else in life. Don't publish that menu link to nowhere. Wait until you have your content ready, and then point your visitors to it. Don't have a forum full of empty topics—not only does it look uninviting, but it can have the detrimental effect of driving people away from your site. Please don't put that giant "under construction" graphic on your pages, hoping that someday it will be filled with glorious content. Wait until that someday arrives. You don't need all the bells and whistles right now, especially if you aren't ready or prepared for it. Your Web site is a long-term commitment, so give it and your audience room to grow.

## Usability: Novel Idea! Users Want to Actually Use Your Site

Usability is the ease with which people can employ a particular tool or other object in order to achieve a particular goal. Usability can also refer to the methods of measuring usability and the analysis of the principles behind an object's perceived efficiency or elegance. In human-computer interaction and computer science, usability often refers to how a Web site or computer program is designed and how the design facilitates users of the program or Web site to accomplish specific tasks or goals.

A number of research studies and books are available on Web usability; one of the most popular online resources is Jakob Nielson's site (*http://useit.com*). Web site usability is a two-part equation.

- How easy is it for visitors to your site to get the information they need or to fulfill the reason they visited your site to begin with?

- How can you, the Web site owner, translate that ease of use into the results you are intending, such as encouraging people to read your content, purchase your product, or visit your physical location?

More usability is better for you and your visitors because everyone has had their expectations met and gets a rewarding experience.

The first usability check for your Web site is to check your color scheme and typography. Are your colors giving your users a headache, or are your colors pleasing? Are you using them effectively to direct people's eyes to the important parts of the page? Is your text easy to read and the proper color for the color of background? Do you have your titles and headings clearly standing out to organize the page's information?

A second usability check is to evaluate your navigation. Are you offering clear navigation that is intuitive on a glance? Do the menu items accurately indicate the content

they are pointing to? Are you giving people too many choices or not enough? Can people get to the information they need in three clicks or less? If you offer a shopping cart,
is the process self-explanatory, or are there too many steps to get to the end goal of
completing checkout? Do you have a clear way for people to contact you or your staff
regarding any questions they may have about your Web site, product, or services?

A third usability check is to make sure your site works across browser platforms,
specifically most modern browsers. That could change if your site is for internal corporate use, because your corporation may be locked into using an older version of a
browser because of program or network compatibility issues. Again, you have to think of
your target audience, but it really is important to note that not all of your users will be
using the same browser or be on the same operating system. You don't necessarily have
to match pixel per pixel in terms of visual display across browsers, because that isn't a
usability issue, although to some it may be an important image issue. Basically, it is
important that all functionality is working; there cannot be an absolute breakdown in
terms of layout or other rendering issues that can cause user frustration or disruption.
Your users need to be able to complete any tasks or processes that you are inviting them
to do.

## What Is Accessibility?

Accessibility is a general term used to describe the degree to which a product, device,
service, or environment is available for use by as many people as possible, or the "ability
to access." Accessibility is often used to focus on people with disabilities and their right
of access, often through the use of assistive technology.

Accessibility should not be confused with usability, although increasing either in most
situations will result in the other also improving.

Accessibility is about making things accessible to all people (whether they have a dis-
ability or not). An alternative is to provide "indirect access" by having the Web site support the use of a person's assistive technology to achieve access (for example, a screen
reader).

Accessibility is an important part of Web design not only because it is a matter of law
in a number of geographic areas but also because the Web has become an assistive technology to a large number of people with disabilities.

In the United States, one of the standards for accessibility is 508 compliance. This is a
set of guidelines for digital and electronic information technology, developed to ensure
people with disabilities have the same access to and use of data compared to people
without disabilities. This set of guidelines refers specifically to governmental sites and
agencies. Outside of governmental agencies, this standard has been picked up as a general
standard of good Web design.

Worldwide, the standards for accessibility are determined by the Web Content
Accessibility Guidelines (WCAG). These guidelines are set by the World Wide Web
Consortium (W3), the international body of member organizations in conjunction with
the public that set all Web standards. It is led by Tim Berners-Lee, the brilliant scientist
who invented the World Wide Web.

WCAG standards are more strict than 508 compliance standards and deal specifically with Web technologies. There are four main points to WCAG 2.0 according to its Web site (*http://w3.org*).

- *Perceivable:* Provide text alternatives for all nontext content, provide content in a way that it can be presented in different ways, and make content easy to see and hear.

- *Operable:* Allow for the operation and functionality with a keyboard, allow enough time for content to be read or used, do not design content in a way that could cause seizures, and make content easy to navigate, search for, and find.

- *Understandable:* Make content readable and understandable, make pages operate in a predictable manner, and help users avoid and correct mistakes.

- *Robust :* Maximize compatibility with current and future user agents and assistive technologies.

Assistive technologies are computer accessories or components that assist people who have disabilities use their computers effectively. Screen readers, eye movement trackers, voice recognition software, large-key keyboards, special trackball mice, and screen magnifiers are all examples of assistive technologies. All of these can present unique challenges to Web and software designers, but for the most part, if good standard design principles and practices are used, these challenges are easily met.

Here are some basic ways to incorporate accessible design and function in your Web site.

- Use tables for tabular data, not for layout or design.
- Use appropriate hierarchical titles and headings.
- Create logical navigation.
- Utilize alternate tags for images and other media.
- Code your Web site to allow for keyboard navigation or navigation with other assistive technologies.
- Structure your content in a logical fashion.
- Use a color scheme that properly utilizes color and contrast to aid in readability.

A good way to test your Web site for basic accessibility is to look at your site with all of the design elements such as images, media, and styling turned off. In Firefox, you can turn off styling by clicking View in the menu and then clicking Page Style and then No Style. Other browsers will have different but similar options to turn off styling. You should now see your raw, unstyled page. You should then ask yourself these questions: Does your content flow logically down the page, and can you tell how the content is organized from the titles and headings? Are you able to see and use your menu navigation to browse your site in a logical manner? Where an image was in your content, can you now see a description of the image and the title of the image? Can you use your keyboard to logically tab through your menu navigation and the links on your page? In analyzing your Web site in that raw state, is your intended message still being conveyed in a meaningful manner?

A good example of an accessible template for Joomla! is included in the core distribution. It is called Beez. It is also relatively easy to customize and adapt, which will be covered in Chapter 5.

# Wireframes, Storyboarding, and Visualization

One way to plan your site is to wireframe, or make a visual diagram of what your site is offering to visitors in terms of structure and navigational needs. It is not concerned with how things are implemented or how they visually look, only with what needs to be present for the site to fulfill its goals. This step allows you to place the functionality visually or create the interactional design. This is the time to ask yourself what the user should be doing on your site and how you can direct users to complete a process that makes both you and the end user happy. This step almost always saves on actual Web development time, because it allows you to make all the mistakes and correct them before one bit of code is written. You can sketch it on a piece of paper or use any number of wireframe programs that are available. Figure 2.7 shows an example of a wireframe.

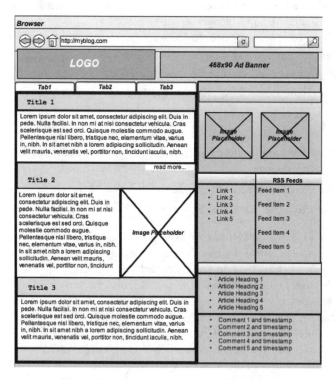

Figure 2.7  Basic wireframe of a Web page

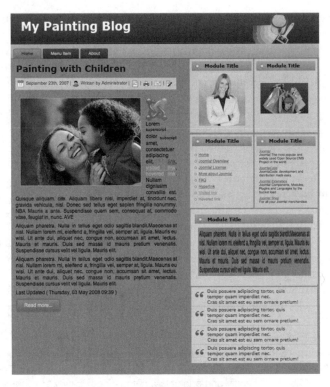

Figure 2.8  Mock-up of Web page

Your wireframes should clearly show the click path of your visitors on any given page, the natural navigation between the pages and areas of your site, and how you are channeling the user to take action, whatever that action may be, without being distracted by design and style.

Once you have your wireframe complete and user interface set, you can storyboard or create a mock-up of your site to incorporate the design and style that will make your site visually appealing. Storyboards or mock-ups usually are a good visual representation of what the site will look like when it is complete, and they can be created with graphics programs such as GIMP, Adobe Photoshop, or Inkscape. Figure 2.8 shows a mock-up based on the wireframe.

# Creating Great Content

Creating engaging content that conveys your message can be difficult. Keeping your content on task regarding your specific subject matter helps build a relationship with your users who will then return and ideally refer friends to your Web site. There are two keys to content creation: relevancy and usefulness. There are two basic types of Web content: foundational and continuous. Your foundational content should be quite narrowly targeted to the subject matter of your site, and it should contain good number of descriptive keywords. Usually foundational content is quite static in nature.

Most Web sites have foundational content that succinctly describes to a visitor who they are, what they do, and why there is a benefit to visitors interacting with them. About Us pages, mission statements, and product and services overview pages are good examples of foundational content. It can set the standard of trust and the importance of the relationship you have with your site visitors. Well-written foundational content is also very important to search engines as they look through your site's content to rate how relevant it is to a specific search term.

Continuous content is relevant, useful content that is updated on a regular basis, such as a blog, press section, product reviews, or news section. This is the content that compels your visitors to keep returning, and it is another way to direct your users to perform an action. Continuous content can also include content such as that from forums, embedded social media, and comments. Continuous content doesn't necessarily have to be generated by you. Your site visitors can be a great resource for content creation. Continuous content is a very important part of creating a great Web site that generates repeat visitors, referrers, and quality links back to your site from other sites that find your content useful. Search engines also like to see fresh new content, because it can indicate that you are current, you are relevant, and you are generating good links back to your site.

> **Tip**
>
> Adding interest to your content with rich-media elements such as images, audio, and video can make the difference between a one-time visitor and a repeat customer. These media elements should be high quality and add value, not just "eye candy," to your site. Podcasts, video casts, and photo galleries that are updated regularly can really improve your site's reach and visitor count.

## Mission Critical: Why Choosing a Good Host Matters

Table 2.1 lists the technical requirements that you need to consider in regard to hosting your Joomla! 1.5 site. (Note that requirements for Joomla! 1.6 are higher.) It is important to discuss with your host these technical requirements to make sure their hosting service supports Joomla!

Table 2.1  **Hosting Requirements for Joomla! 1.5 Web Sites**

| Software | Recommended | Minimum | More Information |
| --- | --- | --- | --- |
| PHP | Version 5.2 + | Version 4.3.10 | *www.php.net* |
| MySQL | Version 4.1.*x* + | Version 3.23 | *www.mysql.com* |
| Apache (with *mod_mysql*, *mod_xml*, and *mod_zlib*) | Version 2.*x* + | Version 1.3 | *www.apache.org* |
| Microsoft IIS | Version 7 | Version 6 | *www.iis.net* |

PHP: Hypertext Preprocessor is a widely used, general-purpose scripting language that was originally designed for Web development to produce dynamic Web pages. It can be embedded into HTML and generally runs on a Web server, which needs to be configured to process PHP code and create Web page content from it.

MySQL is a relational database management system (RDBMS) where data is stored in the form of tables and the relationship among the data is also stored in the form of tables.

Apache is Web server software that runs on a number of different operating systems. Most Web servers running Apache are using the Linux operating system.

Microsoft Internet Information Services (IIS), formerly called Internet Information Server, is a set of Internet-based services for servers created by Microsoft for use with Microsoft Windows.

PHP versions 4.3.9, 4.4.2, and 5.0.4 are releases of PHP that have known bugs that inhibit the installation of Joomla! Zend Optimizer 2.5.10 for PHP 4.4.*x* has bugs, and your host should upgrade the version of Zend Optimizer they are using. Joomla! 1.5.15 and higher are compatible with PHP 5.3. The Open ID Library is not yet compatible with PHP 5.3. Joomla! is not yet compatible with MySQL 6.*x*. Joomla! can run on Microsoft IIS 6, but version 7 is recommended. PHP 5.2 and MySQL 5.1 are required. You may need Microsoft URL Rewrite Module and FastCGI.

Choosing your hosting provider is probably one of the most important decisions you will make regarding your Web site. Your host can either make or break (literally) your Web site and impact your visitor's experience, so it is imperative that you choose wisely. Here are some items to consider and questions to ask before you buy.

- Does the host meet or exceed the recommended technical requirements for running your Joomla! site? With so many hosting options available, there is no reason to choose one that doesn't.

- Does the host offer the customer support options that are important to you such as e-mail, phone, or live chat? Some hosts offer all of these options, and some may offer only one. You should be comfortable with the options they are offering to you. You should also check to make sure that their customer support is timely and courteous. Is their relationship with their clients evident on their Web site, forums, or other communication channels? Does it give an indication of positivity or negativity?

- What is the online reputation of the host? Can a simple search engine search find blogs dedicated to a company's poor service record, or are customer complaints figuring prominently in the first two pages of search results? What is their rating at the Better Business Bureau or other similar consumer protection agency? If their rating is anything but stellar, I would keep on searching.

- What is the host offering in terms of storage space and bandwidth limits? Hosting companies that offer unlimited storage and bandwidth are offering something that they cannot realistically deliver on. Be sure to read the fine print in any host's terms of service, especially if the word *resources* is mentioned but not specifically defined. If it isn't, ask them for a specific definition of what *resources* means. Be careful of "oversellers." Overselling is a term used for shared hosting services companies (many individual hosting accounts share one server) that sell server storage space and bandwidth in excess of the actual capacity they have available, in the hopes that the individuals will each not utilize all of the storage and bandwidth sold to them. Although some very good hosts can effectively juggle this scenario, it is important to consider whether your site is critical for your business. Poorly run, oversold servers will have significant downtime, service lags, or interruptions.

- What are the host's server and service uptime statistics and/or guarantee, as well as security record? Can they articulate their security practices, equipment failure mitigation protocol, data storage, and backup procedures? No host can guarantee 100 percent uptime, and bad days happen to everyone. Ultimately, your site is your responsibility to maintain and keep updated. Back up your site on a regular basis, and download the backup, remembering that you also need a copy of your database. With a current backup and complete database, you will always be able to restore your site in the event of an emergency.

You may have noticed that we didn't include price in the list of considerations when choosing a host. Although price can certainly be a factor, we recommend that it never be a determining factor. There are so many hosts to choose from in various price ranges that you are certain to find one that meets the criteria of a good host and also suits your budget.

### Tip

Content management systems create "dynamic" sites. This means they are able to be utilized in real time, with new content being created instantaneously through a Web browser. This is in contrast to "static" sites where content is created offline and then uploaded to a server via File Transfer Protocol (FTP). For the content to change on a static site, you usually have to download your page, edit it, and then upload the new page to replace the old. Dynamic sites on some hosting accounts can have issues with file ownership and file permissions. Ask your prospective host whether they are running PHPsuExec, suPHP, or an equivalent solution that keeps your files secure and set with the proper permissions and ownership.

## Conclusion

As you can see from the items this chapter has touched upon, there are a number of things to consider when embarking on creating a Web presence. Although some of these things are rather permanent in nature, such as your domain name, other items may be flexible as you work through the process, such as the look of your site and its design elements. The great thing about picking Joomla! is that your design, layout, and functionality are highly flexible and extendable.

# 3

# Installing and Configuring Joomla!

This chapter explains how to download and manually install Joomla! and describes the basic configuration options. The screenshots and instructions reference a common Web hosting control panel called Cpanel. Cpanel is an interface that allows users to have control over the various functionalities of their hosting account. A number of hosts have their own hosting control panel account interfaces that are similar to Cpanel, and your host will have documentation that shows you the equivalent actions and functions that we describe in this walk-through. The main functions we reference are creating a database, accessing phpMyAdmin, and using File Manager. If your host does not use Cpanel, please reference the documentation for each of those functionalities that your host has available to familiarize yourself with them before proceeding. Also note that some hosts may limit your ability to create databases or your access to phpMyAdmin. In that case, you will have to contact your host to get the database name, database username, and database password. You should make sure that the database character set is utf8 and the collation is utf8_general_ci. Having the database set to this character set and collation gives the broadest available use of numerals, alphabetical characters, and symbols across many languages.

In Chapter 2, we discussed how to choose a good host for Joomla! and what the minimum requirements are for running Joomla! 1.5. This chapter requires that those best practices in choosing a host have been followed and that the host offers an optimal environment for running Joomla!

## Downloading Joomla!

Go to *www.joomla.org*, and look for the download link, which at this time looks as shown in Figure 3.1.

When you click the link, it will take you to a page that lists the latest downloads, as shown in Figure 3.2, including a full package, which contains all the files for Joomla!, and a patch package, which contains only files that have been changed since the previous release. If this is the first time you are installing Joomla!, you want to download the full

Figure 3.1  Get the latest version of Joomla!

Figure 3.2  Joomla! download screen showing where to click to get the full
package ZIP file and where to subscribe to e-mail security notices

package (1) by clicking ZIP. Save the file onto your computer in an easily remembered
place such as your desktop. At this time, the page for downloading Joomla! also contains
a lot of other helpful information, including the ability to subscribe to security updates
that will be sent to you in e-mail (2). It is suggested that you sign up for these e-mail
notifications to stay current when Joomla! is updated and to get any security announcements. Enter your e-mail address, and click Subscribe.

Click ZIP to download the Full Package for Joomla! Once you have downloaded
Joomla! and subscribed to the security update e-mail list, you need to navigate using
your browser to your hosting account's control panel, log in to your hosting account
control panel, and use the following steps to prepare your hosting account to install
Joomla! In the examples in this chapter, the screenshots depict the use of Cpanel as the
hosting account control panel. This should be easy to do by logging in to your hosting
account. You should have instructions for this from your host. Some hosts may have an
older version of Cpanel, which will look slightly different but include the same functions.

## Creating a Database

Once you have logged in to administrate your hosting account through your host's control panel or Cpanel, you want to look for the MySQL Database Wizard. Cpanel offers a
Find box in the upper-left corner that allows you to find the function you are looking
for easily. In the Find box, type in **data**. Figure 3.3 depicts using the Find box and how
Cpanel then filters the functions available to show only those that may pertain to

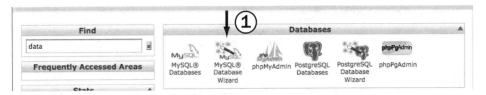

Figure 3.3  Using Cpanel to create a database using the MySQL
Database Wizard

Databases (1). You want to click MySQL Database Wizard to open the database wizard
screen to create a new database.

Once you have clicked and opened the database wizard, you will be walked through
screens to create your database. The first step is creating a database by giving it a name, as
shown in Figure 3.4.

When you go to the next step by clicking Next Step, you will see a confirmation that
a database has been created, and it will confirm the name of the database that you have
just created. Some hosts will combine your hosting account name or another string of
characters, and they will add it to the name that you gave to the database; see the blurred
text in Figure 3.5 (1). It is helpful to keep notes as to what the full database name is,
which is its combined name. It then asks you to create a database username and give the
database user a password. Figure 3.5 (2) points out that you need to have a very strong
password for your database that is a combination of letters, numbers, and symbols to be
the most secure. Do not use a common phrase, name, or easily guessed dictionary word.
Cpanel includes a password generator that you can use by clicking Generate Password. It
will generate a password made up of a random string of letters, numbers, and symbols.
Using Generate Password will open a small overlay window where you can select how
you want the generator to generate the password. Please write down your username and
password for safekeeping. Once the password is generated, you can click Next Step.

Figure 3.6 shows the new user and the password that was entered for that user (1).
The Step 3: Add User to the Database section states the full username of the user and
the full name of the database (2). This is where you attach the user of the database to the
database and assign the privileges that the user has in relationship to the database. For the
purposes of this database used for Joomla!, you want to assign All Privileges by checking
the All Privileges box (3).

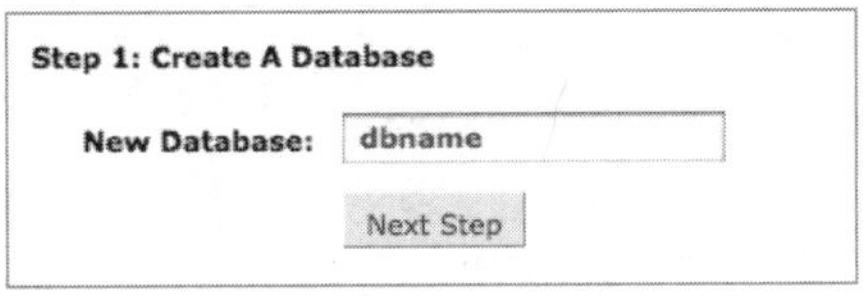

---

**Step 1: Create A Database**

**New Database:**  dbname

Next Step

---

Figure 3.4  Create a new database by entering a name for your database.

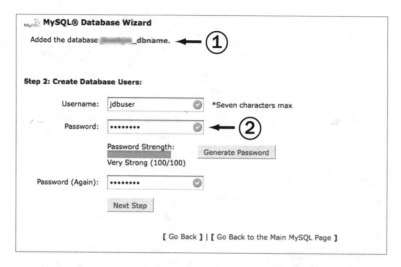

Figure 3.5  Create a user and a password for the new database.

Complete the creation of a database process by clicking Next Step. You will see a confirmation screen, as shown Figure 3.7, that will then give you options to create another database, add another user, or return to the Cpanel home screen. You want to continue to the home screen to start uploading and installing Joomla!

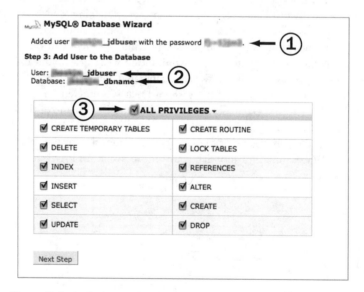

Figure 3.6  Assigning privileges to a database user and confirming the
database full name, full username, and user password

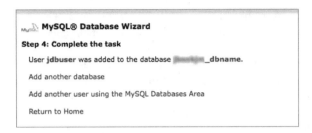

Figure 3.7  Final confirmation screen of creating a new MySQL Database
and assigning a user to database

After you have created your database, you want to check to make sure that the character set is utf8 and the collation of the database is utf8_general_ci. You can see these settings in phpMyAdmin.

Once back at your home page, if you do a search again in the top-left corner for *data*, it will bring up the options you have regarding databases. Click the selection for phpMyAdmin to open it (usually it opens in a new window or tab in your browser). When you open phpMyAdmin, you will see your databases on the left side. Figure 3.8 is an example of the screen that you see in phpMyAdmin. Select the database we just created, and then click the Operations tab (1). The Operations tab shows various information regarding your database, such as the character set and collation. When we created

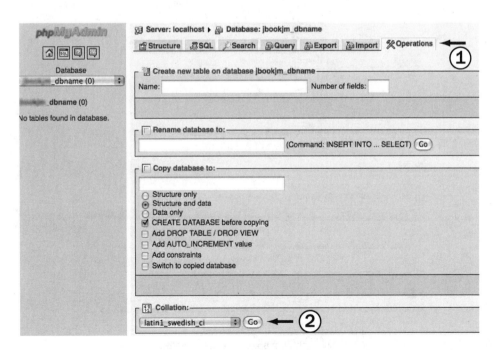

Figure 3.8  Example of phpMyAdmin and where to find the collation information

our database, it was given the collation of latin1_swedish_ci (2). This is a common setting on a number of hosts to have latin1_swedish_ci as the default collation and Latin as the default character set.

The collation can be changed to utf8 to allow the broadest use of characters, because a number of Joomla! extension developers require this for their extensions to work well. Click the collation drop-down to pick utf8_general_ci (see Figure 3.9) as a collation, and then click Go (1).

You will then be presented with a screen that confirms that the change has executed successfully, and as shown in Figure 3.10 (1), the collation is now changed to utf8_general_ci.

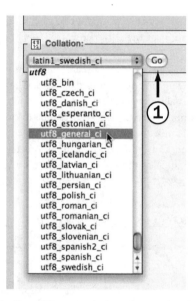

Figure 3.9  Selecting utf8_general_ci to change the character set and collation of a database

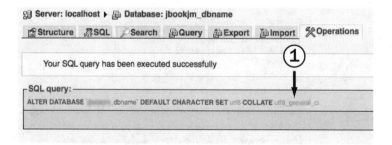

Figure 3.10  Successful change of character set and collation

You can now close the tab or window for phpMyAdmin. The next step will be using the File Manager located in Cpanel to upload the Joomla! zip file we downloaded earlier in this chapter.

## Using File Manager to Upload Joomla!

From the Cpanel home page in the top-left corner, search for *file*, and you will see the options available to work with files using your hosting account. Select and open File Manager. This will open in a new tab or window in your browser. Once File Manager has opened, you want to navigate to your root folder for your hosting account. On most hosts, this is called *public_html*; it can also be called *htdocs* or something similar. Your hosting company should have documentation available to you that states what your root folder is and where you put your Web site files. The root folder of your Web site is the folder you want to upload the Joomla! zip file to. Click Upload in the toolbar located at the top of the screen. This will open a new tab or window where you can then click Browse to find and select the zip file, as shown in Figure 3.11. If you are familiar with the use of an FTP client such as FileZilla, you can use it to upload the zip file, but always wait to unzip until your file is on the server to minimize the risk of file corruption.

Once the file has uploaded, you can go back to the main File Manager screen either by clicking the option to return to the File Manager on the screen or by closing that tab or window. Once you are back in the File Manager, you will see the Joomla! zip file in your *public_html* folder. Select the zip file by putting a check mark in the box (1), and then click Extract (2), as shown in Figure 3.12.

Once you have clicked Extract in the top menu of the File Manager, you will be asked to confirm a path. This path should be in your default root hosting account folder, which is usually called *public_html* or *home*. This may vary between hosts, so you may

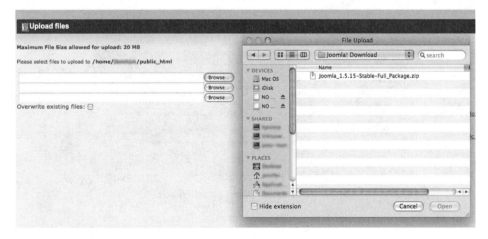

Figure 3.11  Using Cpanel to upload files to your hosting account

Figure 3.12  Using Cpanel File Manager to extract the files from
a zip archive

want to confirm what your root hosting account folder is called with your host before extracting the files. Figure 3.13 demonstrates the extraction path selection.

Figure 3.14 shows the results of clicking Extract File(s).

Upon closing the extraction results screen, you will see that all the files for Joomla! have been extracted into your *public_html* directory. Keep the File Manager open in your browser, either in its own window or on a tab, because you will be using the File Manager in the very last step of installation.

The next step is to go through the Web installation to install Joomla!

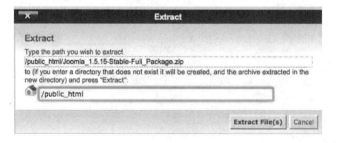

Figure 3.13  Extract path selection screen

```
                              Extraction Results
  X

Archive:  /home/        /public_html/Joomla_1.5.15-Stable-Full_Package.zip
  creating: administrator/
  creating: administrator/language/
  creating: administrator/language/en-GB/
 inflating: administrator/language/en-GB/en-GB.mod_stats.ini
 inflating: administrator/language/en-GB/en-GB.com_content.ini
 inflating: administrator/language/en-GB/en-GB.com_banners.ini
 inflating: administrator/language/en-GB/en-GB.plg_editors_tinymce.ini
 inflating: administrator/language/en-GB/en-GB.com_checkin.ini
 inflating: administrator/language/en-GB/en-GB.com_media.ini
 inflating: administrator/language/en-GB/index.html
 inflating: administrator/language/en-GB/en-GB.com_frontpage.ini
 inflating: administrator/language/en-GB/en-GB.com_search.menu.ini
 inflating: administrator/language/en-GB/en-GB.com_wrapper.ini
 inflating: administrator/language/en-GB/en-GB.tpl_rhuk_milkyway.ini
 inflating: administrator/language/en-GB/en-GB.com_banners.menu.ini
 inflating: administrator/language/en-GB/en-GB.plg_authentication_example.ini
 inflating: administrator/language/en-GB/en-GB.plg_authentication_openid.ini
 inflating: administrator/language/en-GB/en-GB.plg_content_image.ini
 inflating: administrator/language/en-GB/en-GB.plg_search_contacts.ini
 inflating: administrator/language/en-GB/en-GB.mod_status.ini
 inflating: administrator/language/en-GB/en-GB.tpl_ja_purity.ini
 inflating: administrator/language/en-GB/en-GB.plg_xmlrpc_blogger.ini
```

Figure 3.14  Results of extraction

# Joomla! Web Installation

In a new window or tab in your browser, navigate to your Web site such as *www.yourweb-sitename.com*. If your domain has not propagated throughout the Web yet, you can usually use a temporary URL for your site. The temporary URL for your site will be specific to your hosting company, and they will be able to give it to you. Most times a temporary URL for a hosting account will look similar to *http://yourhostingcompanyservername.com/~yourhostingaccountname*.

When your domain or temporary URL has opened, you will be presented with the first Joomla! installation screen, as shown in Figure 3.15, where it asks you to select the language that you want to use while going through the installation. Once you have picked your language, click Next in the top-right corner of the screen.

The next screen is Pre-installation Check (see Figure 3.16), which will help you determine whether your server is optimally set up to install Joomla! The top portion shows items that are required to install Joomla!, and all of the items should have a green Yes beside them. If any of the items in the top box are showing a red No, then you should rectify the situation with your host before continuing. One of the most common issues to show up as No in the top box is that *configuration.php* is not writable. This could be an indication that your host is not running an optimal setup in regard to file permissions and/or file ownership on their servers. To solve this issue if you cannot resolve it with your host, please see Appendix A.

Figure 3.15  The first of seven steps to install Joomla! through the
Web installer

Figure 3.16  Second installation screen: Pre-installation Check

The second set of information relates to specific settings for PHP. Joomla! will install
if these settings are not optimal, but any indication of an issue with the recommended
setting not being present could cause problems with your site in the future.

If you are able to change or have your host change any settings to their optimal selections, you can click Check Again to see whether the changes have taken effect. We
strongly recommend that all of the settings be optimal for your Joomla! site to be successful. If they are not, submit a support ticket with your host asking for assistance in

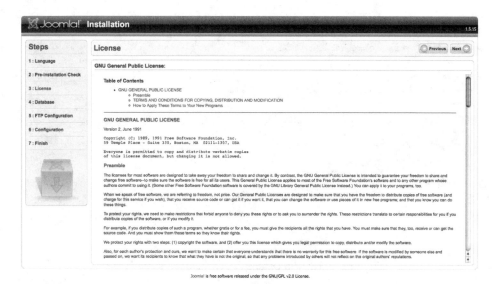

Figure 3.17  The GNU General Public License

changing them. When you are ready to proceed from this screen, click Next in the top-right corner to go to the License screen.

The License screen shown in Figure 3.17 presents a copy of the GNU General Public License and is for informational purposes. When you are ready to proceed, click Next in the top-right corner to go to the Database Configuration screen.

The Database Configuration screen as shown in Figure 3.18 is where you will define the database for your Joomla! site that was set up previously. This is also where you will define the user and the user's password for the database. The first selection box allows you to pick the type of database. The database we set up was a MySQL database, which is the default selection for that drop-down menu.

The second box to fill out is Host Name. This is usually localhost, and if it is not, you will have to get the host name from your hosting provider.

The third box is where you will enter the username for the database that we set up earlier. It is important to remember that your host may have added your hosting account name to the front of the name you set up for your user. You will have to use the entire name for installation to continue (for example, *xxyyzz_dbuser*).

The fourth box is where you will put in the password you created for the user.

The fifth box is where you will enter the name of the database that was created earlier. It is also important to remember that your host may have also added your hosting account name to the front of the name you set up for your database. You will need to use the entire name for installation to continue (for example, *xxyyzz_dbname*).

Figure 3.18 shows the Advanced Settings box in the open position. You can open this box by clicking the title of the box. The advanced setting fields give even more options to define how your database works, such as the table prefix. The default table prefix is

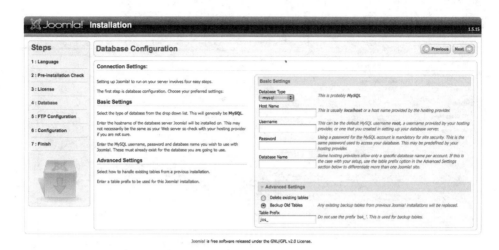

Figure 3.18  The Database Configuration screen

*jos_*. It can be helpful to define a different table prefix if you are limited to one database through your host but want to run more than one Joomla! site. If you do change the default prefix or use another prefix, be sure to include the underscore character. Without the underscore, the prefix letters will run into the database table names. You also have the ability to drop (remove) any tables that may be existing in your database or back up any existing tables. Backup tables will automatically use the prefix of *bak_*.

When you have finished putting in the details of your database, click Next in the top-right corner to go to the FTP Configuration screen.

The FTP layer exists to help with managing your Web site files. FTP is a network protocol used to facilitate a connection between two computers over the Internet. This connection allows users to upload, download, and manipulate files between the two computers. Some Linux-based servers have issues with system permissions and restrictions. The FTP layer in Joomla! 1.5 allows authorized users on hosts with these issues to have access to upload processes available within Joomla! such as installing extensions and uploading images in the Media Manager. If your host is using good practices to manage hosting account file ownership and permissions by using suPHP, PHPsuExec, or a similar solution, you should not have to utilize the FTP layer.

To utilize the FTP layer, you must enable it by selecting Yes to enable it and then fill in the FTP user with your FTP username and your password. Your host can supply this username and password to you, or if your host allows it, you can create an FTP username and password for your account through your hosting control panel. Once you have entered the credentials for your FTP account, you can use autofind to find the path to your directory containing your Joomla! files and verify your FTP settings.

As shown in Figure 3.19 under the Advanced Settings heading, you can specify the FTP host and FTP port, if your hosting provider has a specific setting that you need to

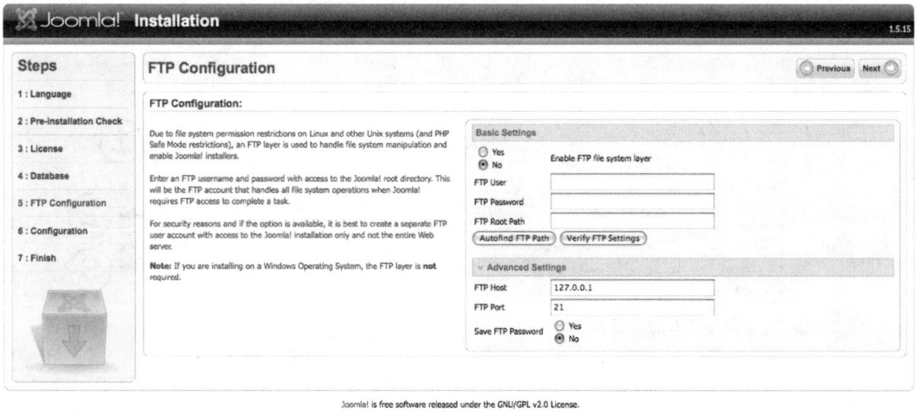

Figure 3.19  The FTP configuration screen

use. You will need to get that information from your hosting provider. You can change the FTP settings through the Global Configuration settings in Joomla!

If you are not using the FTP layer or after you have put in the information needed to make the FTP layer work, click Next in the top-right corner to go to the main configuration screen.

In the Site Name field, put the name of your site; typically this will be your company name, your business name, or the name you want people to associate with your Web site. The Your E-mail field is where you will put the e-mail address that will be the main e-mail address associated with the administrator of the Web site. The Admin Password and Confirm Admin Password fields are for the administrator password, where you will enter the password once and then verify the password by typing it in a second time. This password should be a strong password made up of a random string of letters, numbers, and symbols to make it as secure as possible. You may want to write this password down and keep it with the other important information you should keep for reference purposes for your Web site.

There are three choices you can make when it comes to the Data portion of the installation configuration.

- Install the sample data. The sample data that is distributed with Joomla! is used to give a good general example of how Joomla! works, how content can be organized, and how content can be presented.

- Load the migration script to migrate data from a Joomla! 1.0x site. To utilize this migration ability, you will have had to use migration tools to prepare the old database for migration. Information on these tools and how to use them are available on the *http://docs.joomla.org* site.

- Choose to not install sample data or migration data, and start with a totally blank site (typically used by people already familiar with Joomla! and creating a new Joomla! site).

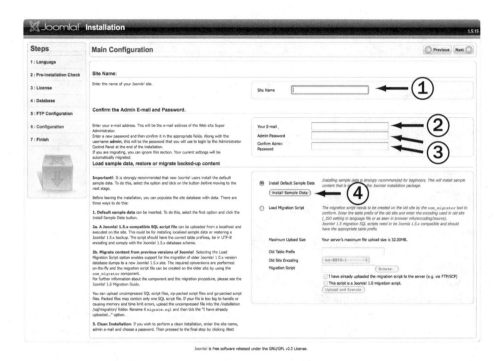

Figure 3.20  The Main Configuration screen

For the purposes of this book, we are starting with a new site and will be installing the sample data that will allow you to have a better understanding of how Joomla! works. As shown in Figure 3.20, click Install Sample Data (4). If the data installs successfully, you will see a confirmation that the data has installed. When you have completed the installation of data, click Next in the top right to go to the Finish screen.

Figure 3.21 shows the final screen for the Web installation of Joomla! There is a "Congratulations!" message as well instructions on how to move forward from this point. This screen also directs you to now remove the installation directory from your site.

Removing the installation directory is imperative for the security of your site, and you will not be able to view or edit your site until you remove the directory. Return to the File Manager browser window, and as demonstrated in Figure 3.22, select the installation directory (1), and utilize the Delete function in the toolbar in the File Manager (2). You will see a confirmation that you want to delete the directory. Confirm by clicking Delete File (3).

Once you have deleted the installation directory, you can return to the browser window showing the Congratulations! screen. Using the buttons located at the top of the screen for either Site or Admin, as shown in Figure 3.23, you can direct your browser to either the front end (Site) or the back end (Admin) of your newly installed Joomla! site.

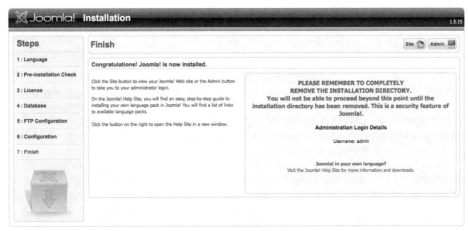

Figure 3.21  The Finish screen

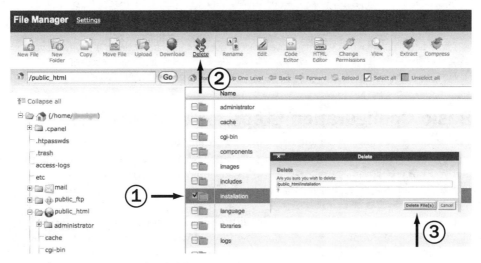

Figure 3.22  Deleting the installation directory

Figure 3.23  Installation is finished, and you can now navigate to your
new site.

In the next portion of the chapter, we will be going through some basic configuration options to set up your site, looking at where some important administrator functions are located and how to set up content.

> **Tip**
>
> A number of hosts make available easy installations of popular Web scripts and programs such as Joomla! through assistive programs bundled in the control panel that they offer to their users. The most popular of these is called Fantastico, which is part of the hosting control panel called Cpanel. These one-click installation routines make installing popular Web programs and scripts an easy process, but unfortunately they don't explain the processes behind installation, and they limit the knowledge you can gain by learning how to install these programs and work with your Web site files. Also, you may be limited to using the same procedure to update your programs or scripts when updates are released, and these updates may not be available through the assistive installation program in a timely manner. You may have to consult your hosting company's documentation to use this functionality.
>
> You can also use these same instructions for installation on a localized server setup on your personal computer. Programs such as XAMPP, WAMP (Windows specific), and MAMP (Macintosh specific) allow you to set up a Web server on your local machine so you can stage Web sites or develop and design without having to do it on a live server at a hosting company. The instructions may differ in that your personal computer may have file and folder permission issues you may have to work out, and instead of using a File Manager, you will be working as you usually do with your files on your computer.  Microsoft Web Platform Installer is also available to easily install Web applications on a Windows computer.

# Basic Configuration Steps for Your New Site

This section will show some basic configuration settings to get you started with your new Web site and is in no way a comprehensive review of all the configuration options that you can take advantage of. As you work with Joomla!, you will be utilizing a lot of the configuration options, but for the purposes of this book, we will only be touching on the basics.

In the previous section at the end of installation, you could choose to click either the Site button or the Admin button of your new Joomla! Web site. If you look at the front end of the site, with the installation of the sample data, you can see the basics of how a Joomla! site looks to people surfing the Web. On first glance, a new site with the sample data installed can look a bit overwhelming, but the sample data is used to show the many different options to display data.

If you haven't already, log into the administrator back end of your site by going to *www.your_domain_name.com/administrator* and entering **admin** as the username and the password you set up in the configuration step during installation.

Upon logging into the administrator back end of your site, the screen that is presented is the Control Panel. Sometimes people refer to this as the admin panel, administrator screen, or various other names, but the name that is associated with it in the Site

Figure 3.24  Administrator back-end Control Panel showing an expanded
site menu

menu, as shown in Figure 3.24, is Control Panel (1). The Control Panel offers some of
the most-used administrator functions in clickable icons in the center of the page and
also offers other choices of administrator functions across the top of the screen as a menu
bar with drop-down menu items. For the purposes of this book, we will explain items
by going to their menu item in the top menu bar rather than the large clickable icons in
the middle of the page.

## Editing the Administrator User

The first stop for configuring your new Web site is to open the User Manager (2) shown
in Figure 3.24, make the administrator account more secure, and set the user settings.

Once you have entered the User Manager by clicking the User Manager menu item,
you will see a list of the users who are currently registered at your site. Because your site
is a fresh site, you will see only one user: Administrator. Changing the name of the
Administrator user helps make your site more secure. To edit a user, click the name of
the user under the Name column. This will open the User Edit screen. This screen will
show input boxes: Name, Username, E-mail, New Password, Verify Password, Group,
Block User, Receive System E-mails, Register Date, Last Visit Date, Back-end Language,
Front-end Language, User Editor, Help Site, Time Zone, and, if linked to a contact,
Contact Information.

At this time, there are only a few things you want to take care of in terms of basic
configuration. The first is to change the administrator name. It should be something that
is relevant to your site if you are planning on having your administrator user be an
author of articles on your site, where you have the article details, such as the author
name, showing on the front end of the Web site. The administrator username, which is
what you use to log into your site, should be changed to something that is not easily
guessed. You can also at this time change your password and verify it, but changing the
password isn't necessary if you created a strong one during installation. If you do change
your password, remember to record it for your records. The only other thing to change is

your time zone to reflect the time zone you want the administrator user to have. Also, you should notice that your group is set to Super Administrator. This means that you have control of the site and all the settings. When this is finished, click Save in the top-right corner of the screen. Saving will bring you back to the User Manager.

## User Groups

You are the super administrator of your site, but you don't want all the users of your site to have permission to do everything, such as changing your design or switching your database. User groups are the way that Joomla! allows you to manage which users can take various actions on your site and who can see what content. As you create new users, you will need to decide what user groups to put them in.

There are three user groups that have access to log in to the administrator back end of a Joomla! site.

- *Super Administrator:* The Super Administrator group has access to *all* the administrator functions in all areas of the site. Your site must have at least one user who is a super administrator. Users in this group cannot be deleted. Only super administrators can grant other users the Super Administrator right by assigning them to the Super Administrator group. Only super administrators can change the group of other super administrators.

    Be very careful who you make a super administrator. This all-encompassing level of access should only be given to those who you can trust your site and site information with. Never give your super administrator username or password on a public forum. Do not give your super administrator username or password to anyone in an e-mail unless you know and trust the person receiving the e-mail.

- *Administrator:* The Administrator group has slightly restricted access to the back-end (administrator) functions, which is better explained by what they cannot do. Administrators cannot add a user to the Super Administrator group or edit a super administrator's account. Administrators do not have access to the Global Configuration settings. Administrators cannot use the mass mailing functions of the site through the messaging system. Administrators cannot manage, edit, or install templates or language files.

- *Manager:* The Manager group is usually used to group together the user accounts that will be managing content items. A manager cannot add or edit users; cannot install modules, components, or plugins; and may have limited access to work with components in the administrator back end.

A second set of four user groups cannot log in to the administrator back end. They have increasing privileges to do things on the front end of your site. You may recognize the names for these groups as their privileges reflect print workflows.

- *Registered:* This group of users can log in to the site and see content that is designated for registered users only.

- *Author:* This group can log in and see registered-only content but can also create new content if you make those options available.

- *Editor:* This group can do everything authors can do and can also edit articles.

- *Publisher:* This group can do everything editors can do but can also change the published state of articles.

### Tip

A common problem that people can have is losing their ability to log into the administrator back end because the password or username is incorrect. This can occur if someone has forgotten their password or if a new administrator is taking over an existing site and the password and username have not been relayed or recorded for reference. Thankfully, there is a way to change the password outside of Joomla! as long as you have access to the hosting account and phpMyAdmin. This technique is explained in Appendix A.

Once you have edited the super administrator user to be more secure, you can move on to the next step of configuring your Web site by configuring a few of the options in the Global Configuration page. From the User Manager screen, you want to go to the Global Configuration page by selecting it from the Site menu drop-down located in the top left of the screen.

## Basic Global Configuration Options

The Global Configuration page comprises three areas.

- Site options located in the Global Configuration affect the Web site at the site or public level, meaning what people see when they browse your Web site. For example. this includes whether the site is online or offline, the default editor you want to use for all users, and the metadata for your Web site. It is also where you can implement some search engine optimization (SEO) settings such as friendly URLs.

- System options are configuration options that affect how the Joomla! CMS program works and that involve some permissions and how some data is handled by the system.

- Server options are configuration options that affect how Joomla! and the settings for your server work together.

On the site level of configuration, you want to change only a few things, as shown in Figure 3.25. The site name should match what you entered in the installation procedure. If you want to change it or if you have changed your mind, the Site Name input box is where you can change that information (1).

The Metadata Settings section has default information about Joomla! You want to change these to be relevant to your site.

The Global Site Meta Description field (2) should be a relatively short sentence that shows a good summary of what your site is about. Try to keep your description to 120

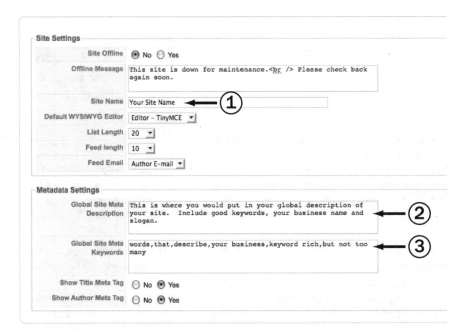

Figure 3.25  Global Configuration site settings to change

characters total to allow your full description to be used by search engines when it is displayed in search results. Use more than 120 to 150 characters, and your description has a chance of being shortened in the display.

The Global Site Meta Keywords field (3) should be a short list of keywords or keyword phrases, separated by a comma. Keywords are best used as two- to four-word phrases that are relevant to your site and more specifically your content. Best practices for using keywords tend toward the importance of quality over the quantity of keywords used. A good place to start with building your keywords is to come up with five basic terms that relate to your Web site and enter those terms into the Global Meta Keywords input box. Next create a two- to four-word phrase using each of those basic terms utilizing words that convey action and plurals and synonyms of your basic five terms.

As your site grows and you have a chance to see statistical data on how people use search engines to find your site and what keywords they use, you can adjust your Global Meta Keywords setting to adapt.

On the right side of the screen are the SEO settings, as shown in Figure 3.26. This is where you can set the URLs for your site to be search engine friendly and more readable by your users.

Dynamic sites like the sites that are created with Joomla! use programming to construct the URLs to the content. Once you turn on search-engine-friendly URLs and

Figure 3.26  Global Configuration site settings to change for
search-engine-friendly URLs

use Apache's *mod_rewrite*, rename the *htaccess.txt* file to *.htaccess*, and add a suffix to the
URLs that are generated by Joomla!, you go from this:

*www.mysite.com/index.php?option=com_content&view=category&layout=blog&id=1&Itemid=50*

to this:

*www.mysite.com/the-news.html*

Three factors go into turning on search-engine-friendly (SEF) URLs.

- *Making the URL readable:* This involves making the URL readable and understandable but also allows you to represent the content you are displaying with an URL
  that will contain appropriate keywords or phrases, giving you an SEO boost.

- *Using Apache mod_rewrite:* This is the underlying server technology that executes
  the commands that create the rewritten URL. To use this, you have to be on a
  server that is running Apache and that has *mod_rewrite* enabled on it. You also have
  to specifically rename the *htaccess.txt* file that is included with Joomla! to *.htaccess*.

- *Adding a suffix to URLs:* Suffixes describe the file type that is being displayed. Web
  pages when displayed would be given the suffix of *.html*.

Figure 3.27 shows the Cpanel File Manager and the *htaccess.txt* file as well as the
default *.htaccess* that a number of hosts put in the root of a hosting account.

| | | | | |
|---|---|---|---|---|
| | xmlrpc | 4 KB | httpd/unix-directory | 0755 |
| | .htaccess | 619 Bytes | text/x-generic | 0644 |
| | CHANGELOG.php | 100.33 KB | application/x-httpd-php | 0644 |
| | configuration.php-dist | 3.33 KB | text/x-generic | 0644 |
| | COPYRIGHT.php | 1.14 KB | application/x-httpd-php | 0644 |
| | CREDITS.php | 14.82 KB | application/x-httpd-php | 0644 |
| | htaccess.txt | 2.71 KB | text/plain | 0644 |

Figure 3.27  Cpanel File Manager showing htaccess.txt and a
default .htaccess file

**Tip**

To rename the *htaccess.txt* file to *.htaccess*, use the File Manager in your hosting Cpanel to locate the *htaccess.txt* file, and use the rename function to rename it *.htaccess*. Alternately, you can open the *htaccess.txt* file, copy the entire contents of it, and then create a new file using the New File command. When the new file opens for editing, paste the information that you copied from the *htaccess.txt* file into the new file and name it *.htaccess*. Some hosts may include an *.htaccess* file in your root directory already. If this is the case, open the *htaccess.txt* file included with Joomla!, copy the entire contents of the file, then open the *.htaccess* file and paste the copied information into the *.htaccess* file, and finally save the *.htaccess* file. Remember to take a backup of the *.htaccess* file before you change it. There may be *.htaccess* rules from the existing file that need to be put back after you replace it with the Joomla! *htaccess.txt*.

In the System portion of the Global Configuration page, there are only two things you may want to change, as shown in Figure 3.28. The first is whether users can register an account on your site (1). Usually this is enabled only if you are planning on having a site where you want people to be able to register to read content or purchase something or have some other need to get details on your users for interactive purposes. If you do not plan on needing this function, it is best to disable registration by toggling the Allow User Registration radio button to No. You can always enable registration at a later time by toggling it to Yes.

The second is to decide whether you want users to be able to see and change user parameters when they are logged into your site. For most sites, we turn this option off to retain consistency, especially if there are multiple users who are creating or editing content. Toggling this option to Hide (2) prevents users who log in to the front end from editing user parameters such as Front-end Language, Back-end Language, User Editor, Help Site, and Time Zone. If toggled to show, as shown in Figure 3.28, the previously listed user parameters will show to logged-in front-end users. If you install a third-party editor, you can set it globally in the site settings that were covered previously in this chapter.

Figure 3.29 shows the front-end view with Front-end User Parameters toggled to Hide.

Figure 3.30 shows the front-end view with Front-end User Parameters toggled to Show.

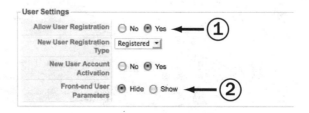

Figure 3.28  Global Configuration system settings to change user settings

Figure 3.29  Front-end view of logged-in user editing their details

Figure 3.30  Front-end view of logged-in user editing their details

Under the Server Settings area in the Global Configuration settings, you will want to set the Locale to the time zone that you want your site to be operating under by selecting the appropriate time zone from the drop-down menu, as shown in Figure 3.31 (1). This completes the basic configuration of your site. There are other options, but for typical users they do not need to be changed.

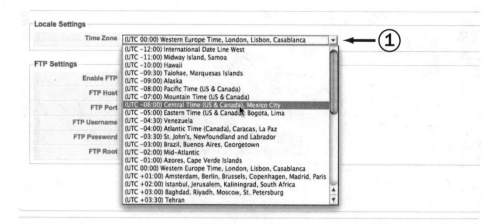

Figure 3.31  Global Configuration server setting to change the time zone

## Conclusion

In this chapter, you installed your very own copy of Joomla! and took a brief tour of how to navigate in a hosting panel and work with file management on a server. Having a good basic understanding of your Joomla! control panel, your database, and how to manage files is important and will empower you to manage your site. With those basic settings set, you are ready to start organizing the structural content of your site and begin working with the sample content and learning how to create your own.

# 4

# Working with and Creating Content for Your Joomla! Site

Now that you have a basic Web site with sample data installed, you are ready to start organizing the structural content of your site using Joomla! In this chapter, we will explain the use of the Joomla! Content component to create articles and organize them into sections and categories. We will use the sample data you installed in Chapter 3 to demonstrate key features and procedures. The patterns you learn in the Content component will apply in other components.

## Defining Content

The Content component is the most important component for creating what visitors and users will see on your Web site. Articles are the basic form of content. Articles are organized into categories, and categories are organized into sections. This terminology comes from traditional print models, where a newspaper might have News, Sports, Business, and Features sections, and those sections might have different categories, such as local and national news in the News section, baseball and basketball in the Sports section, the stock market and retail business in the Business section, and home furnishings and cooking in the Features section. In your site, you may have many sections or just one. You may have many categories or just a few. What is important is to understand how to use the Content component and to have a good plan for organizing your articles.

Working with the sample data is a good way to learn how to work with site content without having to create the content yourself. Once you learn to edit existing articles, create new articles, and manage sections and categories, you will be ready to create your own.

The sample data comes with three sections and nine categories already defined. It also has 43 articles already created. It also shows one article that is not categorized, which means it is not in any category or section. Articles that are not categorized are static content, meaning that their display is managed somewhat differently. However, they are still articles. With a few exceptions (such as for landing pages described later in this chapter), we recommend always putting your articles in sections and categories.

From the Control Panel in the administrator back end, go to the Content menu, and click Article Manager. This will open the Article Manager screen. Figure 4.1 shows how the Article Manager screen is organized and what functions you can perform while in this area of your site, with two main parts that allow you control over your content. The first is the icon menu bar (1), and the second is the filter options (2).

The following are the Article Manager icons.

- *Unarchive:* This allows you to change an article's status from archived to unpublished. If you want an unarchived article to be seen on the front end of your site, you will need to publish it again. You use this by selecting the check box beside an article's title in the list of articles and then by clicking Unarchive. This will work only on archived articles.

- *Archive:* This allows you to archive articles that you want to still be accessible, but only if they are accessed through a specific menu type. You use this by selecting the check box beside an article's title in the list of articles and then by clicking Archive. This will work only on published and unpublished articles.

- *Publish:* This allows you to publish articles, meaning they will be visible on the front end of your site. You use this by selecting the check box beside an article's title in the list of articles and then by clicking Publish. This works only on articles that are unpublished.

- *Unpublish:* This allows you to unpublish articles that have been published. You use this by selecting the check box beside an article's title in the list of articles and then by clicking Unpublish. This works only on published articles.

- *Move:* This allows you to move an article from one section or category to another. You use this by selecting the check box beside an article's title in the list of articles and then by clicking Move. This opens another screen that confirms which article you are moving and asks you to select the section/category that you want to move the article to. Once you have selected the section/category, you then click Save in the upper-right corner.

- *Copy:* This copies an article and creates a duplicate of it. You use this by selecting the check box beside an article's title in the list of articles and then by clicking Copy. This opens another screen that confirms which article you are copying and asks you to select the section/category you want to copy the article to. Once you have selected the section/category, then click Save in the upper-right corner.

Figure 4.1  Article Manager menu icons and filtering options

- *Trash:* This deletes an article from the Article Manager and puts it in the Article Trash. You use this by selecting the check box beside an article's title in the list of articles and then by clicking Trash. This automatically moves the article selected to the Article Trash without any confirmation screen. You can restore an article that has been mistakenly trashed by going to the Content menu item and then clicking Article Trash. From the list of available trashed articles, you can then select the article you want to restore by selecting the check box beside its title and clicking Restore located in the upper-right corner. If you are certain that you want an article permanently deleted, you should delete it from the Trash Manager.

- *Edit:* This allows you to open an existing article to edit it. You use this by selecting the check box beside an article's title in the list of articles and then by clicking Edit. This opens the article in the back-end editing screen. Once you have edited the article, click Save in the upper-right corner to save the article and return to the Article Manager, or click Apply to save your changes but leave the article open for further editing if you want to view your changes on the front end. If you have opened an article by mistake for editing, you can click Cancel to return to the Article Manager. Note that if you select Apply before your article is ready to be seen by the public, you should make sure to change the status to unpublished.

- *New:* This allows you to create a totally new article. You use this by clicking New. This opens the article in the back-end editing screen. Once you have entered the contents of the article you are creating, click Save in the upper-right corner to save the article and return to the Article Manager, or click Apply to save your changes but leave the article open for further editing if you want to view your changes on the front end. If you have created a new article by mistake, you can click Cancel to return to the Article Manager.

- *Parameters:* This is where you can set the global article parameters that affect every content item in your site. Most of these article parameters can be overridden in two places: they can be overridden on individual content items, and some can be set in the menu parameters, which can affect a group of articles that are linked from the menu. This is also where you can set the content filter, which gives you options as to what sort of content can be entered in the Content Editor. To open article parameters, click Parameters, and a small modal box—a pop-up with a dark background that hides the rest of the screen—will open containing the following items.

  - *Show Unauthorized Links:* Allows you to choose whether links to content that is set to the permission level of registered will show or not to people who are not logged into your site.

  - *Show Article Title:* Allows you to set whether the article title will show.

  - *Title Linkable:* Allows you to choose whether the title is made into a link to the full article.

  - *Show Intro Text:* Allows you to choose whether to show intro text of articles.

- *Section Name:* Allows you to choose whether the name of the section will be shown along with the article.

- *Section Title Linkable:* Allows you to choose whether the section name if shown along with the article is made into a link to the section.

- *Category Title:* Allows you to choose whether the title of the category will be shown along with the article.

- *Category Title Linkable:* Allows you to choose whether the category name if shown along with the article is made into a link to the category.

- *Author Name:* Allows you to choose whether the author name will be shown in the article.

- *Created Date and Time:* Allows you to choose whether the time and the date the article was created will be shown in the article.

- *Modified Date and Time:* Allows you to choose whether the article will show if it has been modified or edited and the time and date that occurred.

- *Show Navigation:* Allows you to choose whether navigation between articles will be shown. This shows the last and next articles for people to use to browse your site.

- *Read more... Link:* Allows you to choose whether a "Read more" link will be shown. Used in combination with showing intro text to allow site visitors to browse to the full article.

- *Article Rating/Voting:* Allows you to choose whether to show how an article is rated.

- *Icons:* Allows you to choose whether you want to use icons or text for the PDF, Print, and E-mail functions that can be set to show within an article.

- *PDF Icon:* Allows you to show or hide the ability for visitors to turn the article they are viewing into a PDF.

- *Print Icon:* Allows you to show or hide the ability for visitors to print the article they are viewing.

- *E-mail Icon:* Allows you to show or hide the ability for visitors to send an e-mail with the article information to an e-mail address.

- *Hits:* Allows you to show or hide the number of times an article has been accessed or read, otherwise known as *hits.*

- *For each feed item show:* Allows you to set whether the full article text or just intro text will show if you have turned RSS feeds of your articles on.

- *Filtering options:* These are set to protect your site from possible malicious or dangerous action to your site through the Content Editor when entering an article or other content. By default the super administrator does not have any filter set at all, because the super administrator should only ever be someone who can be trusted with full control over the site. Also, by default all other groups have filtering set to blacklist, which prohibits those groups from entering specific code into the Content Editor that is commonly used in Web site attacks. If you change the filtering options, it will override the default settings because only one rule can be set for content filtering. It is best to leave the default settings as they are, for the most protection. The filter will automatically clean out any prohibited code from a content item whenever it is saved. These are the filter parameters:

- *Filter groups:* These are the groups available to select to apply a filter to.
- *Filter type Blacklist (Default) Whitelist No html:* Blacklist is automatically set to filter out a number of commonly used Web site attacks such as malicious scripts. Whitelist, if selected, allows you to place specific HTML tags in the "Filter tags" box to allow only those tags in content items. Whitelist also allows you place specific HTML attributes that can be allowed in content items.
- *Filter tags:* This is the input box where you would put tags you allow inside your content.
- *Filter attributes:* This is the input box where you would put attributes you allow inside your content.
- *Help:* Clicking this will open a help screen with more information about these parameters.

If you have changed any of the selections from the default selections of your install in the article parameters, remember to click Save at the top of the Article Parameter box that opened when you clicked Article Parameters.

You can also take advantage of various filtering options to find articles quickly when you are in the Article Manager. This is especially helpful for sites with large numbers of articles.

The filtering options are as follows.

- *Filter:* Allows you to input text contained in a title of an article to do a search for any articles that may be using that text as part of their title.
- *Select Section:* Allows you to filter your articles by choosing a specific section to display.
- *Select Category:* Allows you to filter your articles by choosing a specific category to display.
- *Select Author:* Allows you to filter articles by choosing a specific author to display.
- *Select State:* Allows you to filter articles by their state. There are three states that an article can be: published, unpublished, and archived.

To help you get started editing the sample content to suit your own purposes, you can at this time remove a number of the articles, because you need only a few to start out with as examples.

5

apter 4  Working with and Creating Content for Your Joomla! Site

In Chapter 2, we gave you ideas on how to think about your site before you even start, so we hope that at this point you have an idea on how you want to organize your content. In this example, we are going to reference a brochure-type Web site that is relatively simple that has a need for information about the site or business, a blog category where there will be content that is updated on a daily or weekly basis, a press release category where visitors will find press releases regarding the site or business are located, some customer testimonials, and a contact form for visitors to get in touch with the site owner.

# Managing Content

To start, we will show how to remove some articles. From the Control Panel, go to the Content menu, and click Article Manager. This will open the list of articles used in the sample data. Leaving two articles or less in each category will give a good representative group of articles to use and edit.

Using the filtering options from the previous section, you can bring up all the articles in any category, click the Select Section drop-down menu, and choose the last section that is in the list, FAQs. This will show three articles in the category The Project. Select the box that is located on the far-left side of the screen next to the number (#) sign. Selecting this box will select every article shown in the list; then click Trash. This will remove the articles selected and place them in the Article Trash. This will remove all articles from the FAQs section from within all the categories that are assigned under the FAQs section. Click the Select Section filter drop-down again, and return the selection to Select Section. This will clear the filter and return you to a view of all remaining articles.

To see the articles that you have removed and put in the trash, go to the Content menu, and navigate to Article Trash. This will list all the articles that have been removed from the Article Manager. You can restore an article to the Article Manager by selecting the box beside the title of the article you want to restore and then by clicking Restore. This will take you to a confirmation screen that asks you to confirm the article you are restoring. If you want to restore the article, click Restore again, as shown in Figure 4.2. Restored articles are placed back in the section and category they were previously in but in an unpublished state. You will have to publish the article again if you want it to be publicly viewable. If you do not want to restore any articles, click Cancel in the upper-right corner of the screen. This will take you back to the Article Trash Manager.

Figure 4.2  Confirm restore screen

All the articles in the Article Trash must be removed if you are going to remove any of the sections or categories they were previously in. Select the box in the upper-left side of the screen next to # to select all the articles in the list, and then click Delete in the upper-right side of the screen. This will take you to a confirmation screen asking you to confirm that you want to delete all the articles. Click Delete again to delete all the articles, as shown in Figure 4.3. This will permanently delete all the articles listed from the database, and they will not be able to be recovered. Upon clicking Delete, you will be returned to the Article Trash Manager, where you will see that no articles remain.

Next you will start to rename your sections and categories. From the Content menu, navigate to Section Manager, and click it. This will show you all of the sections available:

- About Joomla!
- News
- FAQs

Click the About Joomla! title, or select the box beside the title and click Edit. This will open the section for editing. In the Title input box, enter **Our Blog** or whatever you want to name the section that will hold your company or Web site blogging categories. In the Alias input box, remove all the information, which will automatically replace it with *our-blog* or a lowercase version of what you put in the Title field, with the words separated by a hyphen. Alias is part of what makes up your search-engine-friendly URLs. If you want it to read differently, you can input whatever you want in the Alias field. Best practices would be to make it the lowercase form of your title without any spaces but instead using hyphens. It is also acceptable to use underscores, but you should never use spaces. If the title is very long, you may want to shorten the alias. This alias creation action is consistent across all your articles and article structure, including categories and sections. Published shows whether the category is published by using a radio button you can set to Yes or No. You can set the order of sections using the Order drop-down. Access Level determines whether something is Public, meaning viewable to all who come to your Web site, Register means it will display to only those who have registered and are logged into your site, and Special means it will only show to those who are in the Author user group or higher. At this time, you can put a description and images in the Description text box if you want. Once you have renamed the section to your blog

Figure 4.3  Confirm delete screen

name, click Save in the top-right corner of the window. This will save the section and return you to the Section Manager. Figure 4.4 shows the section-editing screen.

In the Section Manager, click News to open it to edit. In the Title input box, enter **Press and Media**. Remove the text from the Alias input box. In the Description box, remove the text that is already present, and replace it with a sentence that will describe your news, media, and press releases. For example, enter **Our company press releases, news, media and customer testimonials**. Click Save located at the top-right corner of the screen.

Next, the categories need to be edited. Go to the Content menu, and navigate to Category Manager. This will open the Category Manager screen to show the list of all the categories that are already created through the sample data. First we will remove the categories that belong to the FAQs section because they contain no articles, and we do not need that section. Select the boxes beside the category Titles for the following:

- General
- Current Users
- New to Joomla!
- Languages

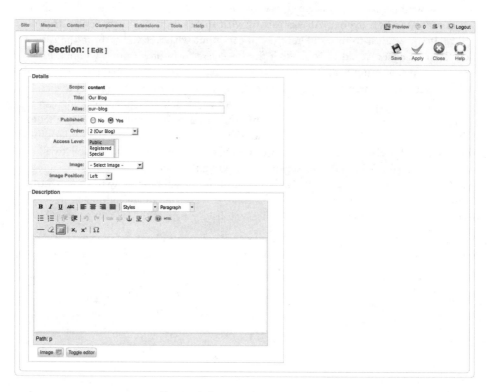

Figure 4.4  Section-editing screen

When you've selected all of these categories, click Delete in the right corner of the screen. This will permanently remove those categories. If you have not removed all the articles that were in the Trash that at one time were in those categories or if there are existing published, unpublished, or archived articles in those categories, you will get a warning that the categories cannot be deleted because they contain articles. As shown in Figure 4.5, the number of articles that are active are shown in the category listing on the right side of the page (1).

Once the empty categories from the FAQs section have been removed, you can rename the categories located in the Our Blog section. They are as follows:

- The Project
- The CMS
- The Community

Click the title The Project in the category list. This will open the category for editing similar to the way we previously edited the section. The Category edit screen has a few more options than the section-editing screen. First in the Title input box, remove The Project, and enter **General** or another name you want to give the general category for your blog. In the Alias input box, remove *the-project*, and enter what you want the alias to be. Or, leave it blank, and it will autopopulate to be the text you have put in the Title input box. In the Section drop-down box, you can choose to assign the category to another section if you want. For the purpose of this example, you should leave it in the Our Blog section. In the Description box, remove the text, and replace it with a sentence or two that describes a general informational blog category for your Web site. You can rename the other categories that are in the Our Blog section using the same steps, or you can unpublish them to use later.

The category Latest should be renamed Press Releases, and the category Newsflash should be renamed Testimonials. Figure 4.6 shows an example of how your Category Manager should look once you have renamed all the categories.

Now that all the categories are renamed and unused categories have been deleted, you can return to the Section Manager and remove the FAQs section. Go to the Content menu, and navigate to Section Manager. Once inside the Section Manager, select the box beside the section FAQs, and click Delete in the upper-right corner of the page. This will permanently remove the FAQs section.

Figure 4.5  Category Manager showing number of active articles and articles in trash

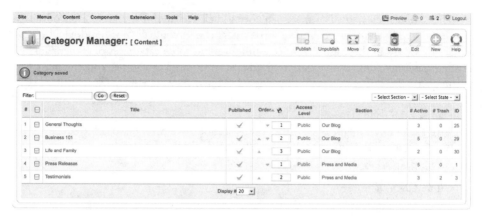

Figure 4.6  Category Manager after editing and renaming all the remaining
categories

The next step is to start to create pages that will be the main landing pages for the
site, such as the first article on the front page, the About Us page, and a Services page.
These items are stand-alone static items that will be specifically linked to a menu, so they
are best left uncategorized so they do not show up in any other layouts other than the
menu item to which they are linked.

Go to the Content menu, and click Article Manager. At the top of the Article
Manager there is an article that is uncategorized, meaning it is not in any section or category. If you don't see the article called Example Pages and Menu Links at the top of the
list of articles in the Article Manager, you can use the filter to find it by searching for
part of the title.

This is the article we will edit to become the article on the front page of the site to
be our introduction to Web visitors. Click the title of the article, or select the box beside
the title and click Edit in the upper-right side to open the article for editing. The Article
Edit screen has quite a few options available, but for beginning purposes, we will only be
covering the most important parts of the screen to get you started in an in-depth way
and giving basic information regarding the more complex items. As you get more familiar with Joomla! and content editing, you will be able to decide whether the complex
items are a benefit to your site.

The first input box is the Title box. This is where the title of your article goes.
Because this page will be the introductory article to our site, we should make the title
something relevant to our site but that does not duplicate our site title, which is typically
the business or Web site name. Some people like to use a witty headline or informational
blurb in the title, making sure it isn't too long.

After editing the title in the Title input box, as shown in Figure 4.7, remove the existing alias so that the alias can autopopulate from the words used in the Title box (1). The
Section drop-down is showing that the article is in the Uncategorized section (2). This

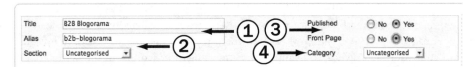

Figure 4.7 Top box of the article-editing screen

article is already published; we are going to change Front Page to Yes so that the article will show on the front page of the site (3), and the category is Uncategorized (4).

Below the top box of the editing screen is the default editor that is installed with Joomla! It's a very popular Web Content Editor called TinyMCE. As shown in Figure 4.8, across the top of the editor you can see icons that represent the different editing capabilities that the editor has, which are very similar to the editing icons in most word processing programs and office suites. Hovering your mouse over each of the icons in the editor toolbars will supply a tool tip that will tell you what the editing function does (1). Underneath the editor toolbars is a large text input box (2). This is where you edit the content that is already in the box describing the example pages, with some text introducing visitors to your site and what your site is about. The next step is using the Media Manager to upload and place an image in the content you have now edited by changing the text.

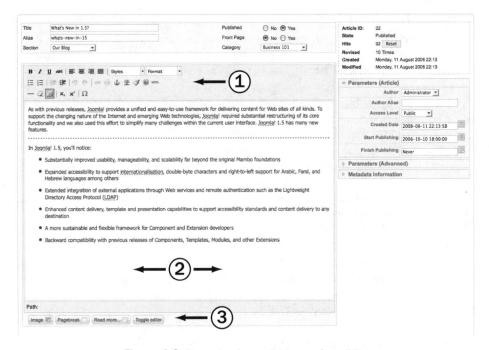

Figure 4.8 Example of an article open for editing

Underneath the content text box are a number of buttons (3).

- *Image:* This is the button for the Media Manager that will allow you to upload images to your Web site; you can also use it to place the images you have uploaded into your Web site, or you can use the "insert picture" icon from the editor toolbar to place the picture.

- *Pagebreak:* This is how you can break very long content items into a number of shorter pages that can be navigated through inside the article itself. Joomla! will automatically create a navigational table of contents for your article using the page breaks to define the sections of the article.

- *Read more:* This is how you put a link to the rest of the article if you want to show some introductory text instead of the full article on every page. Using "Read more" allows you to have teaser text to draw people into your site by encouraging them to click to see more of an article.

- *Toggle editor:* This button toggles the editor between What You See Is What You Get (WYSIWYG) mode, which is a visual layout, and a code view mode, which shows your content item with the HTML tags that direct how the content will display. If you are familiar with simple HTML, you can format your content code using HTML tags.

# Working with the Media Manager and Inserting Images

Inserting pictures in the default installation of Joomla! requires two steps: You have to upload using the Media Manager, and then you have to manipulate the picture properties with the "insert picture" editing button from the editor menu when adding or editing an article.

Clicking the Image button at the bottom of the editor will open the Media Manager, which will allow you to upload images. You can also access the Media Manager from the top main menu by selecting Site and then Media Manager.

To insert an image into an article, you must first have an article open for editing. Once you have opened an article, click the Image button (below the editing text area). You can either upload a new image or select an existing image, as shown in Figure 4.9.

Image Description is the text that will appear if the page is the alternate text that will show upon hovering over an image.

Image Title is the text that will appear if a user moves their mouse pointer over the image. This is also the text that is used for the image caption if the Caption box is selected.

Align is the location of the image on your page. Aligning an image to the left or right will place your picture to either the left or right side of the text that is next to the image, allowing the text to wrap around the image.

To give the image a caption, just select the Caption check box. This will use the text entered in the Image Title field as the image caption, displayed below the image.

Figure 4.9  The editor Media Manager screen

In the full Media Manager that is accessed through the main menu, you can do the three actions outlined here.

- *Upload:* Click the Upload icon to transfer an image/media file from a local computer to the *root/images* directory.
- *Create:* Click the Create icon to create a new directory. This will create a new directory in the *images/stories* directory.
- *Cancel:* Click the Cancel icon to exit the Media Manager and return to the editing screen.

After you have inserted an image using the Image button at the bottom of the screen, you can further manipulate the image using the "Insert/edit image" function accessed through the editor buttons located at the top of the editor screen; just select the image in the article, and click the small picture icon in the toolbar. This will open a dialog box that will offer a few more options to manipulate the image such as dimensions, borders, and vertical and horizontal space. Vertical and horizontal space is the amount of space that is around the outside of the image. Figure 4.10 shows the options available in the "Insert/edit image" dialog box.

On the right side of the articles that are open for editing are the article parameters where you can change the author of an article or use an author alias. An author alias is used to designate an author who cannot be selected from the group of authors who are enabled on a site. The access level allows you to select whether an article is publicly

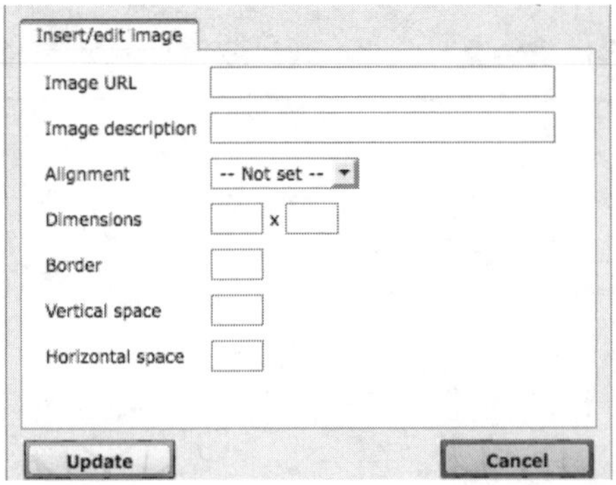

Figure 4.10  The "Insert/edit image" dialog box

viewable, viewable for registered users and above, or seen only by those with special permissions, which is Publisher user level or above. You can alter the date an article was created, set the date you want the article to be viewable on the site, and set when you want the article to be unpublished if you have articles that are valid for only a specific time period.

The advanced parameters for articles are all the global parameters for articles. You can adjust these on an article-by-article basis. To view and set article parameters globally for the entire site, you can assess the Parameters area from the main Article Manager screen by clicking the Parameters icon in the upper-right side of the screen. Most of the parameters are simple toggles to turn something either on or off or to show or hide a given item. The last three items are a bit more complicated. Language allows you to select the language of an article if you have more than one language installed on your site. If you do not select any language, the default language is used. Key Reference is a way to refer to an article with a text string rather than by an ID number. Alternative Read more:text allows you to specify the specific "Read more" text you want to show on any article. The default text is "Read more" followed by the article title.

Metadata Information allows you to set the description, keywords, robots, and author metatags for articles on an article-by-article basis. Using these can be beneficial for search engine optimization.

Once you have finished editing your article and setting any parameters for the article individually, you should save the article. This will bring you back to the main Article Manager screen.

### Tip

If you are editing a particularly long or complicated article, it is best practice to use the Apply button to apply any of the changes you are making periodically. This will prevent you from losing the work you have completed if your session time expires. Apply applies your changes and keeps the article you are working on open so that you can continue to edit the article.

# Menus and Menu Items

The sample data comes with a number of menus already set up and configured with menu modules. You can use these existing managers as examples of how to create the navigational links you need for your site.

## Menu Manager

You can access the Menu Manager by navigating to Menus in the top menu of the control panel and by clicking Menu Manager. The Menu Manager will show the existing menus that were created for the sample data in a table. The table columns show data associated with each menu.

- *Title:* This is the name of the menu. You can edit a menu by clicking its title.
- *Type:* This is the unique name of the menu. Each menu must have a unique name.
- *Menu Items:* This icon, when clicked, will take you to the menu item–editing screen for that specific menu.
- *Published:* This is the number of published individual menu items.
- *Unpublished:* This is the number of unpublished individual menu items.
- *Trashed:* This is the number of individual menu items that have been deleted but not yet removed from the menu trash.
- *Modules:* This is the number of modules a specific menu is associated with. Menus are displayed on a site using modules.
- *ID:* This is a unique number that is assigned to each menu.

### Tip

Do not delete the main menu or the menu that contains your default or home menu item. This will cause the front end of your site to show a 404 error message, meaning the page is not found (this pretty much means all pages will not be found, without a home menu item to reference to). To remedy this, if you have deleted the main menu or default home menu item, simply create a new menu item and assign it as the default menu item, or use an existing menu item and assign it as the default menu item.

## Menu Items

To access a menu's menu items, you can either click the Menu Items icon or navigate to it by using the top menu and going to Menus and then selecting the menu you want to edit from the drop-down list of existing menus.

Once you have selected a menu to edit or add to, the Menu Item Manager screen for that selected menu will open. This will show you a list of existing menu items, if any, and allow you to edit, create new, copy, or move menu items. The copy function is useful if you have a number of menu items that are similar in terms of their parameters, because you can create one menu item with all the parameters set and copy it any number of times, allowing you to quickly edit the menu item name and the article or component item you want it to link to. The move function is also useful if you need to reorganize your menu items and move them from one menu to another.

In the Menu Item Manager, click New in the upper-right side of the screen. The screen that appears will allow you to choose the type of menu you want to create from the four main types.

- *Internal Link:* This is the most common type of menu item type. These are links to content contained on your domain or inside your Web site.
- *External Link:* This allows you to create a menu item type that links to a Web link outside your site.
- *Separator:* This creates a menu item type that acts as a spacer between other menu items. You can apply a graphic or text to it.
- *Alias:* This allows you to link back to an existing menu item.

Note internal links also have the following subtypes available:

- *Articles:* This allows you to create links to individual articles or to groups of articles grouped by section, category, and front page. If you select a group type of section or category, you can choose a blog layout showing the introductory text of the articles of the group or a list layout, which will show the titles and article information in a tabular list.
- *Contacts:* This allows you to create links to a category of contacts or individual contacts. Contacts are configured using the Contact component located in the Components menu.
- *News Feeds:* This allows you to create a menu link to any news feeds you have configured using the News Feed Manager located in the Components menu.
- *Polls:* This allows you to create a menu link to any poll you have created using the Polls component in the Components menu.
- *Search:* This allows you to create a menu link to a detailed search page.
- *User:* This allows you to create a menu link to items related to users on your site such as login, registration, reminder for lost passwords and usernames, user layout (which allows a site administrator to customize greetings for their registered and logged-in user that displays upon login), and user form (which allows users to edit their profile items).
- *Web Links:* This allows you to create a menu link to all the Web links or category of Web links you have created using the Web Links component located in the Components menu. You can also create a menu item for a submission form to allow users to submit Web links to your site.
- *Wrapper:* The wrapper menu item allows you to display an outside page link inside your site using an HTML iframe. Wrapping an external site inside your site can be useful if you want your users to view and be able to navigate another site but still have your site and its navigation available for them to use.

As you add components and extensions, there may be new menu item types that become available that are specific to that component or extension. After you have selected a menu item type, you will be directed to the screen that allows you to configure the menu item and edit the menu item parameters. These parameters change from menu type to menu type.

### Tip

One thing to note is that the advanced parameters allow you to set at the menu level the article parameters discussed in the previous section. If these menu item parameters are changed to be different from the global settings, the menu item parameters will take precedence. Global article parameters are site-wide and can be altered on an article-by-article basis. If altered, the individual article parameters will take precedence. If the menu item type has alterations to the individual or global article parameters, then the menu item type parameters will be the parameters that will be enforced.

## Menu Item Type Layouts

The most commonly used menu item types for articles are single article, category list, category or section blog, and front page. In this section, we will briefly review these menu item types, giving you a quick rundown on some of the basic parameters for menu items that are common through all the menu item types.

### Blog Layout

The blog layouts will allow you to set up a page that has the introductory text from a number of articles (or content items) in one combined view. They will include a "Read more" link to the full article. As shown in Figure 4.11, you can select the category or section you want to display, specify whether you want the section or category description and image (which would have been set up in the section or category itself) to show and indicate how you would like the articles to be displayed. # Leading is the number of articles that are at the top of the page and featured in full width even if you are using more than one column to display the other articles. # Intro is the number of articles that have their introductory text showing with a "Read more" link to the full article (if you have chosen that option). Intro articles will be spread over the number of columns

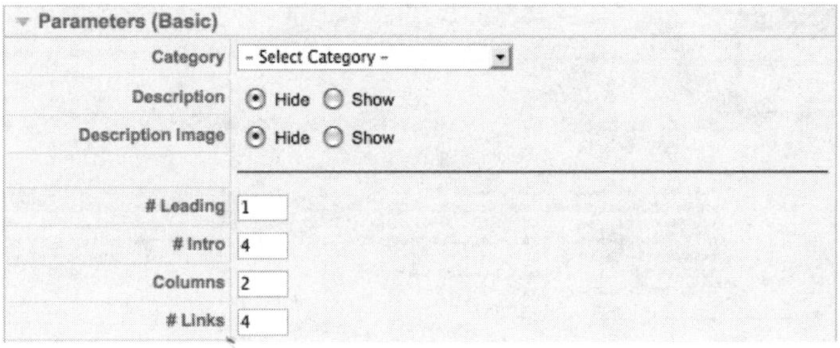

Figure 4.11  Blog layout basic parameters

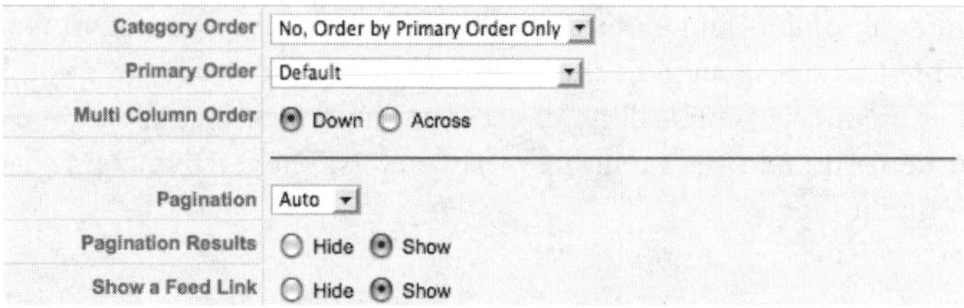

| Category Order | No, Order by Primary Order Only ▾ |
| Primary Order | Default ▾ |
| Multi Column Order | ◉ Down  ○ Across |
| | |
| Pagination | Auto ▾ |
| Pagination Results | ○ Hide  ◉ Show |
| Show a Feed Link | ○ Hide  ◉ Show |

Figure 4.12  Blog layout advanced parameters

specified in the Columns parameter. # Links is the number of links to the remaining articles that may be in that section or category that you want people to be able to access from that page.

Figure 4.12 shows the advanced parameters. You can set the order of the articles, set whether the article order will flow across the columns or down the columns, and set pagination (which is the numerical linking to the other pages if the number of articles available is greater than the number of articles that are shown on the page). Also, you can show or hide an RSS feed.

A blog layout will yield a page that appears as in Figure 4.13. Experiment with different options for your layout and other parameters to understand how they change the display.

## Category List Layout

Category list layouts allow you to show a list of available articles in a category in a table. Figure 4.14 shows the basic parameters you can set in list layouts such as the category, the number of links you want to display, whether the table should have headings that denote what the data shown in the columns relate to, whether the article date will be shown, and the format of the date. You can also set the filter or sorting function on the

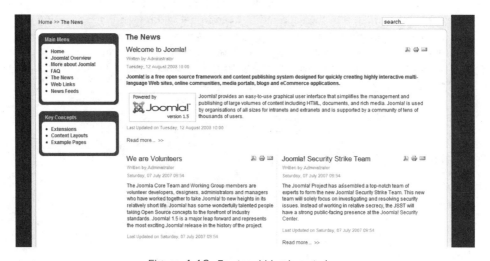

Figure 4.13  Front-end blog layout view

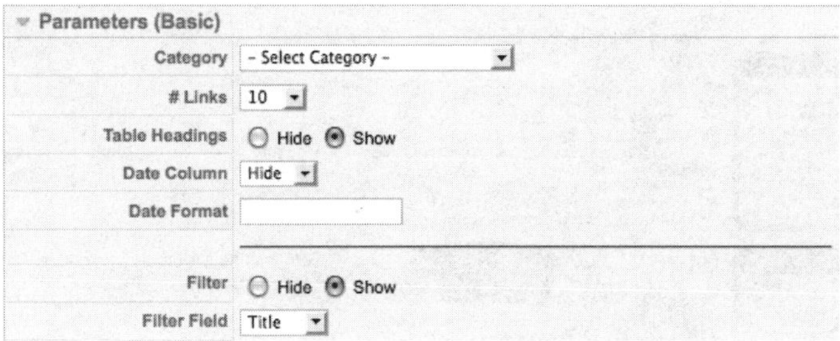

Figure 4.14  Category list layout basic parameters

table column to be hidden or to be shown and select which column you want the filter to be active on. The advanced parameters for the list layouts are similar to the blog layout, allowing you to specify the order of articles, pagination, and feed link.

Figure 4.15 shows a category list layout as it would appear on the front end of your site.

### Section List Layout

The section list layout presents a link list of categories in a section. Clicking the category name yields a category list layout for that category. As shown in the previous Figure 4.14, the menu options are similar to those for a category list layout except that you choose a section rather than a category. Figure 4.16 shows the appearance of a section list on the front end of your site.

### Front Page Layout

The front page layout is similar to the idea of a front page in a print newspaper. It displays selected articles from a number of different sections or categories in a blog-style layout. To place items on the front page, when editing an article, set the Front Page parameter to Yes, as shown in Figure 4.17.

You can manage the order of front page articles using the Front Page Manager, as shown in Figure 4.18. Change the numbers in the order column to the order you want (articles with lower numbers will be displayed first). Then click the disk icon to save the ordering.

Figure 4.15  Category list layout view on the front end

Figure 4.16  Section list layout front-end view

When making a front page menu link, you will have the same options for layout as you have in blog layouts. In the sample data, the Front Page menu item is set as the home or default page. You can tell this because it has a yellow star in the Default column of the Menu Item Manager (see Figure 4.19). You can make any menu link the default page, but it is important to always have a default item, because this is what will display when a visitor visits your *domain.com* without any other page information. If you do not have a default page, your site will not render, and visitors will see a 404 "page not found" error page.

Figure 4.17  Order of articles on the front page of your site

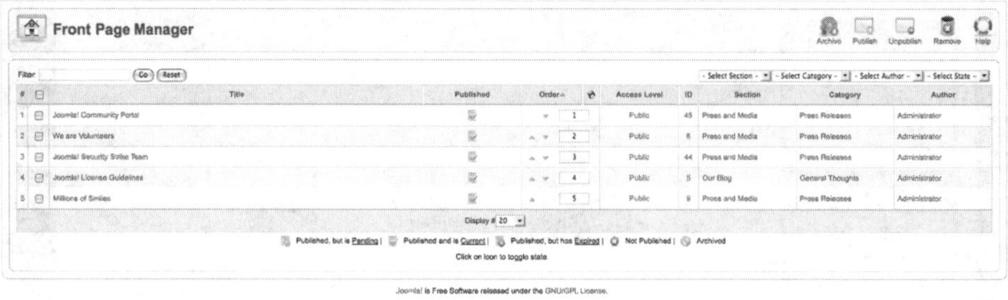

Figure 4.18  Placing an article on the front page of your site

Figure 4.19  Menu Item Manager showing the default menu item Home

If you do accidentally delete the default menu item, simply create another menu item by clicking New in the Menu Item Manager and selecting the menu item type of Article and Front Page Blog Layout as the specific article menu item type. Figure 4.20 shows where this is located in the New Menu Item selection screen.

Figure 4.20  Selecting Front Page Blog Layout for the menu item type

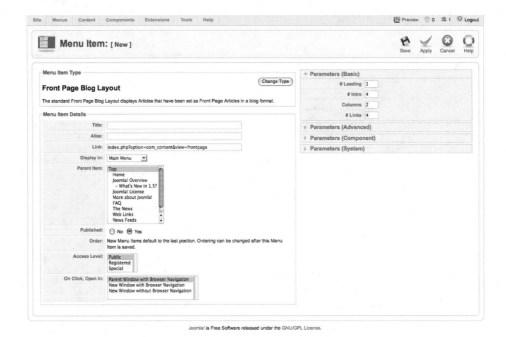

Figure 4.21  Front Page Blog Layout menu item–editing screen

Once you have selected Front Page Blog Layout, you will be presented with a menu item–editing screen that is similar to the other blog layout menu items. Figure 4.21 shows the options that are available for the Front Page Blog Layout option.

## Conclusion

The basic techniques demonstrated in this chapter on how to work with menu items, how to work with content, and how to organize and structure your content are just a starting point. The Joomla! forum and the documentation sites provide a wealth of in-depth resources that can give you insight on how to plan your content structure, as well as assist with any stumbling blocks you may encounter. Chapter 5 will demonstrate how to work with one of the default templates, how to modify the color scheme, and how to customize the images to suit your needs. Chapter 6 will discuss extensions, components, modules, plugins, and languages, with information on installing them and recommendations for some of the best Joomla! extensions available.

# Customizing Templates and the Basics of Templates for Joomla!

Joomla! templates control the look and feel of your site by controlling colors, typography, images, and other elements of design. This chapter will take you through customizing the default template called Beez, and it will provide information on the basic files that make up a very simple Joomla! template. What this chapter will not do is teach PHP, HTML, and CSS, because all three topics are entire book subjects themselves. Also, this chapter will talk about the many available resources the community has regarding template clubs and custom template providers and how you can take the look and layout from a standard static HTML Web site and turn that file into a Joomla! template.

A basic search in search engines for *Joomla templates* brings up thousands of results, which is good news for nontechnical people and those who want a quick and easy solution. There are thousands of templates to choose from, ranging from templates that are very simple to templates that are very high design and those that come with added functionality through extensions. In addition, a massive number of template clubs/professional template developers offer templates at reasonable prices. Along with Joomla!-specific templates, there are thousands of template resources that offer HTML templates that can be converted into the Joomla! templates easily if you know what you need to replace. Joomla! itself comes with three templates already installed ready to use.

- *Milkyway:* A standard three-column layout with left and right columns that collapse, meaning the columns will not display if they have no content in them, allowing the main body to expand into the space where they would be. It has a rounded corner design with six bold color schemes to choose from—blue, red, orange, green, black, and white—as well as configuration settings that will allow you to choose the width of your site.

- *JA Purity:* A standard three-column layout with a right column that is configurable to collapse, allowing the main body content to expand into where it would be. It offers the ability to set the total width of the body of the Web site in a number of different ways, and you can choose a black, blue, green, or red main color, along with whether the secondary elements are light or dark in theme.

- *Beez:* A standard three-column layout with left and right columns that will collapse, meaning the left and right columns will not display if they have no content in them, allowing the main body content to expand into the space where they would be. It was designed to be a template that uses Web and accessibility standards, which also demonstrates the new function in Joomla! 1.5 of being able to easily change the default layouts without changing core files by using template overrides. It has one color scheme that uses a pink/purple monochromatic color scheme with gray as an accent color. It is designed to be a fluid width with a maximum width of 1,000 pixels, which means it will contract and adjust to fit screen resolutions that are less than 1,000 pixels wide.

## Customizing the Default Template Beez

Built into Joomla's administrator back end is the ability to edit template files without any other tools or additional software. With that being said, having a plain-text editor can make it much easier to edit the files, because you can use the added functionality of "find and replace" to edit multiple instances of a change at one time.

Some examples of good text editors to use are Notepad++ (a GPL licensed and free text editor for Windows) and TextWrangler (a free text editor for Mac). A search in any of the search engines will help you find those software programs to download. Follow the instructions to install them. For the demonstrations in this chapter, we will be referencing TextWrangler because we work on a Mac. Windows users should be able to find the editor functions that are referenced in basically the same steps. If you have difficulty, please reference the help files that come with the software you are using.

Another helpful program to use is a File Transfer Protocol (FTP) program. FTP programs allow you to connect to your Web site's server, allowing you to view the files that are on your server and download and upload files. A good example of a free and open source FTP program is FileZilla. It works on both Windows and Mac computers.

Also helpful when editing and designing templates is an extension for the Firefox browser called Firebug. Firebug allows you to examine the code of a Web page to see what code is affecting areas or items on a page. It also allows you to edit this code live while you are viewing it to test what your changes will affect. If you do not use Firefox as a browser but plan on doing a lot of template editing, it is a good idea to have a copy of Firefox installed. Internet Explorer has some tools that can aid in Web site development, as do Chrome and Safari. It is also helpful to have multiple browsers installed on your computer to help you see whether your Web site is consistent across various browsers. There are also some paid services for comparing renderings across browsers, but they are not more useful for basic sites than having the major browsers installed on your own computer.

The first step to customizing any default template that is distributed with Joomla! is to make a copy of template to work with. Making a copy of the template and giving it a new name will prevent any changes you make from being overwritten by any updates that may be done to the template when you perform and update to Joomla! To make a copy of a default template, you can use the same File Manger that should be part of your hosting control panel, as was used in Chapter 3 when installing and configuring Joomla!, to create a copy of the Beez template files and rename the new template to a name of your choosing.

Log in to your hosting account, and navigate to your File Manager. This should open a directory listing of your Web site files. Navigate to your template folder. Once you are in the template folder, use the New Folder (1) function, as shown in Figure 5.1, to create a new folder for your template files. Name this folder something that is relevant to you. In Figure 5.1, the name used is *mynewtemplate* (2).

Once you have created the new folder for your new template, all the files from the Beez template need to be copied to the *mynewtemplate* folder. Navigate to the *beez* template folder. Inside that folder, you will see a series of folders and files, as shown in Figure 5.2. Using the "Select all" function (1), you can select all the files and folders inside the *beez*

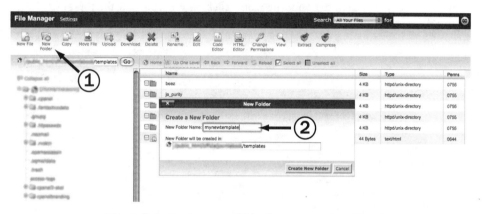

Figure 5.1  Create a new folder for your template files.

Figure 5.2  Copy Beez template files to the new folder, mynewtemplate.

folder, and then using the Copy function (2), you will be shown a new pop-up window that asks you to select the directory you want to copy the files to. Enter the name of your new template folder as shown (3), and then click Copy File(s).

Once all the files from *beez* have been copied to the *mynewtemplate* folder, the last step to finish duplicating the template is to rename the template in the *templateDetails.xml* file. You can edit this file using the Edit function in File Manager by navigating to the *mynewtemplate* folder and then selecting the *templateDetails.xml* file. You can click the Edit button on the top File Manager menu, or you can right-click the file and select Edit from the context menu, as shown in Figure 5.3. This will open the file for editing.

When the file has opened in the editor, look for the `<name>beez</name>` line near the top of the file. Figure 5.4 shows where you change the word `beez` to `mynewtemplate` in the XML file.

After you have changed the template name, click Save Changes at the top of the File Manager Edit screen. This will save the file and return you to the File Manager.

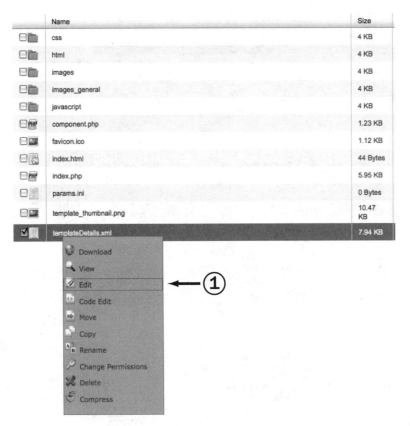

Figure 5.3  Opening the templateDetails.xml file for editing to change the name of the template

```
<?xml version="1.0" encoding="utf-8"?>
<!DOCTYPE install PUBLIC "-//Joomla! 1.5//DTD template 1.0//EN" "http://www.joomla.org/xml/dtd/1.5/template-install.dtd">
<install version="1.5" type="template">
    <name>mynewtemplate</name>
    <creationDate>19 February 2007</creationDate>
    <author>Angie Radtke/Robert Deutz</author>
    <authorEmail>joomla@run-digital.com</authorEmail>
    <authorUrl>http://www.run-digital.com</authorUrl>
    <copyright></copyright>
    <license>GNU/GPL</license>
    <version>1.0.0</version>
    <description>Accessible template for Joomla 1.5</description>
    <files>
        <filename>css/layout.css</filename>
        <filename>css/position.css</filename>
        <filename>css/template.css</filename>
        <filename>css/ieonly.css</filename>
        <filename>css/ie7only.css</filename>
        <filename>css/print.css</filename>
        <filename>css/general.css</filename>
        <filename>css/index.html</filename>
        <filename>css/template_rtl.css</filename>
```

Figure 5.4  Changing the template name in the templateDetails.xml file

When you install Joomla!, the default template that is active is Milkyway, configured to use the blue color scheme. Log in to the administrator back end. In the upper-right corner of the screen there is a small menu/indicator bar, as shown in Figure 5.5 and detailed here.

- *Preview:* Clicking this will open a new tab or browser window, depending on your browser, to show the front end of the Web site.

- *Mail icon with a number beside it:* The number will indicate whether there are any messages for the super administrator(s). Clicking the number will take you to the Messages screen.

- *People icon with a number beside it:* The number will indicate how many people are logged into the site at the current time. You can also see exactly who is logged into the site and what their user group is by clicking the Logged in Users information box located on the control panel.

- *Logout:* Clicking this will log you out of the administrator back end.

In this chapter, we rely heavily on being able to switch between the administrator back end of the Web site and viewing the front end of the Web site to assess the changes we are going to be making. Click Preview to open another browser window or tab in your browser, showing the front end of your site. It should show the Web site you have configured with the edited sample content and the template Milkyway with the blue color scheme. Return to the window or tab that shows your administrator back end.

Once you are back to the administrator control panel, we will start by changing the default template from Milkyway to your copy of Beez *mynewtemplate* by navigating to the Extensions menu and clicking Template Manager. This will open the Template Manager screen, as shown in Figure 5.6. To select a template, you must select it by clicking the

Figure 5.5  Menu/indicator bar

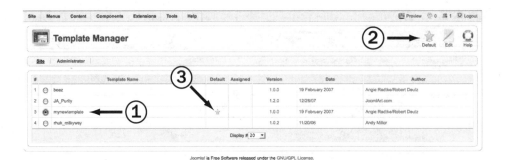

Figure 5.6  Template Manager screen

radio button beside the template name (1). Then you can select the action you want to perform in the upper-right corner of the screen by clicking Default or Edit (2).

- *Default:* Makes the template you have selected the default template of your site.
- *Edit:* Takes you to the template editing screen, showing you the editable parameters of the template if it has them. Also allows you to assign a template to a specific menu item and gives you the option of opening the actual template files for editing.

At this time, click the radio button beside the copy of Beez *mynewtemplate*, and then click Default. The default template is signified by a gold star in the Default column (3). There can be only one default template at any given time.

## Beez Color Scheme

Once you have made your new template the default template, return to the tab or window that shows the front end of your Web site, and refresh or reload the page. You should now see the copy of the Beez template applied to the Web site.

Beez uses a monochromatic color scheme in a pink/purple color spectrum, along with some gray/charcoal accents, as shown in Figure 5.7. (If this image is being shown as a black-and-white image in your copy of this book, please go to *The Official Joomla! Book* Web site at *http://officialjoomlabook.com* to view the color version of this image.)

As you hover your mouseover menus and links on the screen, you can see certain effects such as color changes when you "roll over" a menu item (switches to gray) or that link colors change to indicate that you are hovering over a link (switches to white text on a pink/purple background).

Chapter 2 discussed color schemes, what they are, and how to design a color scheme. For demonstration purposes, we will be changing the Beez color scheme from a pink/purple monochromatic color scheme with gray accents to a blue color scheme, leaving the gray accents, as shown in Figure 5.8. (If this image is being shown as a black-and-white image in your copy of this book, please go to *The Official Joomla! Book* Web site at *http://officialjoomlabook.com* to view the color version of this image.)

# BEEZ COLOR SCHEME

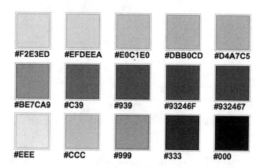

Figure 5.7  Beez color chart

# BLUE COLOR SCHEME

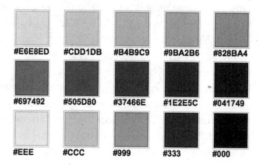

Figure 5.8  Blue monochromatic color chart

From the administrator back end, navigate to the Extensions menu, and click Template Manager. Click the radio button beside the name of the new template, and then click the Edit icon in the upper-right corner of the Template Manager. This will open the template-editing screen, as shown in Figure 5.9.

The template edit screen has a number of menu items.

- *Preview:* This allows you to preview your site inside the Joomla! administrator back end. Once in the preview screen, you have the ability to click Back to return to the template-editing screen.

- *Edit HTML:* This opens the Template HTML Editor, which shows the template's *index.php* file in a editable text box. Be very careful when editing the *index.php* file. Missing code or incorrectly placed code can break your site. If you do want to edit the *index.php* file, it is a good idea to make a copy of the code it contains so that you can return it to the original state if it is not working correctly after editing. One way to do this is to copy the whole file into a file in your text editor

Figure 5.9  Template-editing screen

(not a word processor). The menu options available are Save, which will save your edits if you have made them and return you to the Template Edit screen; Apply, which will apply your changes saving them without returning you to the template-editing screen; and Cancel, which will return you to the main template-editing screen.

- *Edit CSS:* This opens the Template CSS Editor, showing a list of all available CSS files that are in a given template. You can select a CSS file to edit by clicking the radio button beside a CSS file's name and then clicking Edit. This opens that specific CSS file for editing in a text input box. It is a good idea to make a copy of the CSS code it contains so that you can return it to the original state if your template is not working or looking like it should after you have edited it. You can do this by copying the whole file into a file in your text editor (not a word processor). Once you have finished editing the CSS file, you can save your changes and return to the Template CSS Editor screen; apply your changes (which does not return you to the Template CSS Editor screen), allowing you to continue making changes; or cancel, which returns you to the Template CSS Editor screen.

- *Save:* This saves any changes you may have made to menu assignment or parameters and returns you to the Template Manager screen.

- *Apply:* This applies your changes by saving them without returning you to the Template Manager screen.

- *Close:* This closes the template-editing screen and returns you to the Template Manager screen.

- *Details:* This shows the name of the template being edited and a description. The description may include developer notes and instructions.

- *Menu Assignment:* This shows the available menu items a template can be assigned to if that function is allowed. Because we have set the copy of Beez to be our default template, it cannot be assigned to a menu item, because by default it is assigned to all of them already.

- *Parameters:* This is where a template developer will put any configurable parameters for their template such as choosing a color scheme if more than one is available, the width of the template, or any number of options that they may have included in the template. Some templates have very extensive parameters that can be set, and the template developer usually includes help files or instructions as to what each parameter does and how you can set it.

A lot of templates use CSS to control the color scheme. Those are the files we are going to edit to change the Web site to a blue scheme. Figure 5.10 shows what the template looks like before editing.

Figure 5.11 shows the colors that are going to be changed from pink to blue in the CSS files. Colors in CSS are represented by hex codes, which is a number (#) symbol and a six-digit code represented by a combination of the letters A–F and the numerals 0–9. (If this image is being shown as a black-and-white image in your copy of this book,

Figure 5.10  Beez before editing

## COLOR SCHEME CHANGES

Figure 5.11  CSS color changes to change the pinks to blues

please go to *The Official Joomla! Book* Web site at *http://officialjoomlabook.com* to view the color version of this image.)

From the Template Edit screen, click Edit CSS. This will show a list of eight CSS files that can be edited.

- *general.css:* This contains the CSS for general elements that are used throughout the Web site such as buttons, tool tips, and system messages.

  #F2E3ED: Three instances to change to #E6E8ED.

  #93246F: Nine instances to change to #1E2E5C.

- *ie7only.css:* This style sheet is used to control how Internet Explorer 7 specifically displays some elements. It does not have any instances of color that we will be changing.

- *ieonly.css:* This style sheet controls how all versions of Internet Explorer specifically display some elements. It has two instances of color that we will be changing.

  #CC3399 (same color as #C39, just written in a longer form): One instance to change to #505D80.

  #93246F: One instance to change to #1E2E5C.

- *layout.css:* This style sheet is used to control the look of the layout for the template. There are 61 instances of color that we will be changing.

  #F2E3ED: Four instances to change to #E6E8ED.

  #EFDEEA: Seven instances to change to #CDD1DB.

#E0C1E0: Six instances to change to #B4B9C9.

#D4A7C5: Two instances to change to #828BA4.

#BE7CA9: One instance to change to #697492.

#C39: Eight instances to change to #505D80.

#939: Two instances to change to #37466E.

#93246F: Twenty-six instances to change to #1E2E5C.

#932467: Five instances to change to #041749.

- *position.css:* This style sheet controls the position of the main elements of the template such as where the columns are located and the widths of them. There are four instances of color that we will be changing.

  #F2E3ED: One instance to change to #E6E8ED.

  #EFDEEA: One instance to change to #CDD1DB.

  #DBB0CD: One instance to change to #9BA2B6.

  #D4A7C5: One instance to change to #828BA4.

- *print.css:* This is the style sheet that controls how a printed page will look when the print item function is enabled for an article. There is one instance of color that we will be changing.

  #93246F: One instance to change to #1E2E5C.

- *template.css:* This is the style sheet that controls how a few specific elements, the content pane, and the tool tips are formatted. There are no instances of color to change in this style sheet.

- *template_rtl.css:* This is the style sheet that changes the template text from reading left to right to reading right to left. There are five instances of color that we will be changing.

  #EFDEEA: One instance to change to #CDD1DB.

  #BE7CA9: One instance to change to #697492.

  #939: One instance to change to #37466E.

  #93246F: One instance to change to #1E2E5C.

  #CC3399 (same color as #C39 just written in a longer form): One instance to change to #505D80.

Once all the CSS color changes have been done and saved, the template will show the blue color scheme with only a few more changes to images to complete the switch to blue. Figure 5.12 shows what the template looks like after editing. (If this image is being shown as a black-and-white image in your copy of this book, please go to *The Official Joomla! Book* Web site at *http://officialjoomlabook.com* to view the color version of this image.)

Figure 5.12  Beez after editing the color hex values in the CSS files, leaving only images to replace or remove to complete the color scheme change

## Adding Your Own Logo

All the images in the *images* folder need to be changed to match the new blue color scheme. A number of options are available to change these images, such as downloading all the images and replacing or removing the colors that do not match in your image editor of choice, or you can create new images. An important thing to note if you create your own images is that the naming convention of your new images has to be the same as the existing images, because they are linked in the various CSS files. Also, the dimensions of the images should stay the same to keep the look and layout consistent. Images that are not the proper dimensions may look skewed or may break the layout and move elements out of place.

Figure 5.13 shows the images used in the Beez template unedited.

The logo image is called *logo.gif*. This is the image you must change to include your own logo. The dimensions of the *logo.gif* image are 300 pixels by 97 pixels. Those are the dimensions and filename you should use for your logo file. (This is the simplest method. You can also edit the filename using the HTML editor.)

You can create and edit image files using a number of programs. Aviary is an online image-editing software suite located at Aviary.com. You can upload your images to edit or create new images using its online service and then download your edited or created image for use on your Web site. Picassa is an photo-editing program you can download that is distributed by Google and is mostly used for editing photos and photo galleries. It has an excellent feature that allows you to batch process a group of images at one time. Adobe Photoshop is a very popular commercial image-editing program. It has a lot of functions available in it including batch editing and replacing color. Gimp is an open source alternative to Adobe Photoshop.

Figure 5.14 shows the images edited to match the blue color scheme.

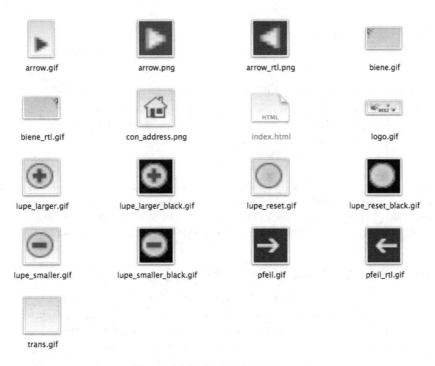

Figure 5.13  Original Beez images

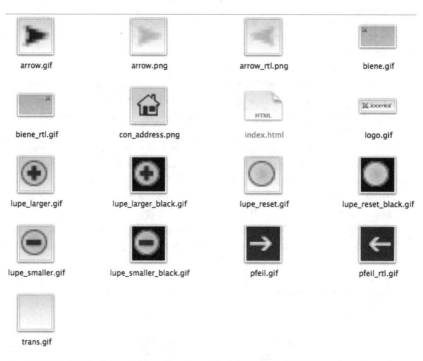

Figure 5.14  Original Beez images edited to match the blue color scheme

Figure 5.15 shows the final template switched to a blue color scheme with all the edits complete, including images. (If this image is being shown as a black-and-white image in your copy of this book, please go to *The Official Joomla! Book* Web site at *http://officialjoomlabook.com* to view the color version of this image.)

> **Tip**
>
> It is important to always back up your template files before you begin to edit them in case you need to revert a change you have made. This is especially important when modifying the default files because these may be changed as part of a Joomla! update. Such changes, though rare in Joomla! 1.5, can cause your customization to be overwritten.

# The Basics of Joomla! Templates

Joomla! is designed to effectively allow people to update or change the look and feel of their Web site in an easy-to-manage way. A template change can be as easy as installing a new template that is already created and then assigning it as the default template for the site. Another great function is the ability to install templates and assign them to specific menu items, giving flexibility to show specific content in a specifically styled way through assigned templates.

**Figure 5.15** Final changes complete to a blue color scheme including images edited to include a new logo

## Design Styling and CSS

Joomla!'s template system allows for a lot of flexibility when it comes to the look and feel of a Web site. It also makes it easy to change the design and style of an entire Web site by simply switching the template. The Cascading Style Sheets (CSS) language is the main technique used to design the visual appearance of Joomla! Web sites.

A helpful tool to use to help in understanding how CSS works is Firebug (an extension for the Firefox and Chrome browsers). Firebug allows you to actively look at the CSS that has been applied to an element of a Web page, adjust that CSS, and preview how the changes you have made will affect the elements on the page.

Creating a CSS style requires two parts to complete the syntax: a selector, which is the (X)HTML element, ID, or class you are wanting to style; and a declaration, which is how you want to style the selector. Common (X)HTML selectors found in a style sheet would be headings such as `h1` or paragraphs, which in HTML are indicated by a `p`. Joomla! has a number of specific classes such as the component heading, which is indicated in style sheets as `.componentheading`. Some designers such as the designers of Beez divide their CSS across many individual style sheets or organize them in terms of the items that they style, such as the position of elements, or if a style is only pertinent to a specific browser, while other designers use one style sheet for the entire template.

A great place to find out more about CSS is the W3schools.com Web site, which gives excellent explanations of how CSS works and how to use it with hands-on tutorials. There are also a number of great software programs that can be helpful when working with CSS such as CSSEdit by MacRabbit for Mac and StyleMaster by WestCiv for both Windows and Mac.

## Simple Template Files

Templates for Joomla! can be very simple all the way to very complex. All templates have some basics that are consistent throughout all templates. In the *templates* folder, you will find the *rhuk_milkyway*, *beez*, and *ja_purity* folders, representing each of the three templates included in Joomla! 1.5. Each of these is structured in the same way. The structure is outlined in the following list.

- *index.html:* This is a blank index file that aids in securing the template directory.
- *index.php:* This is the file that contains the structure of the site, including the code that pulls the Joomla! content into various elements.
- *templateDetails.xml:* This file contains all the information about the template itself, the author, and the version of Joomla! template it is for, as well as a listing of all files and folders that are contained within the template and the positions used by the various Joomla! elements.
- *images folder:* This is the folder that will hold all the images that are used in the template. It should also contain a blank *index.html* file to secure the directory.
- *css folder:* This is the folder that will hold all the template style sheets. It should also contain a blank *index.html* file to secure the directory. Many templates contain multiple CSS files.
- *template.css:* This file should be in the *css* folder, and it will hold all the template CSS code.
- *favicon.ico:* This is an icon file that you can customize to suit your page that shows in browser address bars and when viewing favorites or bookmarks. You can create favicons online using a number of different services such as www.htmlkit.com or www.dynamicdrive.com.

## Template Positions

Template positions are statements inside an *index.php* file that indicate where Joomla! elements will be output in the file. They are implemented using a statement called a *jdoc statement*. Some examples of jdoc statements that you will find in the *index.php* file of your template are as follows.

- `<jdoc:include type="head" />`: This tells the file to get the output of the head information such as page tile, description, and keywords. These are not visible in the body of the Web page.

- `<jdoc:include type="modules" name="user3" />`: This gets the output of the modules that are assigned to the position of *user3*. You can use the positions that are defined in any template, or you can create your own and create a new jdoc statement in your *index.php* file in the place where you want the output of the position to be displayed.

- `<jdoc:include type="message" />`: This gets the output of any messages that have been defined, such as not being authorized, an action has been completed, or there has been a problem with an action. It is usually placed above the component output so that it is easily seen by the users of the site.

- `<jdoc:include type="component" />`: This gets the output of the main content of a site such as the articles of content; it also is where the output of any installed components is outputted, such as Web links or forms.

- `<jdoc:include type="modules" name="debug" />`: This gets the output of the information that can be used to debug a site and is turned on in the global configuration. Most times you will leave debugging off unless your site is in development.

For most people managing a Web site, the most important of these statements are the ones that create named positions to which modules are assigned. There are some position names that are commonly used in Joomla! templates. They are as follows:

- `top`
- `left`
- `right`
- `breadcrumb`
- `user1`
- `user2`
- `user3`
- `user4`
- `syndicate`
- `debug`
- `footer`

However, it is important to know that the names of positions may not accurately reflect where they are on the page. There are several ways to see where positions are actually located. In the Template Manager when you have selected a template to edit, there is Preview link. Clicking this will show you the template with the positions overlaid. In the front end, you can visit any page and add *&tp=1* to the URL, and the positions will be displayed. Finally, you can read the *index.php* file. This has the advantage of helping you understand how the code works.

You can control how modules are outputted by adding to a jdoc statement the module chrome, in other words, by adding `style ="chromestyle"` to the jdoc statement. An example is

```
<jdoc:include type="modules" name="user1" style="chromestyle" />
```

There are six default module chrome styles, and Joomla! offers the flexibility with its templating system to create your own custom chrome styles. The six default module chrome styles are as follows:

- `<jdoc:include type="modules" name="user1" style="rounded" />` rounded: This wraps the module output in a series of container `divs` that you can style with CSS to show rounded corners or other wrapped edge styles. This is the chrome used in the default Milkyway template for the rounded corners on all the modules.

- `<jdoc:include type="modules" name="user1" style="table" />` table: This wraps the module in a table-based layout.

- `<jdoc:include type="modules" name="user1" style="horiz" />` horiz: This wraps the module in a horizontal table-based layout.

- `<jdoc:include type="modules" name="user1" style="xhtml" />` xhtml: This wraps the module in a `div`-based layout.

- `<jdoc:include type="modules" name="user1" style="none" />` none: This strips items from the module such as title; it presents the module similarly to the `horiz` style but without the table-based layout.

- `<jdoc:include type="modules" name="user1" style="outline" />` outline: This wraps the module in the display layout used for previewing modules.

You can also create your own module chrome style by creating a general module override for your template using a *modules.php* file. Examples of this can be seen in each of the templates distributed with the core. You can also create specific overrides for individual modules using the layout override system, which we will explore in the next section.

## Template Overrides

A new development in Joomla! 1.5 is the addition of the ability to use template overrides. Template overrides allow anyone to change how the components and modules display by overriding their display layouts with new layouts in the template. Overrides work by creating a file with the same name as a file in the core of Joomla! and placing it in the appropriate location in your template directory. Joomla! will always check to see whether your template has a replacement for a core layout file when it brings together your template and your database to create the Web pages that your site visitors see.

These overrides are usually contained in a folder called *html* in an individual template's directory. This is demonstrated in the Beez template. Beez was the first template included with Joomla! that utilized the ability to override the default layouts and has served as the model that many template developers use to create their own override packs.

Beez contains a large number of overrides for the Joomla! core components and modules. The content overrides are a representative example. The basic structure of overrides of articles in the Beez template is as follows.

- */templates:* This is your main template directory that contains all the installed front-end templates available to use on your site.
- */beez:* This is the *beez* template directory.
- */html:* This is the *html* directory inside the *beez* directory.
- */com_content:* This is the directory that matches the name of the component you are want to override (in this instance, *com-content* is the component that controls how content is output and displayed).
- */articles:* This is the directory that contains the files that control the view.
- *default.php:* This is the file that actually does the overriding because it is the file that contains the code for the view for the default layout of an individual article.
- *form.php:* This is the file that actually does the overriding because it is the file that contains the code for the view for the article submission form.

A number of template clubs offer their own specialized override packs for their templates, and most commercial templates will include overrides of various types. Because Joomla! is open source, you can make your own overrides and add them to any template. This lets you have a great deal of flexibility and control over how your site appears.

## Conclusion

Templates are an extremely complex subject, and this chapter has touched on only a portion of what Joomla! templates can actually achieve. The template forum at *http://forum.joomla.org* is a very active forum where questions regarding XHTML, HTML, PHP, and CSS are asked and answered by the hundreds every month. Although creating your own template if you are a new user can be intimidating, there are thousands of templates available to choose from, be they templates from template subscription clubs, individual templates offered by developers, or templates that have been developed by users and shared with the community. The Joomla! Resources Directory (JRD) offers many templates and Joomla! professionals who can assist you in creating the perfect template for your site's needs. There are thousands of tutorials on creating Web pages. There are also HTML/CSS layout tutorials with which you can build your Joomla! template by using the HTML/CSS as a base and then "Joomlafying" it by converting it to a PHP file and adding the appropriate `<jdoc>` statements where you want your content to display.

# 6

# The Basics of Joomla! Extensions: Components, Modules, Plugins, and Languages

A lot of the power behind Joomla! comes from the ability for developers and users to extend and build on its framework and functionalities. Chapter 1 described what extensions are and defined components, modules, and plugins. Installable language packs are another extension type; they translate the text used throughout Joomla! and in components, modules, and plugins into other languages.

Joomla! comes with a number of built-in extensions such as the Web Links component, the Latest News module, and the TinyMCE editor plugin. You can extend the functionality of your site by installing additional extensions that are produced by independent developers. This chapter will discuss best practices in using the core extensions, choosing additional extensions, using the Joomla! Extension Directory, and installing extensions, as well as give you recommendations for some very useful extensions that every site can benefit from or that are extremely popular in the Joomlasphere.

## Core Joomla! Extensions

The extensions that are included with a basic Joomla! installation provide everything you need to create a basic Web site.

## Components

Joomla! comes with four major extensions used to produce content: Content, Contact, Web Links, and News Feeds. In addition, Search, Banners, and Polls produce front-end displays, but these are most often presented in modules. It is a good idea to understand and use these extensions first, before adding new ones for specialized purposes. This will keep the management of your site as simple as possible, and you can be assured that these have had the widest possible testing and support by the Joomla! project developers.

## Content

We covered the use of the Content extension in Chapter 3. In this section, we will highlight one additional but vital function: the ability to create articles from the front end of your site. This is extremely powerful because it allows you to enable users who do not have access to your site administrator to create and manage articles.

In Joomla! 1.5, each user is assigned to one user group. The following are what controls the ability to work on articles in the front end.

- Authors can create new articles and edit any articles they have written.
- Editors can do anything an author can do but can also edit articles written by other people.
- Publishers can do anything an editor can do but can also publish an article, which means that it is available for visitors to your site to see (assuming that the access level is set to Public).
- Managers, administrators, and super administrators have the same rights as publishers in the front end.

By utilizing the sample data that has example menus already created and logging into the front end of the site, you will see a menu that is visible only to logged-in users. Clicking the Submit Article link will open a blank editing screen. Using the editor is the same here as in the administrator. As the administrator, you can insert images, a "Read more" link, and page breaks. You select a category, whether an article is assigned to the front page, and whether it should be published. If you want to save your work but are not ready to publish yet, you should change the state to unpublished. Users who are authors or editors will not have the option to publish an article. This is useful when you want to have content reviewed or proofread before it appears on your public site. If you want your users to be able to publish their articles, you can make them publishers; however, be aware that this will allow them to edit and change the publication status of other articles in your site. Figure 6.1 shows what the front-end article-editing screen looks like when submitting a new article, as would be shown to a publisher who has the permissions to publish articles.

Users who are allowed to edit an existing article will see an edit icon when they view a page with that article (this could be the article itself, a category or section blog, or a category list). Clicking the icon will open the same editing screen.

The Content component gives you many options. Most importantly, within each article, section description, and category description, you have the flexibility to design your content the way you desire it.

The Content component offers the widest variety of ways to present your content, called *layouts*, that can be linked from menus.

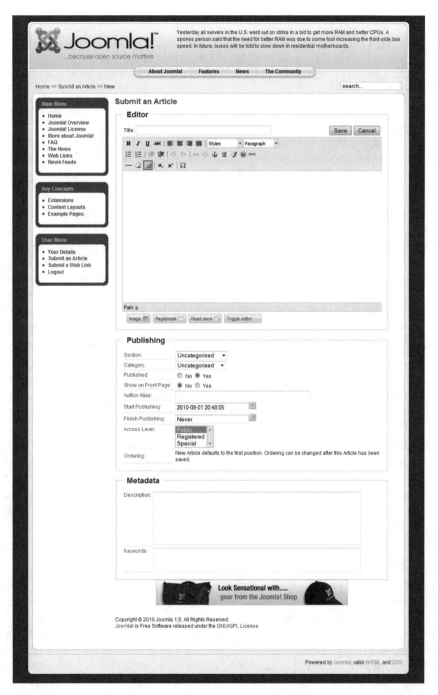

Figure 6.1  Front-end article submission form

- *Single Article:* This displays one article.
- *Category List:* This displays a list of all nonarchived articles in a category that a user is allowed to see (for example, only publishers and editors can see unpublished articles that they have not written). Clicking the article names leads to a Single Article view.
- *Category Blog:* This displays the introductory text (everything before any "Read more" link that you have inserted) for nonarchived articles in a category that a user is allowed to see. Parameters allow you to control the number of columns that these are arranged in as well as other layout details. Clicking the "Read more" link or a linked title (you must select these options in the parameters) will lead to a Single Article display.
- *Section List:* This displays a list of categories in a section. Clicking the category names leads to a Category List display for that category.
- *Section Blog:* This displays the introductory text (everything before any "Read more" link you have inserted) for nonarchived articles in a section that a user is allowed to see. Parameters allow you to control the number of columns that these are arranged in as well as other layout details. Clicking the "Read more" link or a linked title (you must select these options in the parameters) will lead to a Single Article display.
- *Front Page:* This displays the introductory text (everything before any "Read more" link that you have inserted) for articles designated as Front Page that a user is allowed to see. Parameters allow you to control the number of columns that these are arranged in as well as other layout details. Clicking the "Read more" link or a linked title (you must select these options in the parameters) will lead to a Single Article display.
- *Archive:* This displays articles that have had their status changed to Archived. These articles do not display in lists or blogs but are able to be searched. You can create a display of archived items by creating a navigational link, such as an Article Archive menu item, by using the Archive module, or by linking directly to an article in another article.
- *Article Submission:* This displays the edit screen for creating a new article.

## Web Links

The Web Links component provides a simple way to organize information that involves links to other sites. Each item consists of a URL (the link) and optional text. Individual links must be assigned to categories. As with creating articles, one powerful aspect of Web links is that they can be submitted by users who are authors, editors, or publishers in addition to being created in the administrator by a person with back-end access. However, a limitation is that they cannot be edited in the front end after they have been submitted. Web links are organized into categories (which are required for all links), and

Figure 6.2  Front-end editing screen for submitting a Web link

there are no sections. Figure 6.2 shows the front-end editing screen for submitting a
Web link.

There are three layouts for Web links that you can link from a menu.

- *Category List:* This displays a list of all of the Web links in a selected category along
  with any description for the link. Clicking the link will take you to the link
  location.

- *All Categories:* This gives a list of all the categories in the Web Links component
  that a user is allowed to see. Each title links to a Category List layout.

- *Web Link Submission:* This displays the submission form for creating a new Web link.

There is no way to directly display a single Web link with its descriptive text.
However, you can achieve this effect by making a category with a single Web link in it
and using a Category List layout. If you want a menu link that goes directly to another
site, you should use the External Link menu item type.

The Web Links component is a good solution for managing and displaying a number
of different kinds of content. For example, a common use is to have links to external
sources of information about a topic. It can also be used to present a directory of vendors or others who may even pay to be listed. It can also be used to display the Web sites
of your members or a blog roll (list of blogs that you recommend). It can even be used
to manage links to documents and other areas of your site.

Figure 6.3  Creating a new news feed

## News Feeds

News feeds are ways that you can display content from another Web site on your Web site. The News Feeds component gives you an easy way to do this. You simply take the feed URL from a site with a feed you want to include and put it into a New Feed item. To obtain the URL of a feed, look for a feed link or an RSS Feed icon or symbol indicating a feed link on the site that you want to have a feed from. News feeds are organized into categories but not sections. Figure 6.3 shows the screen shown when creating a news feed.

It is important to be careful when selecting news feeds to add to your site. Most sites have terms of service for their feeds, and you should make sure to review them carefully. Some feeds are solely designed for personal use in news readers, not as Web site content. These providers may disable feeds to your site if they detect misuse. Do not give in to the temptation to use content from other sites as a substitute for original content.

One very useful way to use the News Feeds component is to display your own feeds from any social networking site that allows this. For example, you can include your personal feed or the feed for your friends' tweets from Twitter. Simply look for the RSS Feed icon or symbol.

The News Feeds component offers three layouts that can be linked from menus.

- *Single News Feed:* This displays the latest content from one news feed.
- *Category List:* This displays a list of all the news feeds in a selected category that a user is allowed to see along with any description for the feed. Clicking the link will take you to the Single News Feed layout.
- *All Categories:* This gives a list of all the categories in the News Feeds component that a user is allowed to see. Each title links to a Category List layout.

## Contacts

One of the most important kinds of information that your Web site can provide is how to get in contact with you or other people in your organization. The Contacts component provides a useful way to organize and present contact forms, contact directories, and profiles. It contains a large number of fields that you have the option of using or not using. These include complete address fields, an image field, a free-form "miscellaneous" field, and the ability to create an e-mail contact form for anyone listed. Although the component's interface makes it seem complex, you can ignore any part of it that you are not interested in using.

Individual contacts can be created only in the administrator. Each contact must be placed into a category. One benefit of the category structure is that it can allow you to use different features of the component in different categories. For example, you might have a category that consists solely of information about contacts, another category that can include only contact forms, and another that may only include the miscellaneous field, which can serve as an informational page.

The Contacts component has three layouts that can be linked from menus.

- *Single Contact:* This displays the latest content from one contact.

- *Category List:* This displays a list of all the contacts in a selected category that a user is allowed to see. You can select specific fields such as name, position, and phone number to include in the display. Clicking the link will take you to the Single Contact layout.

- *All Categories:* This gives a list of all the categories in the Contacts component that a user is allowed to see. Each title links to a Category List layout.

If you are using contact forms, we suggest adding an antispam extension such as those that utilize a captcha method of determining whether the entity filling out the form is human or mechanical in nature. It is also generally preferable not to show the e-mail addresses of your contacts.

Figure 6.4 demonstrates the contact-editing screen in the administrator back end.

## Banners

Although it can be used in other ways, the Banners component is primarily designed to manage advertising. This can be advertising that you sell to earn money or simple marketing of specific events or sections of your site. The component allows you to set up images or Flash media that when clicked take users to specific URLs. It tracks the number of click-throughs that the banner receives, which allows you to use it for pay-per-click advertising.

Figure 6.5 shows the administrator back-end editing screen for creating an instance of a banner.

The Banners component cannot be linked directly from a menu. Instead, banners are displayed using the Banners module.

## Search

The Search component provides basic search functionality for your site. Articles, category and section descriptions, Web links, and contacts can be searched. What is searched is controlled by the use of search plugins for specific areas.

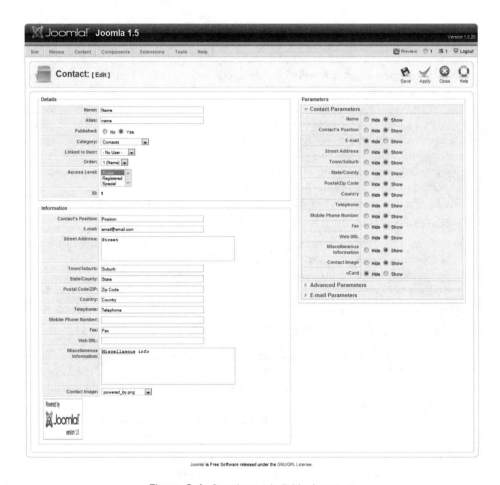

Figure 6.4  Creating an individual contact

- Search has one layout that can be linked from a menu. It displays a search form.
- Search forms are also displayed in search modules.

## Polls

The Polls component allows you to set up one-question multiple-choice polls. This can be a good way to engage your users. Each poll must be in a category. Poll questions are displayed in a poll module. Figure 6.6 demonstrates an example poll set up in the sample data.

The Polls component has one layout that can be linked from a menu.

- *Poll Layout:* This layout displays the results of a selected poll.

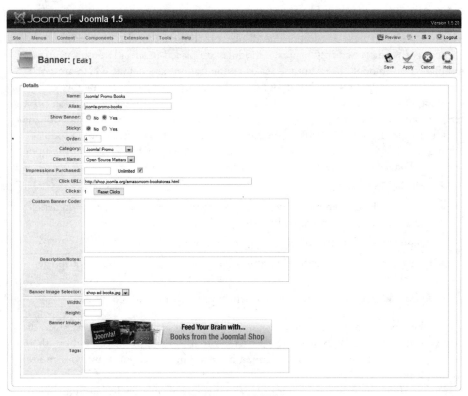

Figure 6.5  Creating a banner with the Banners component

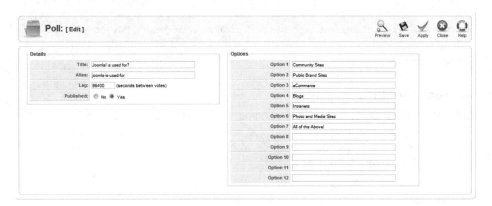

Figure 6.6  Creating a poll with the Polls component

# Modules

Modules are small areas of content that display on your page in the space around your component. As discussed in Chapter 4, modules are placed in specific positions in your template. Each module has a unique set of configuration parameters, which are documented in the help screens. The modules can be grouped into several categories: Content, Display, Utility, User, and Navigation. All modules have some common parameters, although they all have parameters that are specifically related to their functionality.

The common parameters for all modules are found in three areas of the module-editing screen, which you can find by clicking the name of any module. On the upper left is the Details box. You can do the following:

- Edit the title
- Enable or disable the module (similar to publishing and unpublishing an article; if you select no, the module will not be visible on the front end of your site)
- Assign the module to appear in a position in your template
- If there are multiple modules in a position, place it in a particular spot in the module order
- Assign an access level to determine who can view the module

On the lower right is the Menu Assignment box. You can decide what pages to display your module on: All, None, or Select Menu Item(s) from list. If you choose the last option, you can highlight any pages defined by menu links that you want your module to appear on.

On the right, the Advanced Parameters allow you to enable or disable module caching. For most sites, we recommend disabling caching for all modules. Caching is the process by which data is stored for a period of time, which allows a Web site to display content faster. If caching is on, it means changes to content displayed in modules will not immediately be apparent and could be confusing. The content data will not be refreshed if caching is on until the caching time has expired. In very large and/or very busy sites, caching can improve Web site performance considerably, but for most sites, caching turned on does not give appreciable improvement. Figure 6.7 shows the module-editing screen for the Banners module.

## Content Modules

Content modules display information about articles, sections, and categories for the Content component. For many of them, you will need to know the category ID or section ID for the content you want to display. You can get these from the content Category Manager and Section Manager.

- *Latest News:* Displays a linked list of the most recent articles from selected sections or categories. The links lead to a Single Article layout.
- *Most Read:* Displays a linked list of articles based on the number of times the article has been viewed. The links lead to a Single Article layout.

Figure 6.7  Editing screen for the Banners module

- *News Flash:* Displays the introductory text, either the most recent articles or a randomly selected article. The links lead to a Single Article layout.

- *Related Items:* When displayed on a single article page, displays a linked list of other articles with the same metadata keywords. The links lead to a Single Article layout.

- *Archived Content:* Displays a linked list of months in which archived content was published. The links lead to an Archive layout for that month.

- *Sections:* Displays a linked list of all the content sections. The links lead to a Section List layout.

## Display Modules

Display modules display content other than that from content.

- *Banners:* Displays one or more banners managed by the Banners component.

- *Feed:* Displays the content from one of the news feeds managed by the News Feeds component.

- *Poll:* Displays one of the polls created by the poll component.

- *Random Image:* Displays an image randomly selected from a folder in the menu manager that you select.

- *Footer:* Displays the Joomla! site credit. You are free to disable this module.
- *Custom HTML:* Displays content that is created directly in the module using your site editor.

## Utility Modules

Utility modules provide specific functionality for your site.

- *Search:* Displays a search box.
- *Syndicate:* Displays a link that allows other people to take a feed of your site's content. This can be a good way to keep your visitors up to date with your site content. You should consider posting a copyright policy for use of your site's content on other sites.
- *Statistics:* Displays some simple statistics about your site.
- *Wrapper:* Displays a page from another site in an iframe. Some sites have policies that prohibit the display of their content in iframes, and they may block such use through server settings. In general, we recommend against using this module, although there may be some cases where it make sense.

## User Modules

User modules display information related to authentication and logged-in users.

- *Login:* Presents a form for logging into the site with optional links to registration and forgotten password pages.
- *Who's Online:* Displays a list of currently logged-in users.

## Navigation Modules

There are two main types of modules that are used to create navigation for a site.

- *Main Menu:* Displays navigational links. Menus are discussed in more detail in Chapter 3 and in Chapter 7.
- *Breadcrumbs:* Displays the path from the home page to the current page with links to each of the pages in between. This helps users maintain their orientation on your site, especially if you do not have a menu with a home page link on every page.

# Plugins

Plugins are small but powerful pieces of code that carry out a wide variety of specific tasks. Items such as the editors used for creating content are plugins. Each of the buttons below the editor (Image, Pagebreak, Read More) are also plugins. Plugins control everything from authentication to what areas of your site the search component actually searches. Most beginning users do not need to change anything in the plugins that are part of their basic Joomla! installation. However, you may want to add other plugins.

Figure 6.8  Editing screen for the Search Content plugin

To configure a plugin, you go to the Plugin Manager and click the name of the plu-gin; or, select the check box next to its name and click Edit. Most of the time you sim-ply need to either enable or disable the plugin, but with some third-party plugins, there may be additional parameters to set. Figure 6.8 shows the editing screen for the Search Content plugin.

# How to Choose Extensions

Although a lot of Web sites may not need extra functionality outside of what Joomla! provides out of the box, it is important to think about how you may want to extend your site and plan for the functionality you may need. The first best practice to choosing extensions is to know whether you really do need the functionality. It is quite common for people to install extensions just because they can and not because they have a need for them, and although it is good to try things, if you don't need an extension or change your mind about offering or having the functionality that extension offers, you need to remove the extension to keep your site safe. Unused and out-of-date extensions are one of the most common ways that people expose their sites to security issues. If you install an extension, it is important to keep track of the development of the extension and any security bulletins, issues, and upgrades. Upgrading your extensions is just as important as keeping your Joomla! installation up to date.

The second best practice is to pick extensions that have active development. There are a number of extensions floating around in the Joomlasphere that are very old, are out-dated, and haven't had active development or improvement for a long time. These are "dead" extensions, and most likely if they haven't been developed in a long time, they also haven't had a security audit either. If you are unsure whether an extension has active development, look either on the developer's Web site or in the extension files themselves. You should see dates on the files or activity regarding the extension on the developer's site. If you are unsure, it is probably best to look for a similar extension that has the same functionality that is being actively developed.

Another best practice is to try to choose extensions that have good support options. These options can range from developer support that is free to developer support that can be purchased on an as-needed basis or as a subscription or support contract. A lot of extensions offer Web sites that have user-to-user support channels, such as forums, mailing lists, and knowledge bases. The support that comes with an extension isn't always an indicator of how well an extension works or is coded, but it is pretty handy when you run into a problem you need help solving.

Some extensions are all-in-one mega extensions, usually components that can cover a number of different functionalities in one package. Good examples of this are some of the media extensions that allow you to present audio, video, Flash, animation, and image files using one extension. Another example is the various community and social networking extensions that can turn your Joomla! site into a social network that offers messaging, audio, video, profiles, and other extended features. On the opposite side of the spectrum, you have plugins that may do only one thing such as allow you to put an individual MP3 player inside an article. Some people like to get as many things and functionalities in one extension as they can to have fewer extensions to keep up with, while others like to use a number of individual extensions. Both methods have their advantages and disadvantages. The advantage to multipurpose extensions is, as stated earlier, fewer extensions to keep track of for updates; the disadvantage is that if something goes wrong in part of it, it can affect all the other parts. The advantage to individual extensions that are specific in nature is that they tend to do what they do very well; the disadvantage is how it can be difficult to keep up with updates, and sometimes individual extensions can conflict with each other and cause your site to have issues. The decision to use a mega extension or individual extension is mostly about personal preference. One thing to keep in mind regarding mega extensions is that if you aren't going to be using 50 percent of the functionality it provides, most likely you can do with something that is less mega.

## Using the Joomla! Extension Directory

The Joomla! Extension Directory is a directory of third-party developer extensions and tools located at *http://extensions.joomla.org*. To be listed in the JED, an extension has to be licensed as GPL, it must not have any current security issues, and the developer's site and e-mail address must be in working order. The JED is one of the largest and most popular of the Joomla! family of sites, supporting both end users and the developers who support the project with their extensions. There are thousands of extensions to choose from, which cover everything from account access to vertical markets. Extensions can be commercial or non-commercial. The front page of the directory has an extensive menu that helps you navigate through the various categories and highlights what is new to the directory, extensions that have been recently updated, a few randomly selected picks, and extensions that are selected by the JED editors as Editor's Picks.

All the extensions listed have icons next to their names to denote whether there is a component, module, plugin, or language file available. Another important part of the JED is the ability for the community to vote or rate extensions and comment about their experience. Community reviews are a great way to get an idea about how well an extension works and how easy it is for users to use. It is also a nice way for community members to give kudos to a developer of an extension they like particularly well. A listing for an extension will include a link to download the extension, a link to the developer's Web site, a demo if available, documentation if available, and support if the developer offers support in some way for the extension.

While you are surfing the JED for extensions, you may come across helpful notes from the JED editor team that can tell you whether you have to sign up or subscribe to an extension developer Web site to download the extension, whether an extension has been removed from the directory, or whether an extension has additional add-ons. A number of the mega component extensions such as Sobi2, Community Builder, and Virtuemart have vibrant third-party developer communities that specialize in providing add-ons for those specific extensions.

Searching the JED can help you find extensions with a specific functionality, and the advanced search can help you search by category, whether commercial or free, license, or compatibility.

### Tip

Extensions are downloaded as packages, which are archived, compressed files such as ZIP and TAR files. Once you download an extension, do not unarchive, unzip, or expand the extension file unless the developer has given specific instructions to do so. Extension packages are installed using the package file, and the installation process uncompresses the zip file on the server itself.

# Installing Extensions and Viewing Extension Information

The extension installer located in the administration back end of Joomla! sites allows users to install extensions and view information regarding extensions that have already been installed. It is also where extensions can be uninstalled if they are no longer useful or if they have security issues. You will find the extension installer by going to the top main menu, Extensions, and then clicking Install/Uninstall. There are three options available to choose from to install an extension.

- *Upload Package File:* Using this method, you browse for the extension on your computer; then after selecting the extension package file, all you have to do is click the Upload File & Install button. Once the extension installs successfully, you will get a confirmation message that the installation completed.

- *Install from Directory:* Using this method, you can specify a directory on your Web site where you have already uploaded an extension package to install. You can upload the extension using an FTP program or your hosting service's file manager. Once the extension installs successfully, you will get a confirmation message that the installation completed.

- *Install from URL:* Using this method, you can install an extension from any Web site as long as you give the full URL that the extension is located at (for example, *http://somewebsitename.com/extensionname.zip*). This method of installing extensions can be problematic if the extension is large and the connection speed is slow. The length of time it can take to download the extension from the other site to your site can take too long and cause the installation to fail. Once the extension installs successfully, you will get a confirmation message that the installation completed.

Figure 6.9 shows the Extension Manager installation screen.

Some extensions upon successful installation will also give you additional information about the extension you have installed. Those messages can vary from extension to extension.

While on the Extension Manager screen, you can see there are pages you can view such as Components, Modules, Plugins, Languages, and Templates. Each of these menu items when clicked will bring up the screens that reference the installed items of that kind. Figure 6.10 shows the component screen with a table-based layout of all the components that are currently installed. It details the component name, whether it is enabled, the version number, the date of the extension as specified in the component's XML data file, the developer who created the extension, and its compatibility with the installed version of Joomla! The Modules, Plugins, Languages, and Templates screens are similar. You can enable/disable an extension by clicking the icon beside the extension name that is located in the Enabled column.

This area is where you can uninstall an extension you no longer want to use by selecting the radio button by the extension name and then by clicking Uninstall in the top-right corner of the screen. Before installing or uninstalling any extension, it is a good idea to get a full backup of your site files and database. One thing to check after uninstalling an extension is that all the files associated with that extension have been removed, especially if you have uninstalled an extension because of a security vulnerability. You can check this by using the File Manager and going to the appropriate folder in the root of your Joomla! installation such as for components, modules, plugins, templates,

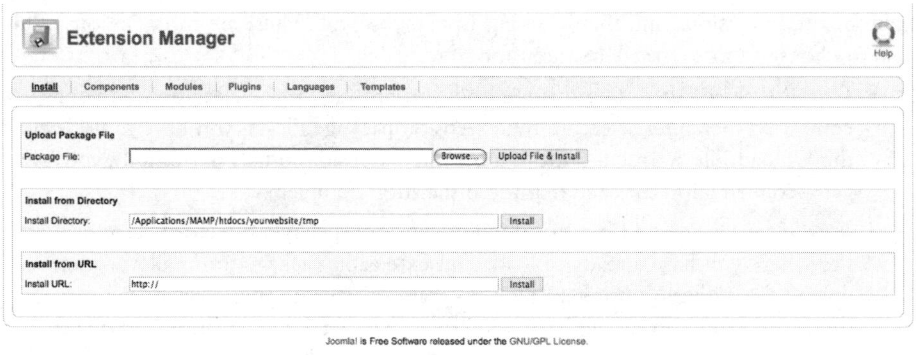

Figure 6.9  The Extension Manager installation screen

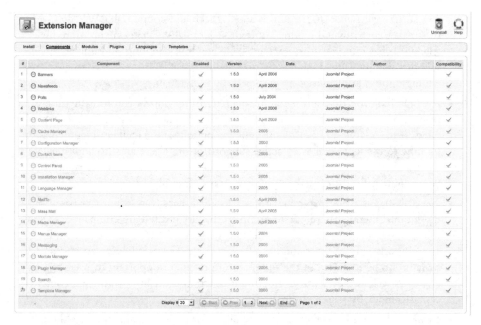

Figure 6.10  The Extension Manager component screen

or languages. You also need to check those same folders located inside the administrator directory to assure that all the related files have been removed from the administrator section of the site.

# Popular Extensions

As mentioned earlier, there is a very large and diverse community of extension developers who contribute to the Joomla! community. We cannot cover all the extensions that are available, but this section is intended to give a list of popular extensions that are helpful to a large amount of sites and popular in the Joomla! community. All of these extensions can be found on the Joomla! Extension Directory.

- *Update Manager for Joomla!:* Formerly known as jupdateman, Sam Moffatt's Update Manager makes updating your Joomla! installation to the latest version effortless. It has an easy-to-use interface, and it is a must-have for all Joomla! Web site administrators.

- *Akeeba Backup:* Formerly known as Joomlapack, Akeeba Backup generates full backups of a Joomla! Web site or can be configured to back up portions of a site. The backups contain a self-installer that is similar to the Joomla! installation process, which allows users to easily restore or move a Web site. It has a very easy-to-use interface and has very good support.

- *Joomla! Content Editor (JCE):* JCE is an advanced and configurable WYSIYG editor that makes entering and editing content on Joomla! Web sites much more user friendly. It has integrated image/media, file and link handling, and uploading and supports plugins. One of the really nice features of JCE is the ability to configure editing options and abilities by groups or by individuals.

- *RokBox:* RokBox is an all-in-one media plugin that allows you to easily insert media such as images, video, audio, files, and even other Web sites into content items. It has a large number of configurable options and excellent documentation on how to use it, as well as an active support forum. There are also additional extensions that have been created for it that allow you to integrate it right into your Content Editor to make using it very user friendly.

- *Xmap:* Xmap is a site map generator for Joomla! that creates site maps based on the Joomla! menu structure. The site maps that are created are compatible to submit to search engine site map submissions such as with Google Webmaster Tools. It also supports plugins for a number of Joomla! extensions, allowing an entire site's structure to be included in the site map. Site maps are important to users as a reference as well as they serve an important function in making your site's content easier to index by search engines.

- *JoomFish:* JoomFish extends Joomla! to allow for multilingual content. Although it does not translate articles automatically, it has a very robust system to help manage and present content in multiple languages and aids in better localizations for sites.

- *sh404SEF:* sh404SEF is an extension that allows you to customize the URLs that your site generates as well as offering some protections against some common security exploits such as flooding attacks or spam input on any forms you may have on your site. Customizing the URLs that your site generates can be very helpful in terms of search engine optimization.

- *BigShot Google Analytics:* BigShot Google Analytics is a very easy and effective way to add your Google Analytics Tracker code to your Web site, reducing the need to manually add it to your template. There are also options available for those who use Woopra, which is another Web site analytics solution.

- *JForms:* JForms is an easy-to-use WYSIWYG forms component for Joomla! Forms allow you to collect data and information from your Web site visitors. It is a great way to add a more robust contact form than what is offered in the Joomla! core. The included plugin allows you to embed any form you create into a content item. There are a number of other form extensions available such as RSForms, ChronoForms, and Fabrik.

## Conclusion

The extensibility of Joomla! is a great part of what makes Joomla! a sensible choice for any use—as well as the supportive and vibrant third-party developers who actively work at making Joomla! better for all users. This means the resources are there to assist you in making your Joomla! site the best that it can be. With thousands of extensions available for any given practical application, the sky is the limit as to what your Web site can accomplish. Chapters 8, 9, and 10 present the practical application of Joomla! in specific scenarios, explain extensions that suit those specific purposes, and provide information on how to use Joomla! and extensions in those scenarios to the best advantage.

# 7

# Caring for Your Joomla! Web Site and Helpful Tips

Once your Web site is created and online, the work doesn't stop. It is important to note that being the administrator of a Web site takes ongoing work to keep it updated, to keep your content fresh, to advertise and market it, and to keep your visitors engaged. Depending on what type of site you have created, the workload may be more or less, but all Web site administrators need to take a proactive approach and stay on top of taking care of their Web site. This chapter will explain some best practices and simple steps to keep up your Web site and to continue growing your visitor exposure and brand reach.

## First Impressions Count: What Your Home Page Says About You

If you browse the Web randomly, you can see examples of all the good, the bad, and the ugly. Some home pages draw you into the site, and others make you wince. Here are some helpful tips on making sure your home page is a winner.

- Avoid splash pages. Splash or intro pages were really popular a few years ago. Usually it was just a page showing an image, Flash media, or video segment with a button or a link that said "Enter" or "Enter site" or "Skip intro." Splash pages really do not offer anything of useful value to your site visitors. They force your visitors to make an unnecessary click just to get to the information they came to your site for in the first place. They also add very little in terms of practical information and relevancy to search engines.

- Make your site navigation easy to locate and use. It can be tempting to be clever with navigation, but forcing users to play a game of hide-and-seek with your navigation will result in lost visitors.

- Blinking, flashing, scrolling, or animated items should be kept to a minimum and should be tastefully done. Items on your page that scroll, blink, flash, or are animated need special care. If items scroll, make sure the information that is scrolling is easily readable, and adjust scrolling speeds as needed. Blinking and flashing items are almost always not good for any site; most people will be turned off by items that are flickering or flashing, and for some people it can induce seizures. W3schools has more information on accessibility and the implications of blinking or flashing at *www.w3.org/TR/WCAG20*. Slide shows or animation should be of high quality, the subject matter should be easily identifiable, and as with scrolling, whatever animation or slide-show speed that is used should be adjusted so that the subject matter is able to be understood by the visitor. Placing what is called "eye candy" on a site simply for artistic reason, without it having meaningful reason to be there such as an actionable item or to impart site information, will distract from the content of your site. Content and information are the two main reasons why people will visit your site.

- Dynamic sites such as those created by CMSs like Joomla! give you the flexibility to showcase new content in compartmentalized areas on the home page such as a list of latest news or updated content and products. This is a great opportunity to guide your visitors into your site and direct them to the actions or interaction you want your visitors to take part in.

- If your site generates revenue with any sort of advertising such as banners, affiliate links, or other advertising such as referrer pay per click, to be effective it needs to be tastefully done (see the earlier comment on blinking and flashing). Experiment with ad placements on your home page to see how your visitors' click patterns work. Ads need to be highly visible but should not interfere with the information you are trying to impart to your visitors and in no way should you be attempting to trick your visitors into clicking your ads by disguising them as your site content. Doing that will irritate your visitors and in some instances get you banned from participating in the revenue programs.

- Don't automatically play video or audio. (Also see the previous comments on splash pages.) There are a number of reasons to not use automatically playing audio or video. You have no idea how loud a visitor's speakers are, their bandwidth limitations, or the speed of their connection. It can be assaultive and intrusive. Another factor is that you don't know where your visitors are when they are browsing your site. If they are at work, it can be disruptive to their workplace or any environment where the visitor is located. You are wasting your bandwidth and also your visitor's bandwidth allotment on their ISP service when you automatically stream audio or video, especially if it is your home page. It can be annoying and frustrating to your visitors who don't want to watch or hear the same thing over and over again every time they visit your page. The best thing to do is to give incentive for people to electively choose to watch the video or listen to the audio; be creative, and give them a reason to click. The absolute worst thing to do is to insist on automatically playing audio or video and give the visitor no way to stop or pause it. That will pretty much guarantee that a significant portion of your visitors will never return to your site.

- Have a search module on your home page and every page in a consistent location. Users generally expect to find this on the top right of each page, so locate it there if possible.

Your home page is the introduction to your brand, your Web site, your work, or your product. It should exemplify exactly who you are and what you do. Depending on their purpose, some sites want the home page to show everything at a glance with details only one click away. Their intent isn't necessarily to have visitors explore the site, but to get the information they need quickly and efficiently. On the opposite side of the spectrum, some sites use the home page to direct visitors to explore and interact, drawing them deeper into the site and the information it contains. You should consider where your planned site fits in this spectrum. Every site wants return visitors; you want your demographic to come back to your site, your work, or your product and become loyal to your brand.

The other important part your home page plays is in search engine optimization (SEO). This page should contain rich key phrases that are relevant to your content and topic. If your site is geographically important, such as offering a service in a distinct service area, you should highlight that geographic service area in text. It makes sense to be targeting search users and visitors from that specific geographical area, and stating the area you service will make it easier for people to find your site. Although keywords and key phrases are important, it is important to make sure they are used in context, in other words, in actual human-readable and enjoyable content. Keyword stuffing (overly repeating keywords for phrases, content that is nonsensical, run-on sentences or just lists of keywords, utilizing keywords that have nothing to do with the site topic) is frowned upon by the major search engines and could harm your search engine rankings.

# Search Engines, SEO, Getting Listed, and Staying There

The topics of search engines, search engine optimization, how to get listed, how to get to the "top," and how to stay there aren't a mystical science or magic. What those topics do involve is having realistic expectations, following a few basic principles, and most of all making your Web site relevant to the people who visit it and who will search for it.

It is a good idea to hold off on making your entire site available to search engines before it is ready or before you have settled on the overall navigation and search-engine-friendly URLs. One way to manage this is to make a single article for the home page of your site that gives a good summary of what the site is about. Keep the rest of your site hidden until it is ready by setting access to all content, menu items, and modules to Registered. Avoid the temptation to have "under construction" pages, since that is what search engines will read, index, and show in search results for your site. That can appear very unprofessional.

As discussed in Chapter 2, write a short paragraph summarizing the purpose of the site in the Global Site Meta Description box found in the Metadata Settings area of the Global Configuration Site tab. This is what most search engines will present to people looking at search results. In the Global Site Meta Keywords field, make a short, general list of relevant search terms that you think people will use to find your site. If your physical location is important information (for example, if you have an actual store), make sure to include that in the keywords. Also select Yes for Show Title Meta Tag and Show Author Meta Tag. Both the description and keyword information entered should be concise and to the point, no more than 100 characters if possible. Stuffing either of these metadata options with excessive information, repetitive words, or incorrect information will not improve your search rankings. If your site is found to be using deceptive SEO practices, it could be removed and/or banned from inclusion. Figure 7.1 shows the Global Configuration – Site screen with the Metadata Settings options.

## Submitting to Search Engines

You don't need to subscribe to a service or hire a SEO professional to submit your site to the major search engines/Web index directories—Google, Bing, Ask, and dmoz (Open Directory Project). Although there are a lot of other search engines and directories out there, those are the top players. Most of the other search engines and directories get their information from them and/or get an amalgamation of information from those search engines or directories; for example, Yahoo! will be getting its search results from Bing starting sometime in late 2010 or early 2011 as a result of their merger (according to their current press releases).

The Web site dmoz.org is the Open Directory Project where Webmasters, Web site owners, and administrators can submit their site to the appropriate category of the directory. Each submission is reviewed by an actual human editor to assure that the entry is

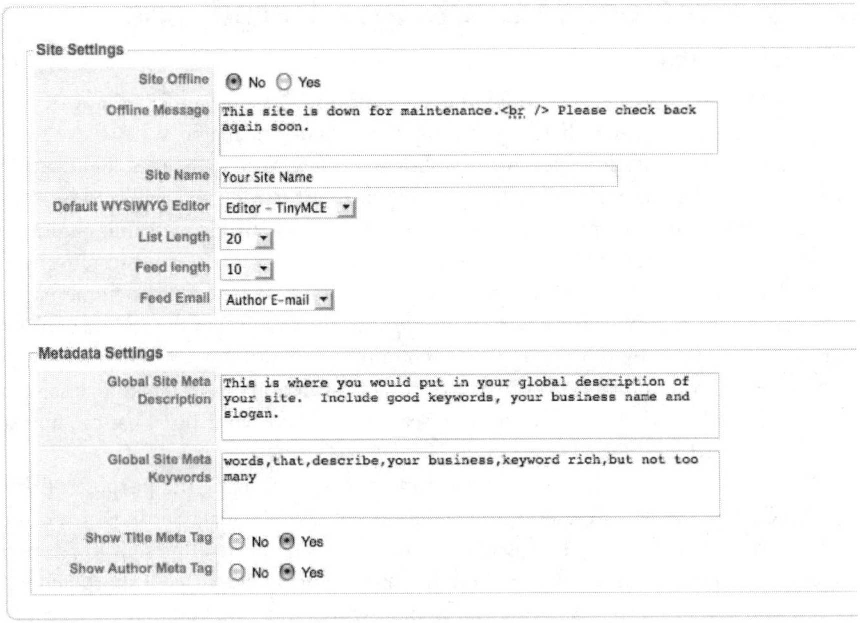

Figure 7.1  Global Configuration – Site Settings screen showing Metadata Settings section

acceptable, that it is submitted to the right category, and that the details submitted are verified. Dmoz.org is regularly scanned and indexed by most of the other major search engines, meaning there is a high level of quality to the information it offers as well as reliability. Having a listing on dmoz.org can be one way to try to get your new Web site picked up by the other search engines.

Google offers a variety of Webmaster tools to facilitate getting indexed and more importantly offers an easy way to submit not only your site but the pages your site contains. Using the extension Xmap on your site, you can submit the site map it generates to your Google Webmaster Tools account, which submits all your pages at one time for indexing. Google Webmaster Tools also offers a number of other services that can help you diagnose search engine optimization issues with your site such as broken links, items that may cause issues like duplicate titles or metadata, and whether any pages in your site are unreachable. Google actively expands the tools it offers. It is also good to have a Google Analytics account so you can analyze the traffic that your site gets.

Ask has a policy of needing a submission of an XML site map. Although Xmap does not generate a site map that is in an acceptable form for this submission, you can utilize free tools online such as the Site Map Generator from *www.web-site-map.com*, which will generate a site map that is in the correct form. Once you have generated and downloaded the site map it creates, you simply upload it using File Manager to the root of your site and then direct the Ask Submission URL to the site map. The URL to submit your site map is *http://submissions.ask.com/ping?sitemap=http%3A//www.YOURSITE.com/sitemap.xml*. Once submitted, you will be directed to a confirmation screen that verifies your site map has been submitted successfully.

Bing has a submission page that you fill out located at *www.bing.com/webmaster/SubmitSitePage.aspx*. Once there, you answer the security question to show that you are human and then submit your Web site URL (*www.YOURSITE.com*); the MSNbot will then index your home page and follow any links that may be located on your home page to other pages on your site. Note that the procedures outlined above may be changed at any time by any of the search engines. Most search engines will provide instructions for submitting sites for inclusion in search directories.

Once you have submitted your site, you can use tools like Majestic SEO or the Google Chrome SEO extension to track how your site is indexed and how many pages of your site have been indexed. Both of those tools also offer quite a few more SEO tools and information that you can utilize to grow your ranking and optimize your site.

Getting your site indexed is only the first hurdle, and sometimes that can take anywhere from 48 hours to 6 months or longer. There are no guarantees regarding submitting your site and getting it indexed quickly, but here are some steps you can take to help your site be indexed.

- Utilize reputable directories that specialize in the same topic as you do, and submit your site to be listed in them. The aim is to get quality linking to your site while targeting your specific audience in order to generate traffic to your site and to have the various search engines find your site.

- Take part in forums and blogs that specialize in the same topic as you do. Follow any rules the site may have about linking to your site or self-promotion. By making your brand and your site more relevant with quality linking and interaction in your target sector, it will help to build your credibility and visibility.

- Join trade organizations, business bureaus, chambers, and local business associations. Most offer listing and linking opportunities that are quality and relevant.

- Don't spam links to your site all over the place or utilize linking schemes or junk "link farm" listing sites. Actions such as these as well as having your site associated with junk link farms will only reduce your relevancy and credibility. Search engines can and do penalize sites for these actions. Nobody likes a spammer.

- Utilize your friends and business associates to try to generate reciprocal linking. This linking should be done in a relevant way, such as someone recommending your services or the information your site offers in the context of their own content, such as in a blog.

Most of all, it is important to be patient. There are thousands of sites being submitted every day.

## Search Engine Optimization

A number of search engine optimization extensions can help with making your Joomla! more search engine friendly. One of the more popular extensions is SEOSimple by Dao by Design. This extension plugin works by taking the first chunk of text in an article or page and then utilizes it as the metadata for the description of the page. This helps sites avoid duplicate metatags on all their pages such as the main meta keywords and description that are present in the global configuration of Joomla! Depending on how your content is written, this can be useful to search engines but also to people who are searching for your site, because it will help them understand what the page link in the search results is about. Search engine result pages typically show the meta description information as the short introductory text of the individual search engine results. SEOSimple also allows you to customize your page titles in various configurations, which can be very advantageous to your search engine relevancy. Having relevant, individual page titles for all your pages is good for your visitors and search engines.

Tags are another way to add keywords and phrases to article content, and some tagging components even allow you to use them as a navigational tool, helping you organize your site content, which is helpful to your visitors to find like content throughout your site. A popular and simple way to use tagging component is Tag by Joomlatags.org. This extension allows you to add keywords or phrases to articles to highlight their main areas of discussion or topic. It has additional modules that allow you to show cloud tags based on the tags you have entered and list articles by tags or phrases. It also can show lists of related content based on tags in an article. A more complex and robust tagging system is offered by Jxtended called Labels.

Although there is a lot of discussion regarding how URLs are formed and how it may create "duplicate content"—defined as content that is exactly the same but accessed through a different URL—the major search engines are well aware of how dynamic sites generate URLs and how different URLs may be generated depending on the click path that people have taken to get to the content. This unintentional duplication of the content in this manner is not penalized by search engines. One way to combat this "duplicate content" is to take total control over the URLs in your site by using an SEF option such as sh404SEF.

Keeping your content fresh and new is an excellent way to ensure your site stays relevant for your topic and demographic.

For more helpful SEO tips, we recommend checking in with Joomla!'s resident SEO expert Steve Burge and his blog Alledia.com. Steve offers regular blogs and articles on Joomla! SEO as well as extension comparisons and other Joomla! news.

# Using Navigation

Site navigation includes all the links that a user can click to move from page to page in your Web site. Navigation should be easy to understand and apparent to the visitor without being overwhelming. Nothing can be more confusing to a site visitor than having to search for the navigation links of a site, having links whose purposes are not clearly identifiable, or having an overwhelming number of menu navigation links. Useful and effective sites have consistent and helpful navigation as a central element of their design. Navigation should make it easy and pleasant for your users to find the information they came to your site to find. Site navigation should be central to the structure and design of your site from the beginning. As your site develops, the demands on its navigation will grow, so it is important that this be designed in a thoughtful way.

The default home page for your site may contain many navigation elements. These could include the following:

- Top menu
- Side menus
- Pagination
- Linked article titles in the Latest News and Most Popular modules
- "Read more" links
- Links inside of articles
- Links in the footer
- Links connected to the buttons in the Login and Polls modules

All these links manage how your users move around your site. As you develop your site, you should always be considering how the addition of new content or features should relate to your navigation. By looking at the front page of a Joomla! site that has the sample data installed, you can see all the different areas that contain navigation from the list noted earlier. Figure 7.2 shows the front page of a Joomla! site with sample data and the Milkyway template.

Figure 7.2  Home page of a Joomla! Web site with sample data installed
demonstrating navigation

The most important thing you can do in designing your navigation is to imagine yourself in the role of your users. If you have several different groups of users, you need carry out this process for each of them. What do they want to find when they come to your site? What words do they use to describe those things? Ideally you will talk to users, but at a minimum try to imagine yourself as a member of each group. Web designers will often talk about how many clicks on links it takes to get to a specific piece of information. The more clicks it takes to find something, the more likely it is that the user will abandon the task of looking for something without completing it. You want the number of clicks to be as small as possible. Visitors should stay on your site because they are finding useful and interesting content, not because they have to spend a lot of time finding what they are looking for.

You should follow a number of principles.

- Make sure that it is easy for people to get to the home page. The first link on your main navigation should be to the home page. If there is a logo on the top of the page, clicking it should send users to the home page.

- Provide "you are here" information for every page to help users know where they are. This doesn't necessarily have to be "breadcrumbs," which are a series of text links like the default Joomla! breadcrumb module. Your visitor should have some sort of cue as to the section or area of the site they are currently visiting.

- Remember that people entering your site via a search engine will often not be entering from the home page, especially if you have a large number of your site pages indexed.

- Never use only an image as a link with no text to indicate what it links to. No matter how obvious you think the image's meaning is, it will not be obvious to some of your visitors.

- Don't require users to use their mouse or keyboard to discover key information. Users will be frustrated if forced to hover over an item in order to obtain important information. An example of this would be forcing the user to hover over an image to trigger navigational links.

- Use standard terms for items, not cute short forms, acronyms, or organizationally specific terms that are understood only by yourself or your team.

- Use meaningful terms in your text to convey your message.

In Joomla! the main navigation is usually controlled through menus and menu modules. The menu system is perhaps the most important part of your Joomla! site besides the actual content because it controls four elements:

- What template is used when a linked page is displayed

- What modules are displayed on the linked page

- How content is laid out

- The URL of the page, which relates to search engine results as described earlier in this section

In Chapter 3, we covered how to assign a template to a menu item and how to create menu items for content. In Chapter 5, we reviewed the other types of menu items available in the core. The menu items themselves along with the parameter options you select control how the article is laid out. The menu item alias controls the search-engine-friendly URL for the page linked.

The Menu module, working in conjunction with the CSS in your template, controls the appearance of the menus on your site. Each time you create a new menu, a corresponding module is automatically created. You may want multiple copies of some menu modules, and you may want several separate menus, as illustrated in the sample data.

The Menu module works like all other modules. It has some important options that can help you manage your site navigation effectively. For example, in the sample data in your Joomla! installation, you will notice that the main menu has a link called Joomla! Overview. As you can see in Figure 7.3, the default main menu in the sample data shows a simple list of links. Figure 7.4 demonstrates what happens when you click Joomla! Overview; a submenu with a new link appears.

This is one of many ways the flexibility of the Menu module can be used to make the navigation of your site more usable. In this way, you can have a longer menu that is not overwhelming to site visitors.

Figure 7.3  Default main menu that is set up in the sample data showing
the menu item Joomla! Overview

Figure 7.4  Default main menu showing a child menu item that is
revealed after clicking a parent menu item

You set up a menu that utilizes showing child menu items (such as What's New in Joomla! 1.5 in this example) after you click. Follow these steps:

1. Create a menu item and then make that new menu item a child of an existing menu item, which is called the *parent item*, as demonstrated in Figure 7.5, which shows the What's New in 1.5? menu item editing screen.

2. In the Menu Manager, identify a child menu of a parent because of the display. Figure 7.6 demonstrates how What's New in 1.5? as a child of Joomla! Overview, which is the parent item.

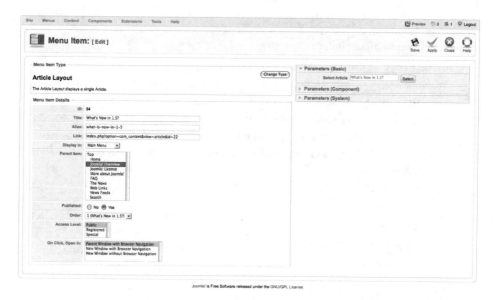

Figure 7.5  What's New in 1.5? menu item editing screen showing the selection of Joomla! Overview as the parent item of the menu item

| # | | Menu Item | Default | Published | Order▲ | Access Level | Type | ItemID |
|---|---|---|---|---|---|---|---|---|
| 1 | | Home | ☆ | ✓ | ▼ 1 | Public | Articles » Front Page | 1 |
| 2 | | Joomla! Overview | | ✓ | ▲ ▼ 2 | Public | Articles » Article | 27 |
| 3 | | └ What's New in 1.5? | | ✓ | 1 | Public | Articles » Article | 34 |
| 4 | | Joomla! License | | ✓ | ▲ ▼ 3 | Public | Articles » Article | 2 |
| 5 | | More about Joomla! | | ✓ | ▲ ▼ 4 | Public | Articles » Section | 37 |
| 6 | | FAQ | | ✓ | ▲ ▼ 5 | Public | Articles » Section | 41 |
| 7 | | The News | | ✓ | ▲ ▼ 6 | Public | Articles » Category / Blog | 50 |
| 8 | | Web Links | | ✓ | ▲ ▼ 7 | Public | Web Links » Categories | 48 |
| 9 | | News Feeds | | ✓ | ▲ ▼ 8 | Public | News Feeds » Categories | 49 |
| 10 | | poll | | ✓ | ▲ 9 | Public | Polls » Poll | 53 |

Filter: [    ] Go  Reset         Max Levels 10 ▾ - Select State - ▾

Display # 20 ▾

Figure 7.6  Main menu's Menu Manager screen demonstrating the What's New in 1.5? menu item as a child of Joomla! Overview, which is a parent item

To set up the module to show child menu items only upon the click of a parent menu item, follow these steps:

1. In your Menu module, set the first and last levels to 0, as shown in Figure 7.7.

2. Set Always show submenu Items to No, as shown in Figure 7.7.

One way to get visitors to browse your site in depth is to have clear and simple navigation that then expands to show more options as they navigate pages. This can be done by showing new navigation menu items that are pertinent only to the page a visitor is currently browsing. Joomla! has a great way to do that using Menu modules via the split menu technique of showing second-level and beyond menu items only on pages to which they are assigned.

To set up a split menu, follow these steps:

1. Make a copy of the Main Menu module as in Figure 7.8.

2. You will now have a module named Copy of Main Menu. Click the name to open the copy. As in Figure 7.9, enable the module, set the title to show, set the Start Level option to 1, and set the End Level option to 1.

3. Because you only want this menu module to show when the Joomla! Overview menu item is clicked, assign it just to the Joomla! Overview menu link, as shown in Figure 7.9.

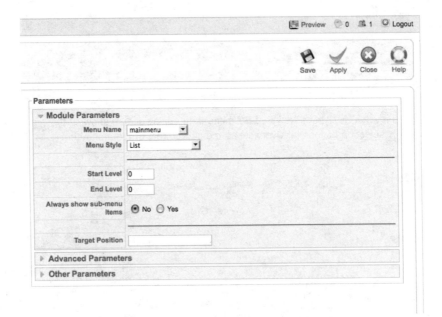

Figure 7.7  Main menu module editing screen showing how to set the
values for Start, End, and Sub-Menu settings

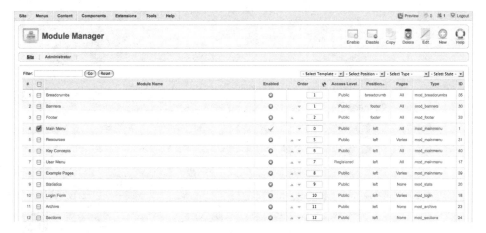

Figure 7.8  Module Manager screen showing how to copy the Main
Menu module

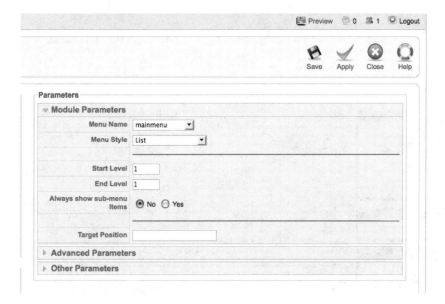

Figure 7.9  Module-editing screen showing how to set a menu module to
show a split menu

4.  Open the original Main Menu module, and change End Level to 1, as in Figure 7.10.

Now when you click Joomla! Overview in the front end of the site, a second menu
will appear with just the relevant submenu showing as a separate menu module, as
shown in Figure 7.11.

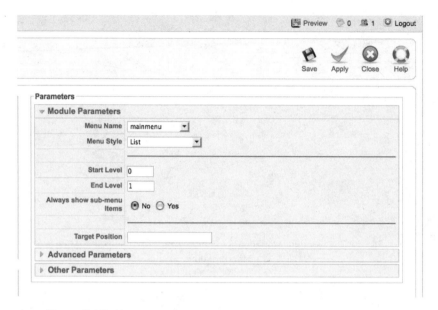

Figure 7.10  Module-editing screen showing how to set the Main Menu
module to not show child items

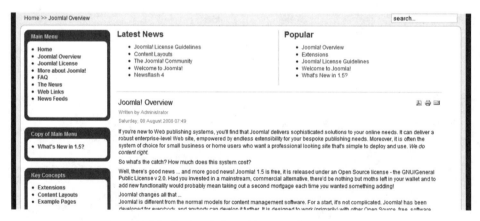

Figure 7.11  Front-end view of how a split menu displays

If you have submenus for all your main menu items and want to use the split menu technique, you should assign the module used for the split menu to all the relevant parent menu items.

There are many options for enhanced menus available in the Joomla! Extensions Directory. Usability research has shown that many complex menus with excessive reliance on drop-downs and special effects can make your site more difficult for visitors, so use any special effects in moderation and for good reasons.

# Engaging Your Visitors and Keeping Your Content Fresh

One of the best ways for any site to keep their target audience as repeat visitors is to keep the content on the site fresh and updated. Whether your site is strictly informational or meant to be a portal where visitors take part in action items on the site, without updated, fresh, new, and interesting content, eventually your audience is going to get bored and click away, or they will find the information they are seeking elsewhere. Here are a few suggestions to keep people coming back.

- Start a blog. Starting a blog is a great way to add new content to a site that is mostly information or to a brochure-type site. Blogging about happenings in your industry, new events, or happenings in your company can add a human touch to your site as well as keep people informed with up-to-date news and information. One basic good practice to follow is to set a schedule for blogging and keep to it.

- Add a news and press release section to your site, and offer it as a news feed. Find sites in your target topic that accept news feeds to aggregate. It can be a great way to drive traffic to your site.

- Add your Twitter and other social networking streams to your site. Create profiles for your Web site/business to further your exposure on social networking sites such as Facebook.

- Offer special deals, coupons, and discounts to your Web visitors. Make sure to keep any coupons or deals up to date. Nothing will annoy a Web visitor more than downloading a coupon or deal only to realize that it has already expired.

- Add a mailing list. A number of mailing lists work with Joomla!, and there are many third-party mailing lists that you can integrate with your Joomla! site. Please don't spam people. Utilize a legitimate mailing list of people who want to get your e-mails. It is extremely important that you keep your site from getting blacklisted as a spam site. As your mailing list grows, it becomes essential that you use mailing list applications that do effective throttling (limiting the number of e-mails sent in one blast) both to avoid spam labeling and to ensure that you do not run into mail capacity limitations that your host may have in place. Your host should have a policy regarding e-mail that is sent through their servers as part of their terms of service.

- Add questionnaires, polls, or surveys to engage your audience, and report the results.

- Add commenting. Allow your visitors to comment on your content, blog, polls, and so on. This can be both a good thing and a bad thing. It is a good way to engage your visitors, but commenting systems do not monitor themselves, so you will have to monitor your site and monitor your visitor's comments. Assess whether the time spent having to manage a commenting system versus the value of the comments to see whether it is an option that works for you. A number of comments extensions are available in the JED.

- Add a discussion forum. A forum can be a great way to interact with your visitors or customers/clientele. As with commenting, a forum does not monitor itself; you will have to spend time monitoring your forum and should carefully weigh the benefits versus the time spent on monitoring.

All of these ideas can be integrated into your site to make it more active and attractive to visitors. What is not suggested is to do all of them at once. Find the avenue of engagement that suits your visitors and your brand and time limitations. It really is better to do one thing well than to do five to ten things in a less than stellar manner.

## Marketing Basics and Social Networking

Search engines are very useful for bringing people to your site, but there are many other ways to attract visitors. One of the basic steps of marketing your Web site is to reach out to people offline. There are lots of avenues to market your new Web site in the offline world, such as with direct mailing, real-life social gatherings, meetings, conferences and expositions, and the like. Utilizing the resources in your community such as local papers, targeted mailings, and local organizations will help expand the reach of your Web site into your community. Real-life networking is just as important as online social networking to spread the word of your site. Join local business associations or groups, and attend their meetings to make contacts that can help you bring visitors to your Web site and business. In a world of inboxes full of e-mails, taking the time to reach out offline and sometimes spending the funds to target your audience outside of the online world can give you an advantage of not being lost in the sea of e-mails that everyone receives. Place a small advertisement in a magazine or periodical that relates to your target audience or send postcards, thank-you notes, and flyers with coupons and discounts to turn people into online visitors you may not have reached otherwise. This can be especially helpful to Web sites that have a specific geographical reach.

Social network through sites like Facebook, Twitter, and Google Buzz. New social networking sites are always appearing on the horizon, but be careful to not get social network burnout; concentrate your time on the social network that works best for you. It can be easy to get overwhelmed and over-extended. The plus side of social networking is its ability to exponentially increase your Web site's visibility as you reach out to people who you know and they in turn expand that reach to people they know. The interconnectivity of people and interest groups makes it much easier to reach thousands of people at any given time.

The important part of social networking is the "social" part. It is about creating relationships with people and nurturing that relationship. You want to create fans and loyalty to your brand, which is usually accomplished by cultivating relationships with people who may be interested in what you are offering.

# Why You Need to Keep Your Web Site Up to Date

The biggest security threat to any Web site is to allow the software it runs on to become out-of-date. This applies to hosting as well as the specific software that any site may be running. It is important to use a host that has a good security track record, as well as a knowledgeable staff who stays up to date on industry trends and software. If your host is running out-of-date software and can't explain why, it is time to find a new host.

## Upgrades: Why and How

For Joomla! sites, it is important to subscribe to the news and announcements regarding new releases and any security issues that may have been addressed in the new release. When a new release is issued, it is important to update your Joomla! site as soon as possible. Although some past releases have contained issues that affected existing sites, critical issues are typically fixed quickly with a new release. One thing to check is the developer's site of any extension you may have installed and any issues their extension may have with a new release. If an extension has an issue with a new release of Joomla!, contact the developer and inquire as to when their issue is going to be resolved, and then update both your Joomla! site and the extension. As was mentioned, Sam Moffatt's Update Manager extension is very easy to use and is an excellent way to keep your Joomla! installation up to date.

A number of extension developers include notifications about updates that are available. It is good practice to keep informed on any updates and news regarding the extensions you use on your site. Subscribe to the mailing list, forum, announcements, or news feeds that the developers may offer. When an update to an extension is announced, it is important to update the extension, especially if there is a security issue involved.

As always before updating, be sure to take a full backup of your site's files and database. Do not rely on any backup system your hosting provider may offer. Ultimately, it is your site, and backups are your responsibility. Set up a schedule to take regular backups of your site depending on the rate of change your site goes through in a typical month. If you update content daily and have an interactive site that is active, it may be best to at least get a daily backup of your database and a monthly backup of your site files. If your content doesn't change often, a monthly backup of your full site and database will most likely be sufficient. Be sure to store your back up files off-site. Download them to a local hard drive or disk or store them in a different online location.

A relatively new initiative for the Joomla! project is the Vulnerable Extensions List (VEL) located on the Joomla! Official Documentation wiki at *http://docs.joomla.org/ Vulnerable_Extensions_List*. This initiative was started by a team of interested users who wanted to track vulnerable extensions and has been a valuable asset to the community. You can subscribe to the page's news feed to stay updated on vulnerable extension reports and get extended information on resolutions or ongoing issues.

Any extension that is no longer supported by the developer, as well as any extensions that you are not using but may have installed, should be completely removed from your

Web site. Check to make sure that all related files for any extension that you have uninstalled have been properly removed from your site, because leaving these orphan files on your site could expose your site to a security vulnerability.

## Conclusion

It is important to remember that a Web site is no different from any other part of owning a business or marketing a brand. It takes commitment and regular work to make it work for you. Just as you take care and concern regarding the security of your physical business location, your Web site needs the same care and concern. Marketing and management doesn't stop at the creation of the Web site itself; it is only the beginning of your online marketing strategy. Although for small businesses it can be relatively easy to manage the day-to-day workload of a Web site, sometimes it is necessary to hire professionals to help you. Professionals have emerged in the social networking and marketing field, as well as the SEO field, at an explosive rate. As with any new technology and the professionals who work in an emerging or always-changing field, getting references and samples of past work and understanding exactly what you are hiring the consultant to provide are priceless when it comes to your Web site. Hire a professional to monitor your site and keep it up to date if you do not have the time to commit. It is much less stressful to be proactive than reactive to a bad situation. The Joomla! Resources Directory provides the contact information for professionals who specialize in Joomla! sites and is an excellent reference tool.

# 8

# Practical Application: Joomla! for Business

Free and open source software (FOSS) is good for businesses on a number of levels. Initially, the greatness comes out of the price point. Free or low cost can make the difference in the overall bottom line of a business's financial status. The other advantage is in terms of support. Most FOSS software projects have communities of users and developers that can support the user base. Joomla! is an excellent example of how a community around FOSS software creates, distributes, and supports a software project. Because Joomla! is open source, at anytime you can view, edit, and add to the source code to suit your own purposes. You also can hire someone to do that for you.

The other business advantage that Joomla! offers is the number of available Joomla! extensions, from full-blown e-commerce to client/customer management or data gathering and tracking. This chapter will look at a few practical applications for business and examples of extensions that they would use.

## Basic Planning of Business Sites

The basic principles for creating a business site are simply variations on those for any site. First think about what the purpose or purposes of your site are. Some may be immediate, and some you may want to develop over time as your site evolves. Speak with customers and staff about what they would like in a site in terms of information and interaction. Try to put yourself in the position of a potential customer and think about what information you need.

It is also worth reviewing what information systems your company is using currently, whether Web based or not, and considering whether their use could be enhanced through some integration with your Web site. A system for managing business leads that are linked with contacts that come in via your site would be a good item to consider for integration. Also consider your business's social media presence and how that can be strengthened. If your business doesn't have a social media presence, creating this site will be a good opportunity to implement one.

As you begin to work on the site, gather together materials such as stationery, brochures, fliers, and advertising so that you can ensure that all of these along with your site have consistent and strong branding and messaging.

Finally, in planning your site, make sure to consider the time and effort it will take to maintain a complex site with the potential benefits. Our experience tells us it is better to start small and manageable and then, if it makes sense for your business, expand the site over time in a way that makes sense financially and in terms of the ability of your team to devote the time necessary to manage the site.

# Brochure Sites

Out of the box without any extensions, Joomla! is useful for a brochure Web site. Brochure Web sites are basic sites that mimic the same information that a business would put in a physical paper brochure for distribution or mailing. They usually contain pages such as the home page, an About Us page, a contact information page with a contact form, and a services offered or examples of work page; and it is always a good idea to have a page or pages with client referrals or testimonials. Brochure Web sites can also allow you to have your online catalog available for people to browse or download, as well as specific information to direct new customers to offline purchasing such as store locations and travel directions.

Although Joomla! may seem to be too big of a tool for a simple brochure site, it really isn't. Joomla! is an excellent choice of CMS to use for any business site, in that it can grow and expand easily to suit the needs of any business as the business expands. It gives you as a business owner complete control over your content on your site.

The Joomla! Community Showcase shows some excellent examples of brochure business Web sites (*http://community.joomla.org/showcase/sites/business*).

## Extending Joomla!: Some Extensions to Consider for Business

Some extensions to think about for a simple brochure site (some may be repeats of the basic suggested extensions from Chapter 6) are covered in this section.

### JForms

JForms is an easy-to-use WYSIWYG forms component for Joomla! Forms allow you to collect data and information from your Web site visitors. It is a great way to add a more robust contact form than what is offered in the Joomla! core. The included plugin allows you to embed any form you create into a content item. Brochure sites are an excellent way for people to find your business and have initial contact through your contact form. The content plugin for this extension also allows you to get specific feedback on a content item by allowing you to place a form directly into the content item.

### Very Simple Image Gallery

Very Simple Image Gallery is an easy-to-use picture gallery that allows you to put small picture galleries inside content items through the use of a plugin. It is a great tool to use

to show a portfolio of work or to showcase products. The plugin works by inse
the images in a specified directory (a folder in your *images* directory) in an easy
layout.

The directory should be the name of the folder that contains the images you want to
make into a gallery. Once you have uploaded the photos to this folder, the plugin automatically creates and lays out a very simple-to-navigate and pleasing photo gallery.

The developer's site has very good documentation on how to use the plugin as well
as the different configuration options.

### JoomFB

JoomFB is a component that will work with your Facebook page or Facebook personal
profile to automatically publish your content items right to Facebook. This can save time
in terms of trying to use social media to promote your business, content, or products.
The developer has good support and documentation on their site as well as options for
additional paid-for functionality and support.

### Twitter Status

Twitter Status will update your Twitter account with an article's title and a link to the
article when a new article is published on your site. This is also a great time-saver in
terms of marketing to social media for your site. The developer has very good documentation and support channels to contact for assistance with the extension.

### Facebook Like Box

Facebook Like Box can add a number of Facebook options to your site such as a like
box, a feed of your Facebook updates, or both. It is highly configurable and able to be
styled to suit the available space you have on your site. The developer offers documentation on how to set up the module.

## E-commerce Web Sites

There are many reasons to have an e-commerce Web site. It allows your Web visitors to
browse your products or merchandise and purchase immediately. For some retailers,
online e-commerce has removed the need for a traditional brick-and-mortar storefront,
reducing their business overhead costs, while for others it has opened up sales to a
worldwide market to supplement their sales from their physical location.

Joomla! has a number of options available to expand your Web site into an e-commerce
site. It also has the ability to bridge or connect with any number of stand-alone online
shopping carts and e-commerce solutions.

One of the first things you should think about before setting up your online shopping cart or e-commerce is how you will accept payments online.

## Which Payment System Is Right for You?

If you already have a traditional physical location, you most likely already have a merchant
account through your banking or financial institution. Your bank or financial institution

should be able to advise as to whether there are any steps you need to take regarding accepting online payments and whether they have specific rules for online transactions or a specific set of transaction fees for online transactions.

Fees are a big part of the thinking process for deciding which payment system to use. Some systems charge either a fixed rate per transaction or a percentage of the transaction total, others charge a monthly fee, and still others charge both transaction fees and a monthly fee. Make sure to understand exactly how much money they get and how much you keep. Fees can make or break a new business in terms of profitability.

Merchant accounts work by depositing the money directly into a bank account. This can be very advantageous to new businesses that may be running their finances tightly. The quicker the money is in your bank account, the more quickly you can access the funds. Because these funds go directly into your bank account, your funds in a number of cases are more secure, especially in the United States where bank accounts are insured by the FDIC. On the other side of the equation are payment processors that are not associated with banks, such as PayPal, for example. With these sorts of accounts, your money is held by the payment processor in that account until you transfer that money to your bank account, which can take a number of days. Also, payment processors not associated with banks are not insured. A bonus to online processors such as PayPal is that they are easy to set up, they accept a varied array of payment types and currencies, and you can use your account at various online stores yourself for purchasing.

Regardless of the payment processor or merchant account you may use for your business, be sure to research how each company handles customer disputes or fraud, and be familiar with the process including any notifications you may be required to give your customers.

Another item to note is that some online processors such as PayPal, if they suspect transactions are occurring fraudulently, can freeze your account and block you from accessing any funds you have collected. It is a good idea to have more than one payment option available for you to use. A backup processor is also a good idea in the event of a technical issue.

## Extending Joomla!: Some Extensions to Consider for E-commerce

There are some extensions that are specifically targeted toward business use that perform specific functionalities as e-commerce or shops.

### VirtueMart

VirtueMart is a full-featured e-commerce shopping cart that has been the leader of the e-commerce Joomla! extensions since the beginning of the Joomla! project. A huge third-party developer community is involved in creating extensions for VirtueMart that cover every need for a full e-commerce solution including custom development. VirtueMart also handles inventory and stock. An excellent program is available to businesses that use QuickBooks accounting to integrate their VirtueMart data into QuickBooks for bookkeeping and business operation purposes.

### Magento

Magento is one of the most popular full-featured, stand-alone e-commerce shopping carts. Although it isn't a Joomla!-specific extension, a number of bridges exist to tie your Joomla! site and a Magento e-commerce site together. Magento is available as a free download, and a number of customization and support programs are available. Magento also supports multistore setups.

### FoxyCart

FoxyCart is a popular full-featured, fee-based software as a service (SaaS) e-commerce shopping cart. It is fully customizable with CSS and HTML and was built to integrate with various CMS solutions.

### osCommerce

osCommerce is one of the longest-running open source e-commerce shopping carts. Although it isn't necessarily a solution for inexperienced people, it does have a very large and supportive community that creates extensions and add-ons to functionality. There is a bridge for osCommerce to integrate it with Joomla!

### Tienda

Tienda is a new full-featured shopping cart extension developed especially for Joomla! It was designed and developed from scratch based on Joomla!'s coding standards, framework, and MVC method. At the time of the writing of this book, Tienda was still partially in development but has released a relatively popular and stable e-commerce platform. Tienda is definitely an extension to keep an eye on as development progresses.

### RokQuickCart

RokQuickCart is a very simple shopping cart component that easily works with PayPal and Google Checkout. If a full-featured e-commerce solution is too much software for the type of shop you need for your site or you have a small number of products, it is a great option. It is very simple to customize the look and feel of the cart to suit any Joomla! template.

Another option if you already have a PayPal site is to simply create content items and place buttons created in PayPal for your items. There are also a number of ways to integrate a PayPal shop with Joomla! such as wrapping it using the wrapping feature in Joomla!

## Other Business Site Extensions

While brochure sites and e-commerce sites are some of the most prevalent types of business sites, some businesses have other needs such as client management or customer support and project tracking. Joomla! can also be used to provide intranet or extranet for your company; do scheduling, project management, document management, and contact management; and fill other common business needs.

### MaQma

MaQma is a full-featured ticketing and customer support portal extension that allows you to organize your customer support with FAQs, a knowledge base, a ticketing system, and client management.

### Project Fork

Project Fork is a project management extension that can be configured to work as an internal company project tracking system or as a BaseCamp-like project tracking that clients and customers can interact with. There are a number of add-ons for Project Fork as well as theme packs to integrate it with your Joomla! site.

## Joomla! Authentication Tools

Many businesses already have servers with user accounts set up for their staff members. Joomla! Authentication Tools allows you to use that database rather than the Joomla! user system for logging into your site. This can substantially improve the ease of use for your site by eliminating the need for multiple logins and passwords.

Many businesses find that Web-based applications provide a good way to manage lead and customer contact information. Several Joomla! extensions provide this functionality, and some also allow you to link information collected through your Web site to be integrated into an enterprise resource planning (ERP) or customer relationship management (CRM) application. For example, there are a number of ways in which your site can interact with SugarCRM, Alfresco, webERP, vTiger, and others by using Joomla! extensions designed for this purpose.

The Joomla! Extensions Directory also features numerous solutions for specific business sectors such as restaurants, real estate, booking, auto sales, and other specialized areas. It is well worth checking the directory for extensions designed for these. Even if they do not perfectly match what you need, the fact that they are open source and licensed under the GPL means that you can modify or adapt them as you need or pay the original developer or another professional to do the modifications for you.

## Business Web Site Demo

You can visit this site at *http://officialjoomlabook.com/business*.

This illustrates the creation of an enhanced brochure site using the example of a toy shop that specializes in handcrafted wooden toys.

### Phase 1: Brochure Site

A basic brochure site will have about five pages:

- Home page
- News
- A second page with more information

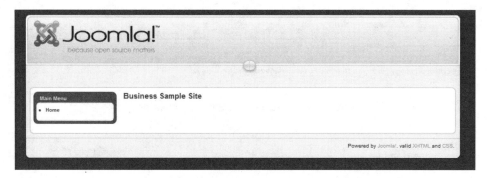

Figure 8.1  Front page view of a new Joomla! installation without sample
data installed

- Contact page
- About Us page

Using a content management system to make this type of site will allow it to develop
over time. This site uses a modified version of the Milkyway template that comes with
your Joomla! installation. We started by installing Joomla! with no sample data, as shown
in Figure 8.1.

### Creating a Home Page

First, we added content. Our first goal was to create a simple but attractive home page
that gives basic information about the shop and features some of the products. For the
home page, we decided to use the Very Simple Image Gallery plugin, which we downloaded from the developer and installed using the installer.

To install the plugin, navigate to the Extension Manager. Click Choose File to find
the package that you downloaded from the developer, and then click Upload File &
Install, as shown in Figure 8.2. You should get a success screen as in Figure 8.3.

Next, navigate to the Plugin Manager, and enable the Very Simple Image Gallery
plugin by clicking the red icon in the Enabled column. This will enable the plugin and
turn the icon you clicked into a green check mark, as shown in Figure 8.4.

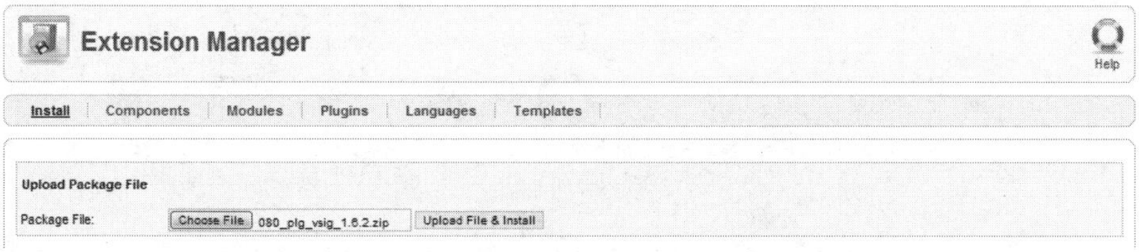

Figure 8.2  Installing Very Simple Image Gallery plugin

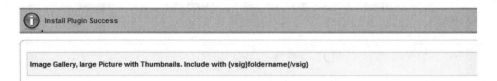

Figure 8.3  Install Plugin Success message

Figure 8.4  Plugin Manager screen showing Very Simple Image
Gallery enabled

In the Media Manager (as shown in Chapter 4), create a folder called *toys* in the
*images/stories* folder to hold the images, as shown in Figure 8.5, with the images to be
displayed on the home page. In our case, we used eight images. We uploaded these to the
folder as explained in Chapter 4 and shown in Figure 8.6.

Figure 8.5  Media Manager showing how to create a new directory for toys

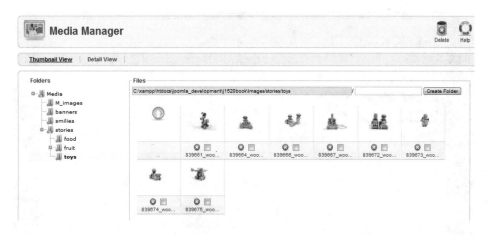

Figure 8.6  Media Manager showing all the toy pictures uploaded into the
toys directory

**Tip**

We found the images to use in our shop by going to Stock.xchange (*http://sxc.hu*). This
site is a great way to find stock images for your Web site. On the site you can find royalty-
free images under various licensing terms. It is important to look at the licensing terms for
any photo or graphic you want to use. The Web site also has stock imagery that you can
purchase for use. The photographer of the toy images is Cecile Graat; she is from
Netherlands and has a Web site (*http://gracedesign.nl*). You can find her Stock.xchng
profile at *www.sxc.hu/profile/Cieleke*.

We then navigated to the Content Manager. First we created a section (Shop) and a
category (Shop) in the section. Then we created a article in the Article Manager with
some text and `{vsig}toys{/vsig}`. This will insert an image gallery created from the
images in the *toys* folder. We called this article Come and Play.

Going to the Menu Item Manager for the main menu, we changed the menu item
type to Single Article (see Chapter 4) for the Home menu item and selected the article
we created. The home page now looks like Figure 8.7.

To further enhance the home page, we then removed the author and date from the
page by changing the menu parameters, as shown in Figure 8.8.

Most extensions have many options that allow you to manage their appearance and
functionality, and Very Simple Image Gallery has many, as shown in Figure 8.9. These can
appear overwhelming, but often you do not need to change many of them.

Figure 8.7  Front-end view of the new home page

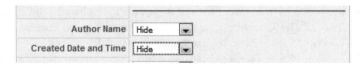

Figure 8.8  Menu Item Manager editing options to hide the author and
date on a specific menu item

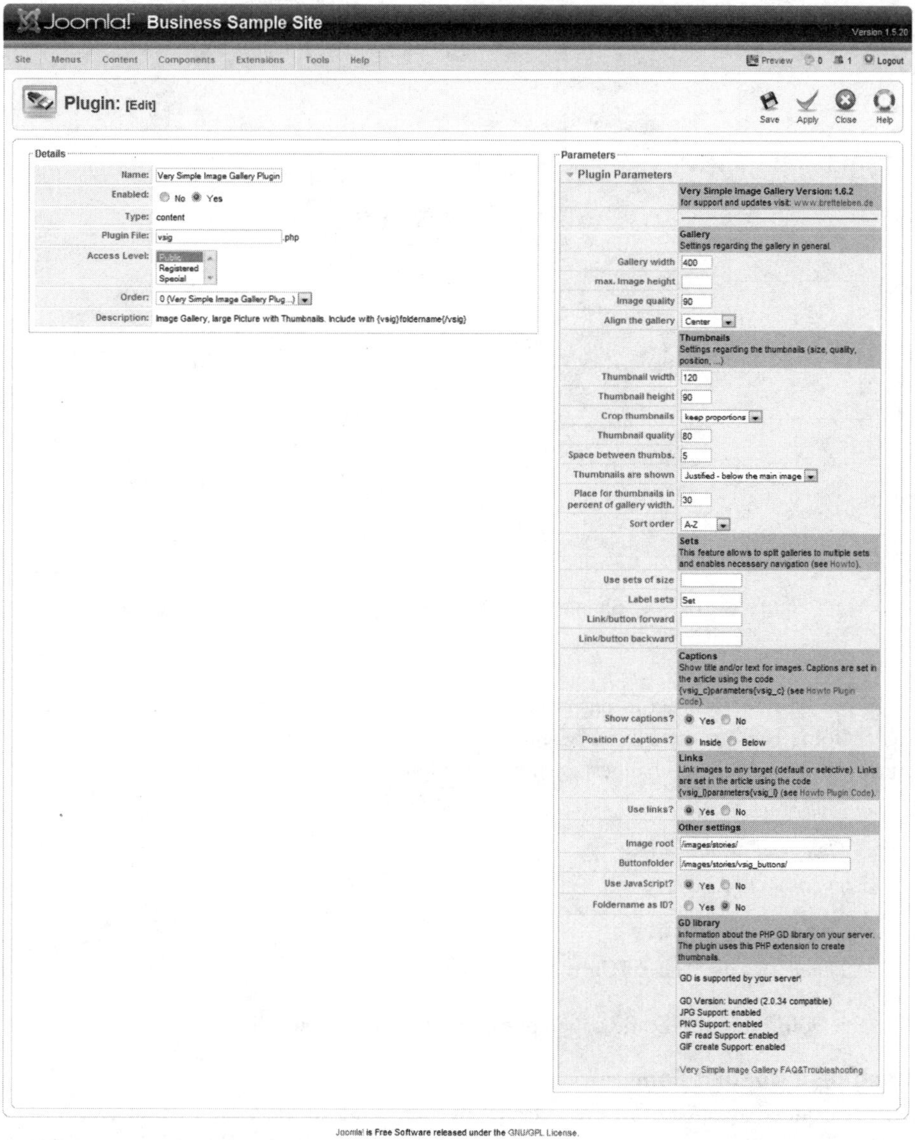

Figure 8.9  Very Simple Image Gallery plugin configuration parameters

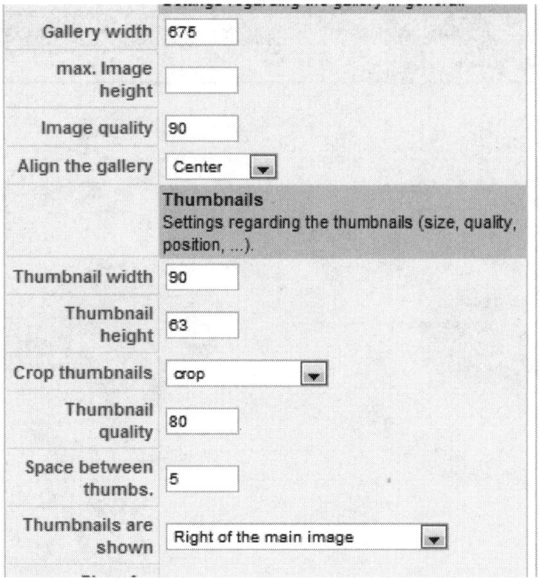

Figure 8.10  Very Simple Image Gallery plugin configuration parameters
that were changed

In our case, we wanted to rearrange the small images to be in two columns on the right. Going back to the Plugin Manager, we opened Very Simple Image Gallery for editing and made these changes, as shown in Figure 8.10:

- *Gallery width:* 675
- *Thumbnail width:* 90
- *Thumbnail height:* 63
- *Crop thumbnails:* Crop
- *Thumbnails are shown:* Right of the main image

After doing this, the home page appears as shown in Figure 8.11.

## Creating a Contact Form

Next we added a contact form. We started by navigating to the Contact Manager found in the Components menu. First, we created a category, Toy Shop. This is just like creating a content category as explained in Chapter 4. Then we created a contact within that category, as shown in Figure 8.12. One thing to notice is that we used some HTML in the Miscellaneous Information field. This is not necessary, but it makes the page look better in this site.

Figure 8.11  Front-end view after configuration of Very Simple
Image Gallery

Add a standard contact link to the main menu. Make sure to have a working e-mail address that will receive the messages. Nothing frustrates a potential customer like sending a message and not getting a reply. Figure 8.13 shows the contact form.

### Additional Content Items

We created two more articles in the Shop category. One is a more detailed product description, and one is an About Us page. We linked each of these from the main menu.

We also created a new category called News and one article in it. For that we made a Category Blog menu link so that whatever the latest news item is will display. Since we do not expect there to be a lot of news articles, we set the display to 2 Leading, 0 Intro, 1 Column, 2 Links. Later, if it turns out that there are frequent updates, this can be rearranged easily by changing the menu link.

### Using Custom HTML Modules

By far the most important piece of information about your business is its name. If you have a physical store, the address is also of vital importance since your goal is to attract customers to your location. The last step of creating content for this brochure site is to add that information to all the site's pages.

We created two Custom HTML modules for the header of the site. To create a Custom HTML module, navigate to the Module Manager, and click New. Then select

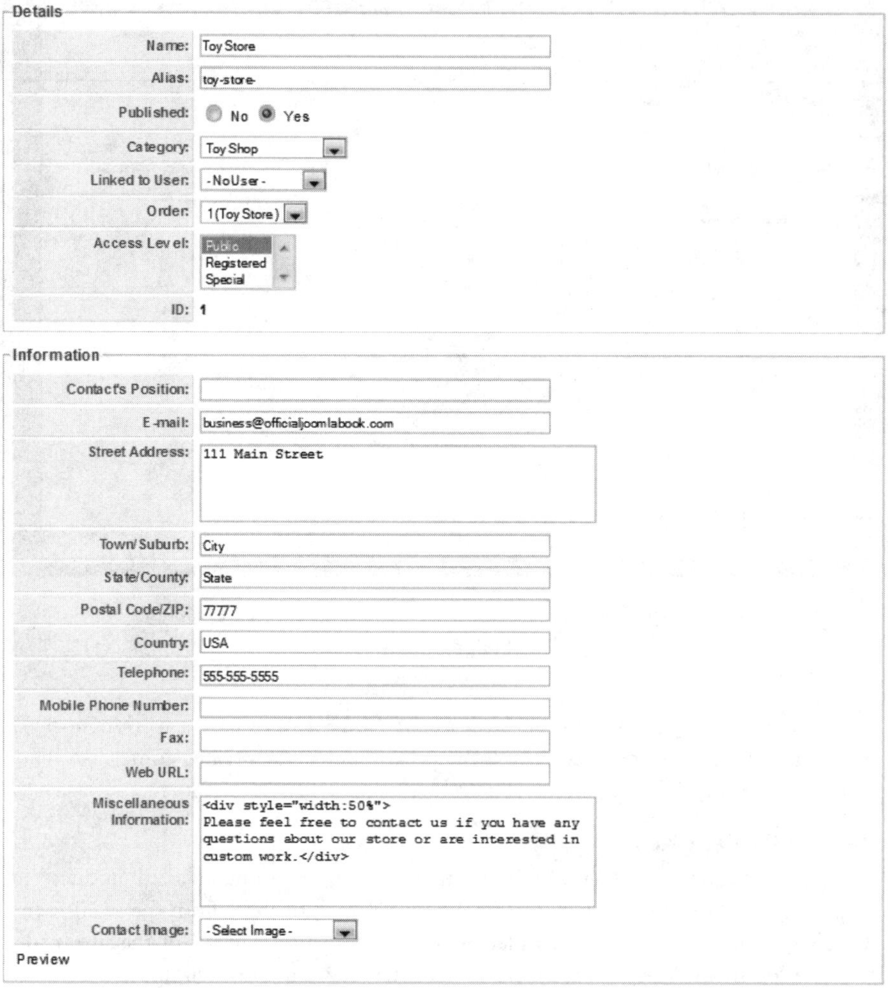

Figure 8.12  Contact-editing screen showing HTML in the Miscellaneous
Information field

Custom HTML from the list of module types available, as shown in Figure 8.14. Then
click Next.

In the Details area of the screen, we typed **Header** in the Title field, changed Show
Title to No, and made the Module Position Top, as shown in Figure 8.15.

We moved to the editor area at the bottom of the page. Here we clicked the Toggle
Editor button and entered our text as shown in Figure 8.16. We did this in order to
enter some HTML that controls the basic layout of text on the Web. The text is simply
the name and address of the shop. Some things to notice are that the name and the street

Figure 8.13  Front-end view of the contact form

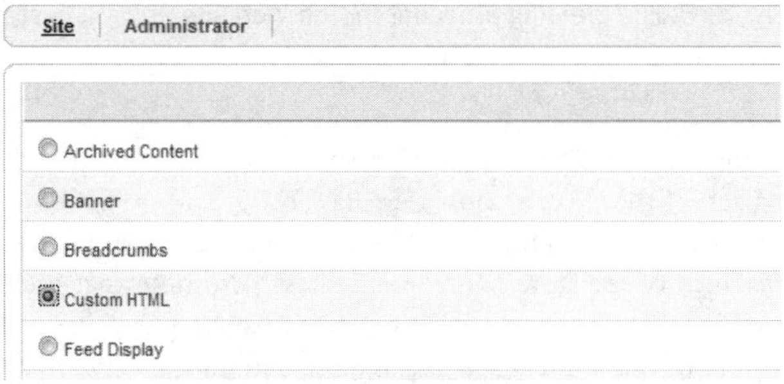

Figure 8.14  Creating a new Custom HTML module

Figure 8.15  Custom HTML module parameters

Figure 8.16  Creating a header for the Web site using a custom
HTML module

address are each enclosed by a pair of tags: `<div></div>`. These define different areas on your Web page. Each of the `<div>` containers has an ID: `id="siteheader"` for the name and `id="sitelocation"` for the address. We will use these in the next section to control the appearance of the store name and address. Also note that each line in the address is enclosed in `<p></p>` tags, which represent paragraphs. Essentially this will ensure that each line of the address appears as a separate line on the Web page. HTML is the basic language of the Web, and as you become more experienced in building your sites, there will be times when you want to use it.

We made a second custom module called Tag Line assigned to position user3 and with Show Title set to No. The custom output contains this:

```
<div>Handcrafted toys to last a lifetime</div>
```

Figure 8.17  Front-end view with custom HTML header

At this point, the page looks as it does in Figure 8.17. All of the brochure content is now in place, and we are ready to work on the site template.

## Customizing the Template

In Chapter 5, modifying templates that are installed with Joomla! is examined in detail. In this section, we will modify the Milkyway template to make it more appropriate for this site. What will be presented are some basic ideas. As you work on your own Web site and gain experience, you will probably want to go much further than this example.

Before beginning work on the template, we created a new image to replace the Joomla! logo in the header. This image should be 298 pixels wide and 75 pixels tall. If you have an image that is close to this size but not exactly the same, that will work. You can create or edit an image by using software such as GIMP or Photoshop or by using an online image editor such as Picnik. In our case, we will be using a photograph of a toy, but if you have a logo or other branding images, you would use that.

Upload the image using the Media Manager. We put the image in a folder called *header*. Our image is called *headerimage.png*.

Also, we removed the blue border around the menu by navigating to the Module Manager and editing the Main Menu module. As shown in Figure 8.18, in the Advanced Parameters section, delete the Module Class Suffix setting (when you open the module, this will say *_menu*).

As mentioned earlier, HTML is the basic building block of Web pages. The HTML that controls the appearance of a site (such as fonts, colors, and background images) is managed by Cascading Style Sheets (CSS). The changes to the template will mainly involve changes to the CSS contained in the template.

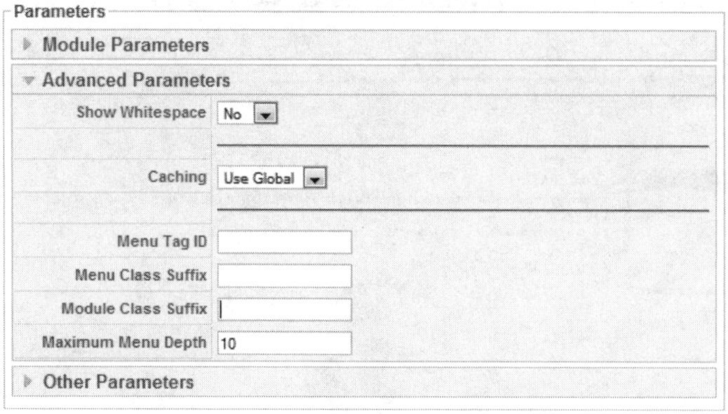

Figure 8.18 Removing the Module Class Suffix setting to change the way a module displays and is styled

When working on a template, you should always start by making a copy. If you do your work on a copy, you will always have the original code if you make a mistake. To copy the Milkyway template, you will need to log in to the control panel of your site, go to the File Manager, and navigate to the *templates* folder. Chapter 3 covers how to use the File Manager in detail. Select the *rhuk_milkyway* folder as shown in Figure 8.19, and click the Copy icon. Copy the folder to a *rhuk_milkyway2* directory, as shown in Figure 8.20.

In your new folder, edit the *TemplateDetails.xml* file by changing the name to `<name>rhuk_milkyway2</name>`.

Finally, navigate to the *css* folder in the *milkyway2* directory, and create a new file called *override.css* by clicking the New File icon as shown in Figure 8.21, and then enter the new file name, as shown in Figure 8.22.

Now return to the site administrator. Navigate to the Template Manager, and make rhuk_milkyway2 the default template by clicking the circle by its name and then the Default icon (a yellow star), as shown in Figure 8.23.

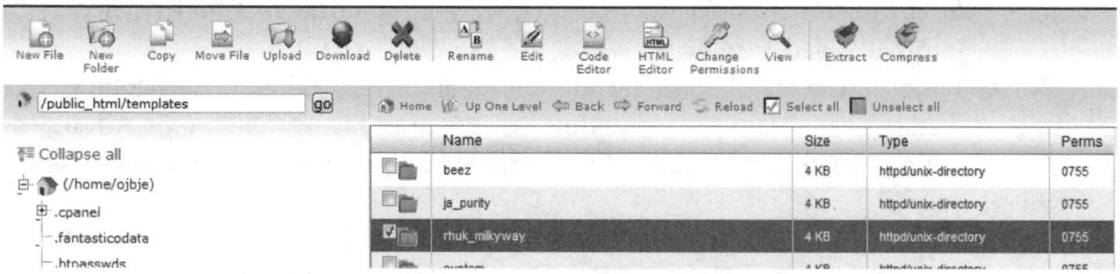

Figure 8.19 Using Cpanel File Manager to make a copy of the Milkyway template

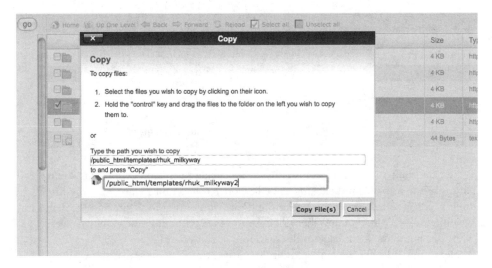

Figure 8.20  Copy dialog box to copy rhuk_milkyway to rhuk_milkyway2

Figure 8.21  Cpanel File Manager New File icon

Figure 8.22  New File dialog box

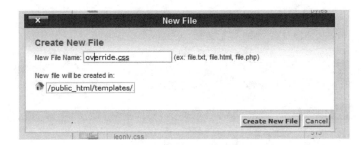

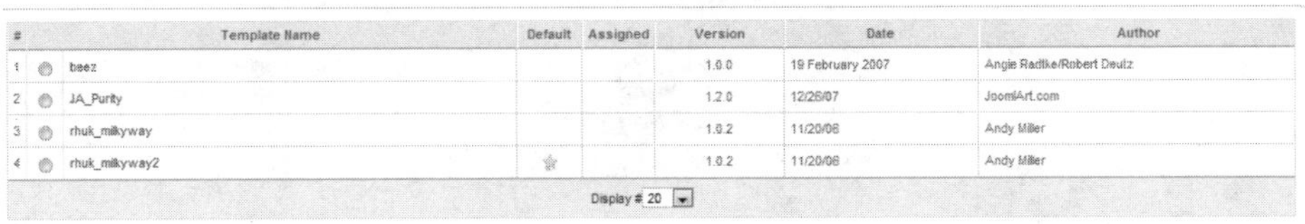

| # | Template Name | Default | Assigned | Version | Date | Author |
|---|---------------|---------|----------|---------|------|--------|
| 1 | baez | | | 1.0.0 | 19 February 2007 | Angie Radtke/Robert Deutz |
| 2 | JA_Purity | | | 1.2.0 | 12/26/07 | JoomlArt.com |
| 3 | rhuk_milkyway | | | 1.0.2 | 11/20/08 | Andy Miller |
| 4 | rhuk_milkyway2 | ☆ | | 1.0.2 | 11/20/08 | Andy Miller |

Display # 20

Figure 8.23  Template Manager screen showing rhuk_milkyway2 as the
default template

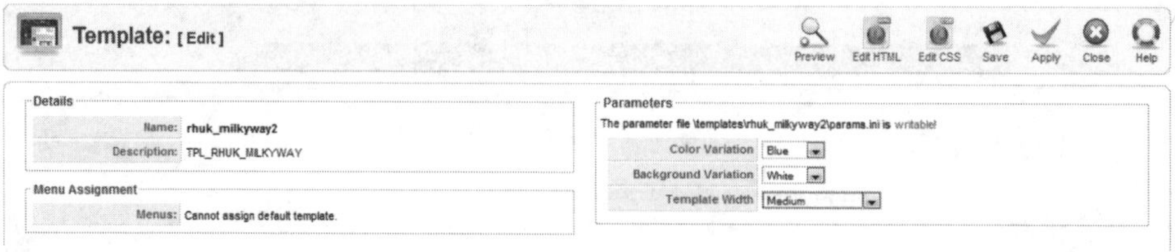

Template: [ Edit ]

Preview    Edit HTML    Edit CSS    Save    Apply    Close    Help

Details

Name: rhuk_milkyway2

Description: TPL_RHUK_MILKYWAY

Menu Assignment

Menus: Cannot assign default template.

Parameters

The parameter file \templates\rhuk_milkyway2\params.ini is writable!

Color Variation    Blue

Background Variation    White

Template Width    Medium

Figure 8.24  Changing the template parameters

Edit the rhuk_milkyway2 template by either clicking its name or selecting the radio button beside its name and clicking the edit icon. As shown in Figure 8.24, the first thing we did was to change the Background Variation setting to White and the Template Width setting to Medium and then click Apply (Save without closing) the changes.

At this point, the front page of the site looks as shown in Figure 8.25.

Next, click Edit HTML, and add this line just above `</header>`, as shown in Figure 8.26.

```
<link href="<?php echo $this->baseurl
?>/templates/rhuk_milkyway2/css/override.css" rel="stylesheet" type="text/css" />
```

This means that the new file you created will be used when your Web pages are rendered. Because this line is going last in the list of CSS files, its instructions will override any others that may have been given in files above it on the list. There are four other instances of `rhuk_milkyway` in the *index.php* file that you will need to change to `rhuk_milkyway2`.

Figure 8.25  Front-end view of home page

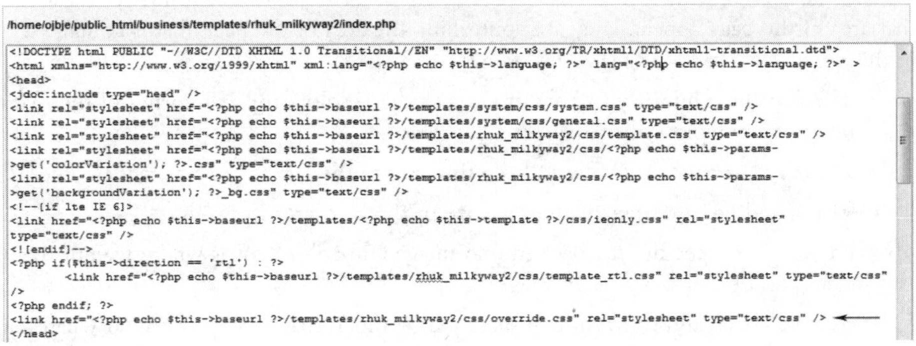

Figure 8.26  Adding override.css to the index.php file

Click Save, and click Edit CSS. As shown in Figure 8.27, you will see your *override.css* file in the list of files. Select the file, and click Edit. You will see a blank file.

To change the header image, add the following code (remember to change "officialjoomlabook.com" to your domain name):

```
div#logo {
    position: absolute;
    left: 0;
    top: 0;
    float: left;
    width: 298px;
    height: 94px;
    background:
        url(http://officialjoomlabook.com/business/images/header/headerimage.png)
        0 0 no-repeat;
    margin-left: 30px;
    margin-top: 25px;
}
```

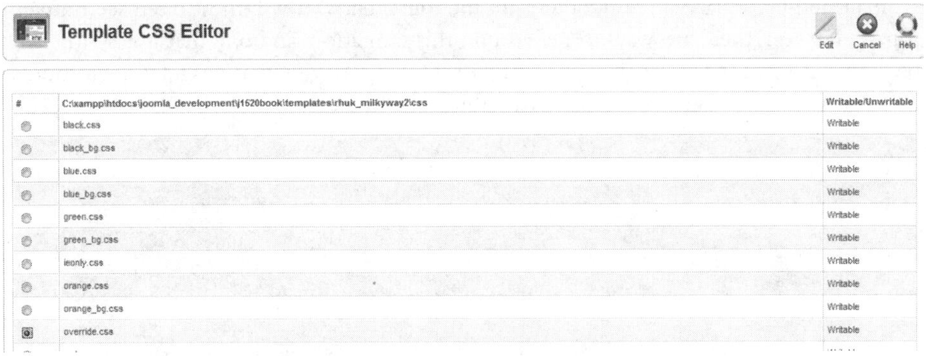

Figure 8.27  Template CSS Editor screen

This looks complex, but it is really just a series of instructions about how to make that area of the page appear. They are controlling the area of the page that is contained in the `<div id="logo"></div>` set of tags.

- The first three lines say to start this area at the absolute top-left corner of the main body of any region of the page it is located in.
- `float: left` means to always keep this area to the left of the area it is located in.
- `width` and `height` specify an exact size of the logo area in pixels.
- `background` specifies the background image and color. This is where we put the exact location of our header image.
- `margin-left` and `margin-top` specify how much space to have around whatever is contained in the `<div id="logo"></di>`.

After applying the changes the file, the header of the site looks as shown in Figure 8.28.

**TIP**

When modifying a template, you can often copy code from the original CSS files to your file. For example, the original `div#logo` code can be copied from the *template.css* file and edited.

Next we wanted to change the rest of the header and decide the color and style of the rest of the site. We wanted the store name to be in the middle of the header and in large type and the address on the right to be in smaller type. Because this is a relatively simple site—and because part of the messaging of the site is that simple toys are good—we decided to add just one additional color to the design and to remove the blue color from the menu links. Using the color of the string connecting the cars in the train in the header image, we decided on the color with this code: #990000.

We also wanted to change the font for the store name and tag line to something more distinctive. If you already have an established font for your business, you would want to use that, but in this case we wanted something new. One issue with font choices on the Web is that there are only five fonts considered "Web safe," meaning they will render correctly in all browsers. They are Arial, Courier New, Verdana, Times New Roman, and Georgia. As a result, these are the fonts that you will most often see on Web pages. However, there are ways to get around this limitation, and one that is easy for beginners is to use the Google Web Font API. This is a service that provides open source fonts for Web site designers. We chose the font called Reenie Beanie.

Figure 8.28  Front-end view of the header logo image

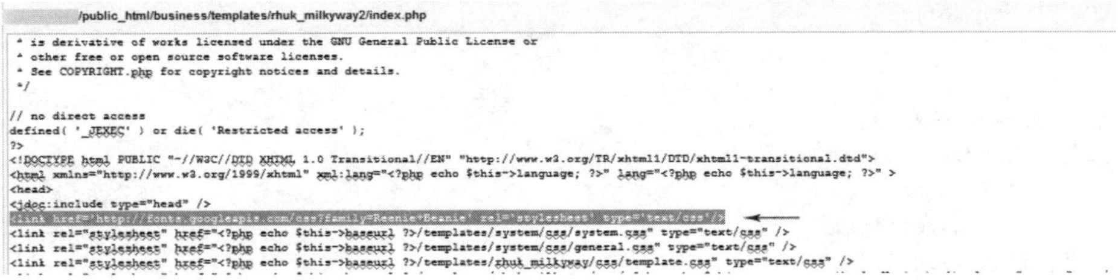

Figure 8.29  Adding Google Font API to the index.php file

To incorporate the Reenie Beanie font in our site, we need to edit the HTML file for the template and add one line at the top of the <head> area, as shown in Figure 8.29.

```
<link href='http://fonts.googleapis.com/css?family=Reenie+Beanie'
rel='stylesheet' type='text/css'/>
```

### Tip

Chapter 5 discusses color choice in depth.

To learn more about the Google Font API, visit *https://code.google.com/webfonts*. There are other commercial and noncommercial font solutions available.

There are more advanced ways to use the Google Font API and other font solutions, but they are appropriate for more experienced users. Documentation for these is widely available.

Remember that earlier in this chapter we created modules for the header and tag line. We want to use the Reenie Beanie font for the name of the store and the tag line and to incorporate our color choice. In the header, we also want to move the address to the right of the store name. To do this, we add to the *override.css* file. The `#siteheader` and `#sitelocation` tags refer to the IDs we created in the custom modules. The `div#pillmenu` ID refers to the area containing the tag line module. The CSS that we added is as follows:

```
#siteheader {
    font-family: 'Reenie Beanie', serif;
    font-size: 80px;
    font-style: normal;
    font-weight: 400;
    text-shadow: none;
    text-decoration: none;
    text-transform: none;
    letter-spacing: 0em;
    word-spacing: 0em;
    line-height: 1em;
    color:#990000;
```

```
       float: left;
  }


  #sitelocation {
       color:#990000;
       float:right;
       font-size:14px;
       font-weight:normal;
       padding-right:1px;
  }


  div#pillmenu {
     font-family: 'Reenie Beanie', serif;
     font-size: 22px;
     font-style: normal;
     font-weight: 400;
     text-shadow: none;
     text-decoration: none;
     text-transform: none;
     letter-spacing: 0em;
     word-spacing: 0em;
     line-height: 1em;
     margin-top: 5px;
  }
```

Next we added CSS to change the colors of various headers and titles that are used in
the site. We also changed the font of the headers from Arial to Verdana with the CSS that
we also added to the *override.css* file:

```
h3, .componentheading, table.moduletable th, legend {
     margin: 0;
     font-weight: normal;
     color: #990000;
     font-family: Verdana, sans-serif;
     font-size: 1.5em;
     padding-left: 0px;
     margin-bottom: 10px;
     text-align: left;
  }


  table.contentpaneopen h3 {
     margin-top: 25px;
     font-weight: normal;
     color: #990000;
   font-family: Verdana, sans-serif;
  }
```

```
table.contentpaneopen h4 {
    font-family: Verdana, sans-serif;
    color: #990000;
}
div#header_r {
    height:90px;
    overflow:hidden;
    padding-left:320px;
    padding-right:50px;
    padding-top:25px;
    text-align:left;
}
a:link, a:visited {
    color: #990000;
}
```

Finally, we added some additional CSS to change spacing and other small elements to styles we prefer. Taking the time to add some polishing CSS will make your site more professional appearing and also reflect your preferences better:

```
div#header_r {
    height:90px;
    overflow:hidden;
    padding-left:320px;
    padding-right:50px;
    padding-top:25px;
    text-align:left;
}
table.contentpaneopen p {
    padding-right: 150px;
}

#leftcolumn {
    margin-top: 10px;
}
td.pill_l {
    background:        url("../images/mw_menu_cap_l.png")
        no-repeat scroll 0 0 transparent;
    height: 32px;
    width: 19px;
}
```

At this point, the site appears as in Figure 8.30. This is a complete brochure site. You can download a complete copy of the *override.css* file from *http://officialjoomlabook.com*.

Figure 8.30  Front-end view of the toy store brochure site home page

## Phase 2: Add a Simple Shopping Cart

As your site develops, you may want to move it beyond a brochure site by adding other features. Many options are available. In this example, we add a simple shopping cart called RokQuickCart.

Find the extension in the Joomla! Extensions Directory, and download it. Then install it using the Extension Manager as explained earlier.

You configure RokQuickCart by navigating to RokQuickCart in the Components menu. Click the Parameters icon as shown in Figure 8.31.

There are many configuration options, as shown in Figure 8.32, but as you set up your shop, the most important will be your payment processor information. For this cart,

Figure 8.31  RokQuickCart Manager screen showing the parameters icon
in the upper-right side

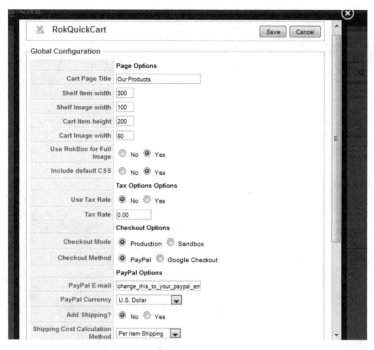

Figure 8.32  RokQuickCart configuration screen

both PayPal and Google Checkout are available. You fill in your account information. While you are working on your site, you should use the Sandbox Checkout Mode. To actually sell items, you would change Checkout Mode to Production.

After saving your configuration, you are ready to add items to your shop. Click the New icon, and add the information you want. In this case, we just added an image and name, but you can also add a description for example. RokQuickCart uses its own folder in the Media Manager so you will have to upload any images that you want to use even if they are already in other folders. When you are done, you add a menu link to RokQuickCart. In our case, we made a new menu called Expansion Menu and made the link there. We also added a custom module with some introductory text about the products and assigned it to the user1 position only on the shop page. Figure 8.33 shows the resulting page.

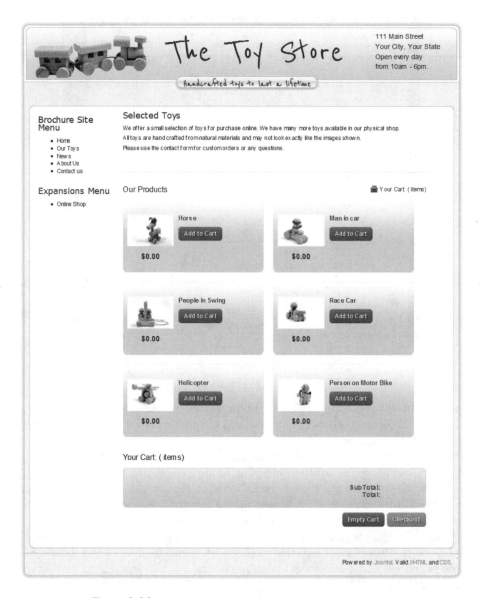

Figure 8.33  Front-end view of the simple shopping cart using
RokQuickCart

# Conclusion

Taking the step to put your business online will open your business doors to the world. An important thing to keep in mind is that you still need to think about demographics and your target audience. Also remember that having a Joomla! site will allow you to steadily grow and expand your Web presence, so you can take your time to develop your site. Joomla! allows you to have control over your site and your content at all times, which gives you the flexibility to be able to plan your Web site rollout in phases or stages to best suit your financial situation, time constraints, or level of knowledge. Professionals are always available for hire to help you make your site the best it can be or if you experience problems. There is also a great group of Professional Joomla! trainers that offer classes all over the world from beginner to advanced. The Joomla! Resource Directory has an ever-expanding list of Joomla! professionals from which to choose. The template forum on *http://forum.joomla.org* is an excellent source of CSS and other design advice.

The step-by-step example shows how to make a basic brochure site for a small business and how to expand it to become somewhat more interactive. As you develop your own site, keep in mind the principles that were explained in earlier chapters including having a well-thought-out organization and design, relating visually and in terms of message to other marketing materials you have, and being realistic about the time it takes to maintain complex sites.

# 9

# Practical Application: Joomla! for NGOs/NPOs, Groups, Clubs, and Organizations

As mentioned in the previous chapter about business applications, Joomla! is an excellent choice because it is free in cost and the code is open source. This makes it a very attractive choice for nongovernmental organizations (NGOs), nonprofit organizations (NPOs), groups, clubs, and organizations. One of the benefits of Joomla! specifically for this application is the collaborative environments that can be set up using Joomla! that help organizations not only connect and organize within their group but also reach out to the greater public and promote their platform or message, gain financial support, and connect like-minded people to achieve a common idea or goal.

## Basic Planning of Group Sites

When creating a Web site for a nonprofit organization or group, whether as a volunteer or paid staff member, there are a few general principles to consider.

- What is the purpose of the site? Is it to give information about the organization, advocate for a specific cause, raise money, attract volunteers, or engage the community of members, clients, or potential clients?

- Is the site envisioned as central to your fulfilling organization's mission? Or is it a brochure site?

- How much interaction will there be between the site visitors and the organization and site visitors and each other?

- Who will manage the site, a volunteer, a staff member, or a team? How much time will they have to devote to it?

As you consider these questions, you will want to discuss goals and expectations for the site with various stakeholders or constituencies connected with the organization or group. Although these groups may create long lists of feature requests, what is most important at this stage is to identify the main purposes, goals, and audiences for your site. You may also want to find out what other solutions are being used within the organization. For example, is there an existing membership list? Is there an e-mail list? How are they managed? Does it make sense to integrate these into the Web site? Keeping focused on the message can be difficult for any organization. Having a clear mission, vision, and strategy can help to solidify your communications and the connection between your organization's members, volunteers, and supporters.

You should also gather together materials such as a mission statement, contact information, images, press releases, printed brochures or stationary, and other materials that may be used on your site. Especially if you are a volunteer, it makes sense to plan to implement a site in stages, starting with a basic site and then enhancing it as time goes on.

If your organization already has a logo or colors associated with it, build on that identity by incorporating them into your site. If the organization does not have these, this can be a good opportunity to develop them. Nonprofit groups can benefit from branding and a strong visual identity just as much as businesses.

## Leveraging Your Site to Raise Awareness and Gain Momentum

Joomla!'s flexibility and ability to be extended makes it easy to use your NGO/NPO or organization Web site as a marketing tool to bring awareness to your cause; attract volunteers, members, or donors; or encourage people to take action. Here are some things to consider to make the most of Joomla!'s marketing advantage.

- Your front page should exhibit a short explanation of the mission or goals of the organization, with easily found navigation to longer mission statements, services, or actions. Utilizing a tag line or slogan that is easily identifiable and memorable is a good way to solidify your brand.

- Visitors should see immediately how to become involved or donate to your mission or cause.

- There should be a news media or press release section of the site to help promote and encourage media outlets to spread your message to encourage new donors and members.

- If you have a physical address that you want people to visit (for meetings or religious services, for example) or regular events, put them on the home page with a link to travel directions and maps.

- Have a general contact form for visitors to get in touch with your organization, making sure that there is someone who will reply promptly. Most hosts provide customers with basic e-mail service.

- Having a latest news or blog section with current and active content will encourage repeat visitors to the site, which in turn will help convert visitors into donors or members.

- Utilize social media to encourage member activity and bring new members or donors to your site. As with any marketing materials, the look and message should be consistent across all platforms so your brand is recognized. Integrate extensions that update social media sites when you post new content.

- An extremely valuable action for any NGO/NPO is to be publicly thankful to those who support it as volunteers or financial contributors. Creating goals and activities to engage visitors or members is important, but it is equally important to acknowledge how goals and activities are progressing. Thanking those who are helping goals to be reached or activities to be successful encourages more engagement from visitors.

## Extensions for Enabling Basic Interaction

As always, extensions for your nonprofit site should be carefully considered. They increase the flexibility and functionality of your site, but they also increase the complexity of managing it. Consider what you want to achieve with your site, explore the options available, and then make decisions. New extensions are always being added to the Joomla! Extensions Directory, and new versions of extensions that add new functionality are continually released.

The following are some extensions to consider that help keep your organization's site focused but improve its ability to be in touch with visitors and membership.

### MadBlanks

MadBlanks is a survey and quiz component that easily allows any Joomla! site to gather detailed survey information or create fun quizzes for their visitors. Surveys can be as simple as yes/no or true/false questions to open fill-in-the-blank questionnaires. MadBlanks is very robust with functionality to create pie and bar graphs based on results, as well as fully customizable results pages. Surveys and quizzes can be an excellent way to listen to your visitors and membership as well as gather ideas. There is extensive documentation available on configuring and using the extension, as well as an active developer and a support forum.

### JXComments

JXComments is a Joomla! component that can enable a site to be more interactive utilizing its three main features: commenting, social bookmarking, and article rating. Comments are a great way to get feedback from visitors or members on the site's content. The social bookmarking is an effective way to allow your site visitors to promote your site's mission and content. Social bookmarking helps bring new users to your site. Documentation is available on configuring and using the extension, and support is available from the developer by e-mail.

## Calendars and Event Registration

Events are an excellent way to fund-raise and raise awareness for any group or organization. Joomla! has a number of extensions that are specific to events, calendaring, and reservations/reservations.

### JCal Pro

JCal Pro is a component calendaring solution that allows a number of advanced functions. Permissions can be set regarding who can post events by access level, and there is the ability to group events into categories, have recurring events based on flexible criteria, and export to iCal—just to name a few of the functionalities available. It uses a templating system that allows customization to match site designs, and the developer offers template packs in a number of color schemes. JCal Pro also has the ability to use the Content Editor to allow images and other media to be inserted into event details. JCal Pro is actively developed, has documentation on use, and offers a support forum.

### GCalendar

GCalendar is a component that integrates the Google calendar system. This can be extremely easy to utilize, especially if your organization is utilizing Google Apps. You can set up individual calendars for specific types of events and enable them to display as individual calendars or display information from multiple calendars in one view.

### Event Registration Pro

Many nonprofits and clubs offer events, whether meetings, service projects, fund-raising events, or conferences. Event Registration Pro makes it easy to schedule events and implement registration, whether paid or free (a number of payment processor options are available). It can also serve as a calendar for your site.

## Forums

Forums have long been a standard part of Web sites because they are powerful and flexible. The help forum at *http://forum.joomla.org* is an example of a large and highly successful forum, but many smaller sites find them very useful for discussing and debating issues, sharing information, providing support, and building connections between community members. Not only does using a forum help visitors and members easily have discussions, but it can also serve as a tool for internal communications for an organization. Forums can also be utilized as a customer or client support system by encouraging users to help each other with issues or activities. One thing to keep in mind, if you do use a forum on your site, is the time investment and labor needed to moderate and manage it. Even the best forums can be targeted by spammers and by "trolls" who cause conflict and destruction and need to be monitored.

Several forums are for Joomla! extensions, where you will be able to build on your knowledge of Joomla! If you choose one of these, it will be easier to integrate the look and functionality of the forum and the rest of your site.

### Kunena

Kunena is a very popular forum component for Joomla! It has a very active development team, detailed documentation, and a large community of users. It was built as a native Joomla! extension and integrates well with your site. It integrates with many other Joomla! extensions.

### Agora

Agora is a full-featured forum that has a large number of users and development team. It integrates with many Joomla! extensions.

Some sites (such as the Joomla! forum) use a stand-alone application, such as phpBB. The Joomla! Extensions Directory contains many extensions that integrate independent forums into Joomla! sites. However, using an independent forum will require you to master a second major application in addition to Joomla!

## CRMs: Constituent/Client/Customer Relationship Management

One of the first options to consider when creating a site for an organization is whether you will need a constituent/client/customer relationship manager (CRM). For the type of application discussed in this chapter, this software is used to identify organization members, their interaction and interests, and their contributions. CRM software is an excellent way to target specific members in an organization for action or activity and to facilitate communication not only from the organization out to their contributors but also in some instances to allow the contributors or members to facilitate relationships and communication with each other.

CRM applications are generally complex but powerful. If your organization has an existing mailing list, fund-raising list, or membership list, you can use a CRM to manage it and integrate it with your site. Moving to Web-based management of this information can also allow additional people to help with it. It also will make it easier for records to be kept up to date by allowing users to self-manage their contact information.

### CiviCRM

CiviCRM is a CRM software that is a specifically designed for advocacy, nonprofit, and nongovernmental groups. It is extremely robust and full featured with the ability to not only be a contact management database but also to assist with online fundraising and donor management, event registration, membership management, mailing list marketing, and report generation by using the additional add-ons that are available. CiviCRM has a very large and active community supporting the software, as well as a large group of professionals who work specifically with CiviCRM installations. It is developed specifically for the two main CRMs: Joomla! and Drupal.

### SugarCRM

SugarCRM is an open source CRM software that is available in three editions. The Community Edition is free to download and use but has specific limitations compared to the Professional Edition and the Enterprise Edition. The Professional and Enterprise Editions are fee based on a per-user basis. SugarCRM has an extensive community that is very active in supporting and extending SugarCRM, as well as professional service providers.

## Creating a Community Portal

Some organizations may not need a full-blown CRM or a forum but instead want to create a community site where members can easily interact and share information with each other. These sites can be very similar to the many popular social networking sites such as Facebook and MySpace. The community aspects of these sites can help your members get to know each other better and can be especially useful when your members, volunteers, or supporters do not have face-to-face interactions, for example if they are spread around the country or the world.

Joomla! has a number of extensions that can facilitate community-style Web sites. Two of the most popular are Jomsocial and Community Builder.

### Jomsocial

Jomsocial is an installable social networking extension made specifically for Joomla! It offers an extensive range of capabilities such as the ability to have member profile pages, groups, messaging, discussions, commenting, integrated event management, and the sharing of media files such as video and photos. It also can connect with the popular social networking site Facebook, giving visitors a unified way to connect using their Facebook account, allowing a user's Facebook content to display inside a Jomsocial community site. Jomsocial also has the built-in ability for social bookmarking, allowing content information sharing on more than 20 social networking and bookmarking sites such as Digg, StumbledUpon, Technocrati, and LinkedIn. It is well supported by the developer and the community that uses it and integrates with many other Joomla! extensions.

### Community Builder

Community Builder is a flexible extension that allows the creation of membership and subscription community- or directory-style sites, as well as sites that need extended user profiles. It allows Web site administrators to extend user profiles to gather expanded data on users as well as organize their users and user data in customized lists or groups. There are a number of extensions for Community Builder that allow for private messaging, paid-for memberships and subscriptions, access control for content and site management, and collaborative content. Community Builder is one of the most well-established extensions for Joomla! and has a large community of users who support and develop for it. Many other extensions have Community Builder plugins that allow integration of users' content with their profiles.

Both extensions are meant to organize users and provide them with rich profiles, but they do it in very different ways. What actions you want your users to take on your site and how you want them to interact with your organization and each other will be the deciding factor as to what extensions you choose on your site.

It is important for a community portal to be about the people in the community and keeping the membership excited and involved. Managing a community takes a lot of commitment in time and resources. If you have an interactive site where members communicate in public spaces with each other such as through commenting, posting, or sharing links, for example, a significant portion of time will be needed to oversee the content that is posted to your site by the membership, as well as keeping the site content fresh and creating community activities.

Recruiting users to help with community management, which ranges from moderating content and dealing with conflicts between users to starting discussion topics and encouraging engagement, is a powerful way to increase engagement with your organization. Watch for people who are active and positive participants in your online community; they are often the best possible recruits to a community management team.

# Fund-Raising

Most nonprofit organizations need to do some fund-raising and often hope to use their Web sites to facilitate that. If you are seeking funds, it is especially important that your site have a clear mission and provide evidence that your organization will use any contributions wisely. Donations can play a huge part in the financial success of any group.

Planning for fund-raising through your site should be done in collaboration with your organization's treasurer so that you can ensure that the bookkeeping and tax records are handled appropriately. Your treasurer will want to review the materials on working with a payment processor in Chapter 8. Some payment processors offer special plans for nonprofits, and you may want to explore them.

There are a variety of ways that an NGO/NPO, group, or organization can raise funds online. Whether you utilize a donation button that simply allows people to donate through PayPal or other online payment system or you use a collecting service, it is important that you are aware of the legal ramifications of soliciting donations and that you are compliant with the applicable rules and laws in your geographical area. Tax status, registration, and licensing for organizations vary widely across the world, so it is best to get the advice of a financial advisor or legal representative before you start to solicit or start planning your funding strategy. Here are some helpful links to fundraising solutions and other nonprofit and organization resources.

- *Guidestar (http://guidestar.org):* Guidestar is an information-gathering and publicizing Web site geared toward encouraging nonprofit and charitable organizations to share information and for donors who want to research charitable organizations. It is similar to a Better Business Bureau for charities. It allows organizations to easily share their organization's reports, share mission and values, and encourage transparency, which assists donors and supporters to make informed decisions.

- *Network For Good (http://networkforgood.org):* Network For Good is an online tool set for organizations, including donation processing services, training, and education on how to effectively fund-raise online. They also offer promotional tools such as integrated e-mail marketing and online surveys.

- *Your Cause (http://yourcause.com):* Your Cause is a site that allows supporters to create a personal page to promote and fund-raise for a cause or charity. It is also a site where organizations can reach out to potential supporters to find volunteers to join and work with their organization.

- *MissionFish (http://missionfish.org):* MissionFish connects nonprofit and charitable organizations with eBay.
- *eBay Giving (http://givingworks.ebay.com):* eBay Giving allows eBay sellers to list their items for sale with the proceeds from the sales going to registered charitable and nonprofit groups. MissionFish collects and distributes the donated funds from the eBay sales and auctions and distributes them to the registered charitable and nonprofit organizations.

# Nonprofit Web Site Demo

You can visit the live version of this site at *http://officialjoomlabook.com/nonprofit.*

This section will explain step-by-step how to create a simple nonprofit site, in this case a site for a club for people interested in rocks and minerals. We had three goals for this site.

- Provide useful information for people who are not club members but who might be interested in joining. In this sense, the site design has elements of a brochure site.
- Provide members with an online community to discuss topics of interest and with up-to-date information about club meetings and events.
- Keep the site relatively easy for a small group of club members to maintain.

## Setting Up the Site and Extensions

We decided on a simple design incorporating GCalendar for presenting information about upcoming meetings and events and the Kunena forum as a solution for creating an online community. There will be four main jobs in managing this site beyond the super administrator.

- Someone needs to manage responding to e-mails sent via the contact forum.
- Someone needs to manage the calendar.
- Someone needs to add news as needed.
- Someone will need to manage the forum. If the forum is successful, this will be the most time-consuming job.

Before beginning to set up the site, we recommend that you create a Google account for the club at *https://www.google.com/accounts/NewAccount.*

Although this account will be tied to one individual as the owner, it can allow you to separate the individual's accounts from the clubs, which will be useful if someone else takes over. The features that you will want to use from this account are as follows.

- An e-mail account for receiving e-mail submitted via the contact form. This can then be forwarded to one or more individuals.
- A calendar used to display club events.
- Google Analytics, which gives you statistics about your visitors and what pages they look at.

- Webmaster Tools, which will assist you in optimizing your site and making a site map for submission to Google.

Google provides very thorough instructions on how to use these applications.

## Settings for the Home Page

The front page features a category blog layout, with the description of the club in the category description, which means it will always be on top. The most recent article will always be on the front page. This is a good solution for sites where there may not be frequent updates. The design is flexible enough that it can be easily made more complex in the future.

## Creating a Contact Form

In your administrator, go to the Contact Manager (from the Components menu), and create a category. We called ours Contact Forms (see Chapter 6 for how to do this).

Create a contact with an e-mail address, a physical or mailing address if you have one, and a brief description. Figure 9.1 shows the contact-editing screen.

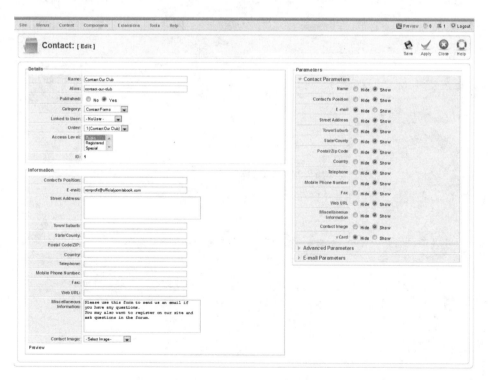

Figure 9.1  Contact-editing screen

Once you have filled out all of the fields, you click Save to save your contact form. To create a Contact Us menu link to the main menu, see Chapter 4 on working with menus and menu items.

## Site Name Custom HTML Module

We created a new Custom HTML module to hold the club's name by going to the Module Manager and creating a new module of the Custom HTML type. As shown in Figure 9.2, we used the Header 1 format for the name and assigned it to the breadcrumb position and all pages.

## Setting Up a Calendar

Because it is relatively simple to manage, we chose to use a Google calendar as the calendaring solution for this site and to incorporate it using the GCalendar extension, which includes a component, plugin, and several modules.

After downloading GCalendar, you will need to unzip it. Then install each of the extensions individually.

Log in to your Google account, and create a calendar for the club. As shown in Figure 9.3, under My Calendar, click Add, and fill in the Calendar Name, Description,

Figure 9.2  Creating a Custom HTML module to display the site name

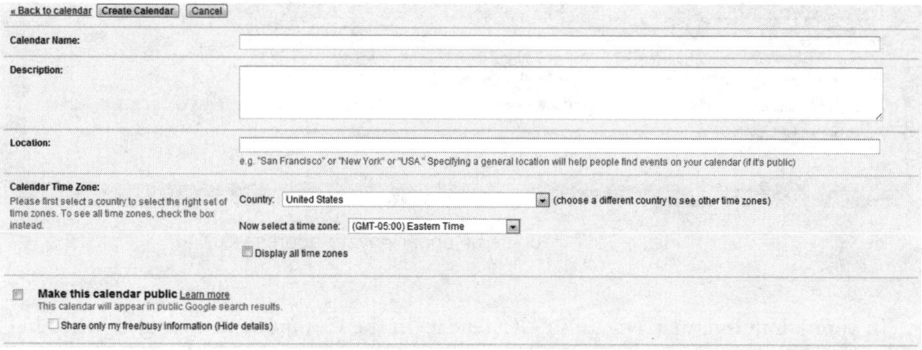

Figure 9.3  Creating a Google calendar

Location, and Calendar Time Zone boxes. Select the "Make this calendar public" box. Then click Create Calendar.

Now that your calendar is created, you want to share it with people and with your site.

Click Settings at the top right of your screen. Go to the Calendars tab, as shown in Figure 9.4.

On that screen, find your calendar, and click Shared: Edit settings, as shown in Figure 9.5.

For GCalendar, you will need the calendar ID, as shown in Figure 9.6. Then for Private Address, click the HTML button to get the information you need for your Magic Cookie, as shown in Figure 9.7. The Magic Cookie is the string of numbers and letters after *pvttk=*. Save this information to put into the GGalendar settings.

Figure 9.4  Google calendar settings

Figure 9.5  Selecting your calendar to edit its settings

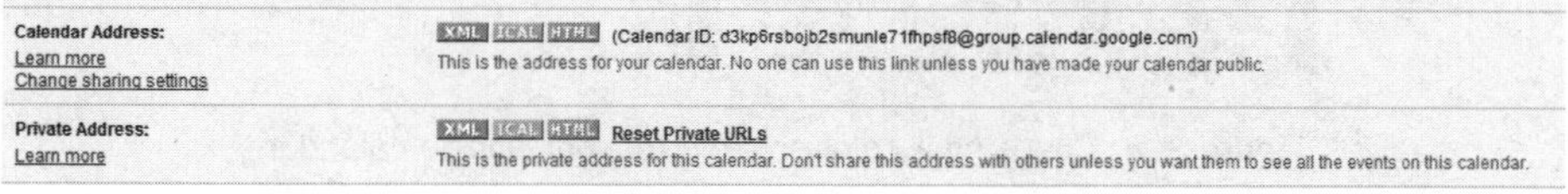

Figure 9.6  Google calendar: the calendar ID

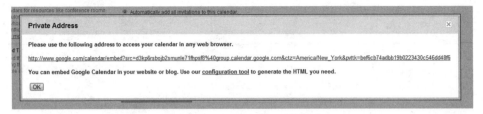

Figure 9.7  Google calendar private address

In your administrator, navigate to GCalendar (in the Components menu) by selecting the GCalendars submenu. Create a new calendar. Fill in a name, the calendar ID, and the Magic Cookie from your Google calendar in the spaces provided. Figure 9.8 demonstrates how to choose a color for your Google calendar. We chose the blue color option that fit with the blue Beez color scheme we implemented in Chapter 5.

Now create a menu link to the calendar from your main menu by going to the Menu Items Manager for the main menu and creating a new menu item.

It is important to note that your time zone settings for your system (which is set in the Global Configuration settings), Google GCalendar, and the GCalendar component match; otherwise, the time display on your site can become out of sync. You can adjust the time zone settings for the GCalendar component in the parameters by clicking the Parameters icon in the top-right corner of the GCalendar component screen. You can also adjust how time and dates display on your site in the parameters using php strftime, which formats a local time/date according to locale settings. There are configuration options to set this in both the component and the modules for GCalendar. You can find more information on formatting the input for strftime at *http://php.net/manual/en/function.strftime.php.*

We also published the GCalendar Upcoming Events module on all pages in the left position. In our case, we chose to show the next two events. As shown in Figure 9.9, we changed the name to Upcoming Events, chose to display two events, and changed the date format by eliminating the year.

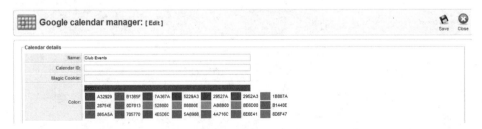

Figure 9.8  Choosing a color scheme for your Google calendar

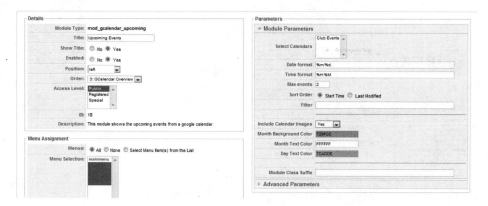

Figure 9.9  Settings for the Upcoming Events module

## Forum

For our forum, we chose to use Kunena. After downloading it, we installed it using the Extensions Manager. Like all forums, Kunena is fairly complex, with many options. Figure 9.10 shows the control panel for Kunena. Starting with a new forum, the two links we used are Forum Administration and User Administration.

Clicking Forum Administration, as shown in Figure 9.11, allows us to create new forums. Here we suggest starting with one or two forums of interest to your group.

Make a link to Kunena from the main menu. Clicking that link on the front end of the site is demonstrated in Figure 9.12.

We suggest "seeding" your forum with a few threads that your membership will be interested in participating in. As your forum grows, you can add more subforums.

Figure 9.10  Kunena control panel

Figure 9.11  Kunena forum administration panel

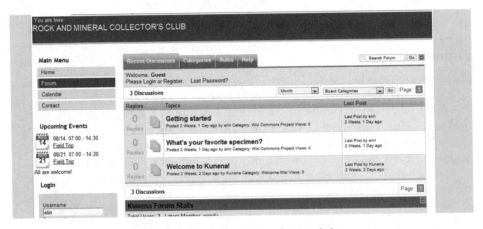

Figure 9.12  Kunena forum front-end view

# Modifying the Template

At this point, we have a Web site with good functionality, but it is not that attractive. So now, we turn to working on the template. For this site, we modified the Beez template to create a simple monochromatic design as was demonstrated in Chapter 5.

## Creating a Copy of the Template

We used the File Manager on our host to begin. Navigating to the *templates* folder, we copied the whole *beez* folder to a new folder called *beez2*, as shown in Figures 9.13 and 9.14.

To finish the duplication of the template, you need to rename the template in the *templateDetails.xml* file. You can edit this file using the Edit function in File Manager by navigating to the *beez2* folder and then selecting the *templateDetails.xml* file. You can click the Edit button on the top File Manager menu, or you can right-click the file and select

Figure 9.13  Selecting the beez folder to make a copy in Cpanel File Manager

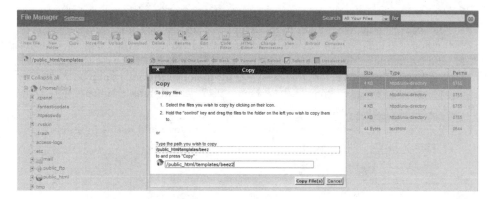

Figure 9.14  Instructing Cpanel File Manager to copy the beez folder to beez2

Edit from the context menu, as was demonstrated in Chapter 5. This will open the file for editing. When the file has opened in the editor, you want to look for the `<name>beez</name>` line near the top of the file. Change the word `beez` to `beez2`.

Now in the Template Manager, we have the new template. Joomla! will find this automatically. We also set it as the default template, as shown in Figure 9.15.

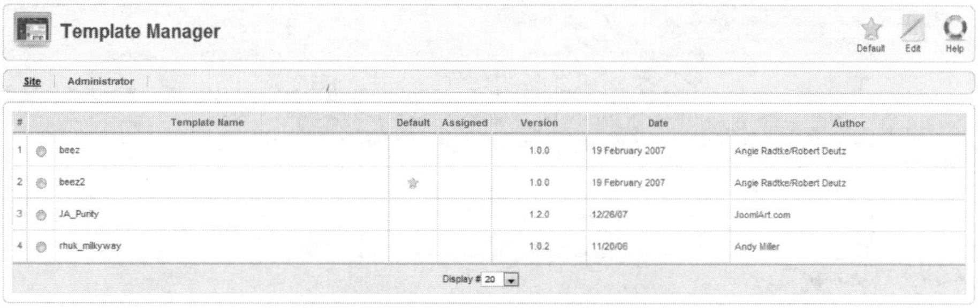

| # | Template Name | Default | Assigned | Version | Date | Author |
|---|---|---|---|---|---|---|
| 1 | beez | | | 1.0.0 | 19 February 2007 | Angie Radtke/Robert Deutz |
| 2 | beez2 | ☆ | | 1.0.0 | 19 February 2007 | Angie Radtke/Robert Deutz |
| 3 | JA_Purity | | | 1.2.0 | 12/26/07 | JoomlArt.com |
| 4 | rhuk_milkyway | | | 1.0.2 | 11/20/06 | Andy Miller |

Display # 20

Figure 9.15  Setting beez2 as the default template

## Changing the Color Scheme

We used the color transformations described in Chapter 5 to change it to a monochromatic blue design.

## Editing the Index File

In general, changing templates to suit your site will mainly involve modifying CSS, but in some cases, you will want or need to modify the *index.php* file that is part of your template. This is accessible via the Template Manager by selecting the template and clicking Edit and then Edit HTML, as shown in Figure 9.16.

We changed the *index.php* file in three places.

- Because we did not want an image/logo at the top of the site, we needed to edit the *index.php* file. We did this in the Template Manager by commenting out the appropriate lines, which you do by adding /* where the part to be ignored begins and by adding */ where it ends. This is a PHP command, and we enclose it in PHP tags. This goes before the area we want to comment out: `<?php / * ?>`. This goes afterward: `<?php */ ?>`. Figure 9.17 demonstrates commenting out the Beez header and logo.

  - We added a `<div></div>` container around the `user3` and `user4` positions. See Figure 9.18.

Figure 9.16  Template Manager: template-editing screen to edit HTML

Figure 9.17  Editing template HTML, commenting out the Beez header
and logo image

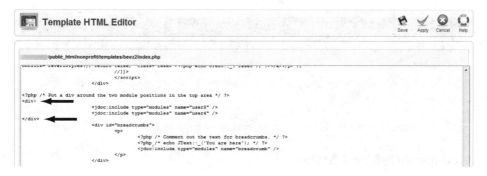

Figure 9.18  Editing template HTML adding a `<div></div>` container
around the `user3` and `user4` positions

- We also did not want the breadcrumb text of "You are here" to be in our template, so we commented out that text, as shown in Figure 9.19.

Save the changes by clicking Save in the top-right corner of the screen. If you want to keep the editing screen open to permit further editing but want to preview your changes, you can click Apply instead of Save and open the front end of your site in a new tab to view the changes you have made.

Before changes were made, the top of the front-end front page looked like Figure 9.20.

Figure 9.19  Editing template HTML, commenting out the breadcrumb text
"You are here"

Figure 9.20  Front-end front page view of the header before changing the
index.php file

Figure 9.21  Front-end front page view after changing the index.php file

After the changes were made, the front-end front page looks as shown in Figure 9.21.

## Modifying CSS and Styling

Next we modified the CSS. CSS is what controls most visual elements of your site. We have already changed a number of the CSS files by changing the colors from pink to blue following the instructions in Chapter 5. Next we wanted to add some additional styling to the site.

First we created a new file called *override.css* in the File Manager in the *templates/beez2/css* folder. (You could also do this on your computer and upload it to the File Manager.) By using an *override.css* file to override the CSS that is loaded by the template, you have the ability to easily roll back a change if you make a mistake. Another option is to edit the existing template CSS files. Remember to download or save a backup of all the CSS files in a template so that you have the ability to return the CSS to its original state if you are editing the original files. Figure 9.22 demonstrates the File Manager showing the *beez2* CSS directory. Click the New File icon in the top-left corner of the screen to create a new file.

Figure 9.23 demonstrates the Cpanel dialog box asking you to enter a filename for your new file. We are creating an *override.css* file.

We then need to tell the template to include this new file. We want this file to be the last CSS file to load because it will always have precedence over any of the other files. Therefore, we make including it the last thing in the <head></head> area. Figure 9.24 demonstrates the addition to the index.php file and where the edit needs to occur.

In the Template Manager, when you click Edit CSS, the new file is now in the list, as shown in Figure 9.25.

Figure 9.22  Creating a new file in Cpanel File Manager

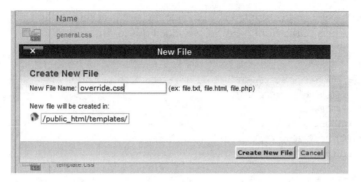

Figure 9.23  Creating and naming a new file using Cpanel File Manager

Figure 9.24  Editing the index.php file to add the link to the style sheet
override.css

### Template CSS Editor

| # | /public_html/nonprofit/templates/beez2/css |
|---|---|
| ○ | position.css |
| ○ | override.css |
| ○ | ie7only.css |
| ○ | template_rtl.css |
| ○ | layout.css |
| ○ | print.css |
| ○ | general.css |
| ○ | ieonly.css |
| ○ | template.css |

Figure 9.25  Override.css showing in the Template CSS Editor screen

Editing the file, we first wanted to eliminate the Beez background image that is used on the first article in the front page. So, we added this to the blank file:

```
.leading {
        background:none no-repeat scroll left top #CDD1DB;
        border:1px solid #CCCCCC;
        color:#000000;
        margin:30px 0 10px;
        padding:20px 20px 40px 30px;
        position:relative;
}
```

This CSS will then override the CSS for .leading from the *positions.css* file (starting at about line 150). Specifying the background as none eliminates the background image from the leading article.

We wanted to fine-tune other elements such as adding some padding (blank space) beneath the font resizer and above the breadcrumbs area. So, we added the following CSS to the *override.css* file:

```
#fontsize {
        padding-bottom:3px;
}
#breadcrumbs {
        padding-top:8px;
}
#header h1 {
        font-size:1.5em;
        font-weight:normal;
        margin-left:20px;
        text-transform:uppercase;
}
.moduletable {
        margin-left:10px;
}
```

The site now appears as in Figure 9.26. The subtle changes make a more polished appearance.

Overall, this site is a good beginning for a dynamic Web site for a club or organization that wants to concentrate its efforts on its core activities, not maintaining a Web site. With one or more people working together to maintain it, the site can be useful and gradually expanded over time if that is desired.

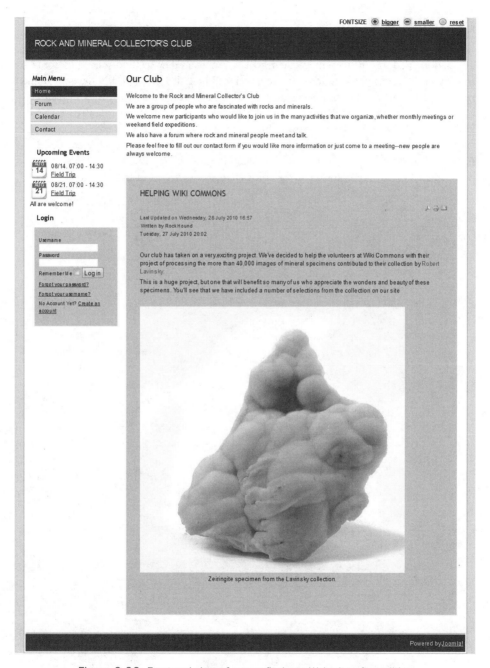

FONTSIZE ⊙ **bigger** ⊙ **smaller** ○ **reset**

**ROCK AND MINERAL COLLECTOR'S CLUB**

**Main Menu**

Home

Forum

Calendar

Contact

**Upcoming Events**

08/14. 07:00 - 14:30
Field Trip

08/21. 07:00 - 14:30
Field Trip

All are welcome!

**Login**

Username

Password

RememberMe ☐ Log in

Forgot your password?

Forgot your username?

No Account Yet? Create an account

**Our Club**

Welcome to the Rock and Mineral Collector's Club

We are a group of people who are fascinated with rocks and minerals.

We welcome new participants who would like to join us in the many activities that we organize, whether monthly meetings or weekend field expeditions.

We also have a forum where rock and mineral people meet and talk.

Please feel free to fill out our contact form if you would like more information or just come to a meeting--new people are always welcome.

**HELPING WIKI COMMONS**

Last Updated on Wednesday, 28 July 2010 16:57

Written by Rock Hound

Tuesday, 27 July 2010 20:02

Our club has taken on a very exciting project. We've decided to help the volunteers at Wiki Commons with their project of processing the more than 40,000 images of mineral specimens contributed to their collection by Robert Lavinsky.

This is a huge project, but one that will benefit so many of us who appreciate the wonders and beauty of these specimens. You'll see that we have included a number of selections from the collection on our site

Zeiringite specimen from the Lavinsky collection.

Powered by Joomla!

Figure 9.26  Front-end view of nonprofit demo Web site after editing the template

## Conclusion

Joomla! provides a huge range of opportunities for nonprofit organizations, NGOs, clubs, associations, and groups to achieve their goals, from awareness to fund-raising to community building. As you develop your site, you will benefit from a clearly developed and realistic plan that matches the needs of your constituencies and that is easy and realistic to maintain. Over time, as your site is used, you can add new features to enhance it. As with all other sites, good design, strong branding, a clear message, and excellent content are the cornerstones of visibility and success. On *The Official Joomla! Book* Web site (*http://officialjoomlabook.com*), you can download the *override.css* style sheet, the icon set used, and a PDF of the color chart for color changes described in this chapter.

# 10

# Practical Application: Joomla! for Education

School Web sites present challenges that are often more complex than those for other kinds of organizations. Unlike a small business or nonprofit with a new Web site, a school starts with a ready-made target audience and, most likely, is not focused on expanding much beyond that audience. Schools have many different constituencies and a variety of communication needs. By following the same basic principles of planning for all Web sites, an educational institution can create an effective communication portal that fits their needs.

## Basic Planning of Educational Sites

The first objective to planning an education Web site should be deciding what type of site to create.

- Is it a site for a single school, a school with several campuses, or a school district?
- Who will the site users be?
- Who will be responsible for creating and maintaining the content of the site?
- Are there any regulatory mandates, governmental standards, or school policies that your site must meet?

In starting to think about your site, you should consider several different groups of potential users of your site:

- Parents
- Students
- Teachers
- Other staff members
- Alumni
- The general public, including community members and potential families
- The news media

You need to consider what kinds of information these groups want and need. Sometimes the information they want most may turn out to be not hard to provide. For example, the school calendar for the current year and the coming year (as soon as it is finalized) is something that all constituencies need for planning their own schedules for vacations and doctor appointments. People often want basic information such as key phone numbers. The general public may need to know the school's address. The news media may want to know enrollment numbers or the name of the school mascot.

It is a good investment to spend some time asking people in these groups questions.

- What are the three most common pieces of information that you need? What are the three pieces of information you get asked for most often? What one piece of important information is hardest to find?
- What information is the school communicating well right now?
- What are the three pieces of information that you think parents should have?
- What are the three most important pieces of information that the public should have?
- What kinds of misinformation do people have?

By taking the time to do this, you will have a good basis for setting priorities for your initial Web site and planning for future enhancements. In developing a plan, it is good to propose phases of implementation because it is more practical and because you are likely to receive many suggestions, not all of which are necessarily practical or useful for the majority of users.

Another set of questions you should explore is where people get the information now. Who is responsible for producing and keeping that information up to date? Will those people be active users of your Web site? If so, you should talk with those people to understand their work processes and procedures. Find out what current software they use and whether they are satisfied with it. Getting this group engaged early with your site design is a good way to help make sure your site actually ends up being used in the ways intended.

You must also consider who will be responsible for maintaining the site, both technically and in keeping the content up to date. If you create a site that is too complex for the time available for supporting it or for the skill level of the staff, it will end up being a frustrating site. Closely related to this is the question of who is going to be allowed to post content on the site and under what rules.

## Extensions to Consider for Education

There are some basic extensions that we recommend installing even if you plan to keep your site fairly simple.

### JCE

JCE, as mentioned in Chapter 6, is a good replacement for the editors that install with Joomla! We have found that with its many plugins, such as the File Manager, Media Manager, and Image Manager, users feel like they are learning one integrated application rather than many separate ones. It is especially useful if you have users who will be uploading many PDF files, something that is common in schools. It also has the ability to group users and set permissions and parameters for groups or individuals, allowing you to separate users and groups into their own folders. This allows you to keep your *images* directory organized and protects files from being altered or deleted inadvertently. JCE is actively developed and has a community forum for support.

## Simple Image Rotator

The Simple Image Rotator module from JoomlaWorks provides an easy way to present a polished set of rotating images. Often, schools use this type of module in the header of their sites, or they may use it in specific sections. The developer offers a community support forum.

## Filtered News

Filtered News is a module that allows you to display linked lists of relevant articles to visitors to various sections of your site. For example, you may want to just display news from a particular grade in one area or just news about sports. It has a number of configurable options for scrolling and image display. It also can be configured to dynamically adapt to display news relevant to the current sections or category that is being browsed. The developer offers some documentation on his site with usage instructions.

## Displaying Documents

Documents can be displayed and organized in a number of ways. For example, users can simply make links directly to the files from content items, create custom modules with lists of links to documents, or use a specific component that specializes in organizing and displaying documents.

### Easy Folder Listing

Easy Folder Listing is a module that utilizes a simple way to display a list of all documents in a particular folder. When uploading files, if you keep them organized in folders, this will provide a nicely formatted display. You should be sure to use descriptive filenames and a module title that describes what the folder contains. You will need to create a separate copy of the module for each folder that you want to display.

An example of a useful way to use this extension is to insert the module into a content item using the loadposition plugin. For example, if you had a group of PDF lunch menus, you could load them to a folder called *menus*. Assign the module to the `lunchmenus` position (which is not a position in your template), and then in a content item called Lunch menus, type the following:

```
{loadposition lunchmenus}
```

Make sure that the module is set to display either on all pages or on the menu link for the lunch menu page (the latter although slightly more complicated will make your site run faster). The developer offers documentation for installing and using the module.

### DOCman

DOCman is a full document repository and download component that can help organize and display most common formats of documents, audio files, and visual files. It also has built-in logging to track file statistics such as views and downloads, including tracking specific user information. A number of third-party extensions have been developed for DOCman to extend it. It has an active development team, as well as support and a community of users on its forum.

### RokDownloads

RokDownloads is a component that provides a simple-to-use interface that allows you to manage your files and folders, publish them, and make files available to users to download. The development team is active and has a community forum for support.

## Calendars

One of the most useful and flexible extension types for a school site is a calendar. From displaying the basic school opening and closing schedule to listing sporting events and school board meetings to reserving space and equipment, and even displaying lunch menus, a calendar system that is actively used can be very powerful.

In choosing a calendar solution, the following are some things to keep in mind.

- You should have the ability to specify public and private events.
- You should be able to have multiple calendars managed by different people.
- Site users should be able to integrate the calendar into their own calendaring systems, such as those integrated into their e-mail systems, smartphones, or other devices.

### JCal Pro

JCal Pro is a long-standing component calendaring solution that allows a number of advanced functions such as setting permissions on who can post events by access level, grouping events into categories, having recurring events, exporting to iCal, and others. It is uses a templating system that allows for customization, and the developer offers template packs in a number of color schemes. JCal Pro also has the ability to use the Content Editor, allowing images and other media to be inserted into event details. JCal Pro is actively developed, has documentation on use, and offers a support forum.

### GCalendar

GCalendar is a component that integrates the Google calendar system. This can be extremely easy to utilize, especially if your school or district is set up on Google Apps. You can set up individual calendars for specific types of events or information purposes to display each calendar separately or display information from multiple calendars in one view.

## Contact Information and Staff Pages

Joomla! comes with a basic contact form system that can be especially useful for general information e-mails. However, it is difficult to use if you want to provide contact information for a large number of users that is searchable and that provides flexible listings. In our experience, the simplest solution to this is to use the Community Builder extension with a number of specific Community Builder plugins.

## Community Builder

Community Builder is a flexible extension that allows you to create membership and subscription community sites, as well as sites that need extended user profiles. It allows Web site administrators to extend user profiles to gather extended data on users as well as organize their users and user data in customized lists or groups. In terms of school sites, Community Builder (CB) really shines for its customizable user profiles and lists.

CB has a built-in system for its own plugins and comes with a number of plugins that are installed automatically. Examples of plugins for CB include templates that style your CB profile pages, content helpers such as the author plugin that lists articles on a user's profile, and languages that translate CB's individual pages to other languages. Also included are plugins that integrate with other third-party extensions for Joomla! The following sections covers some Community Builder plugins to consider installing to expand its capabilities.

## ProfileBook

ProfileBook is a Community Builder plugin that adds a configurable guestbook-like tab on a profile. The use for schools isn't really as a guestbook where visitors can post, but it can be very easy for staff who are inexperienced computer users to use this plugin as an announcement board or lesson plan list. You can use multiple instances of this plugin to give you many different areas of text-based communications, from the teacher's profile to parents and students.

## ImageGallery

CB ImageGallery is a simple-to-use image gallery plugin built specifically for Community Builder. Administrators can control the number and size of all images loaded, and it has a moderator function that allows all images to be screened for approval. This plugin is useful for teachers to show activities in their classes, field trips, or class projects. One thing to note for school settings where children are minors is that the school should get a consent form signed by parents, allowing images of their child to be published.

## Public Mail

Public Mail is a plugin that allows a small e-mail contact form to be placed on each staff member's profile. It has a configurable option to track users sending e-mail through the form and can send a copy of the e-mail to the sender.

## CB Captcha

CB Captcha puts a spam protection element into forms that are used in Community Builder, for example the Public Mail form. Captcha protects forms from being used by computer-generated spammers, also called *spambots*. The aim is to make sure that a human is filling out the form.

Community Builder's lists have the functionality to generate member lists based on items in their profile, and it offers two ways to configure how Community Builder uses profile information to generate them. The first simple way is to select an individual profile field and create a list of people who are using that profile field. This works well when a profile field is one singular item. The other way to create a list is by using a specific query of the database. This is a good way to create a list that may have profile items that are multifaceted, such as multiselect (a field in which users can select more than one item). An example of this would be if a staff member worked at a number of campuses, but you want to create lists of staff by campus location.

Community Builder offers a subscription service that gives access to a very detailed manual for use, as well as a very large community forum based on user-to-user support and assistance.

# Additional Tools

A number of additional tools are available for Joomla! that can enhance your site by extending its functionality. They do require more time to implement, in large measure because you will need to train and support users.

## LDAP Authentication

Many schools have existing intranets that their staffs can access. If you already have a database of staff members stored in an LDAP system, then using the LDAP authentication plugin supplied with the Joomla! installation can be a good solution. We also recommend using Sam Moffatt's authentication tools suite to help manage this.

## Bulk Import of Users

Often you may have a spreadsheet or database listing of staff members, students, or parents who you want to be registered users on your site. A few extensions to consider for this purpose are User Loader, Userport, and Jbupload.

## ProjectFork

ProjectFork is a project management suite that is useful for collaboration and project organization. It is a very good extension to use if a group of users is working on a particular project. It has task tracking, time management, calendars, a file repository, and goal tracking built in. It provides a range of tools and has an easy-to-use interface. A number of extensions, as well as template themes, are available to make ProjectFork more productive.

## Access Management

Joomla! 1.5 has a basic access management that allows you to control who can see what on your Web site and who can do tasks such as creating new articles. For many schools, this system proves inadequate, because they have areas that may be for staff members only, areas that are for parents, and then areas for students but to which parents and staff will have access. Joomla! 1.6 will introduce fine-grained access control, but for Joomla! 1.5 a number of solutions are available to address this.

### Control and Content Manager

Control and Content Manager from Art of Joomla extend the built-in access control system in Joomla! Control lets you add new access control levels and edit access control levels, permissions, and user groups. Content Manager is a front-end editing solution that works with Control so all custom user groups can add and edit content according to defined access levels. The combined effect of these two extensions makes it very easy for school sites to assign content areas to a specific editor, publisher, and author groups or individuals, as well as customizing what parts of content items Content Editors can alter or use. Both extensions have documentation regarding installation and use on the developer's site, and there is a group e-mail list to discuss usage and issues.

### CiviCRM and CiviSCHOOL

CiviCRM is a complete free and open source constituent management system aimed at the civic sphere that integrates with Joomla! It offers a set of tools specifically designed for schools, such as for managing after-school programs, applications, and health forms. CiviSCHOOL is an emerging project but does have a large development and support community.

## Accessibility

Schools have a vital stake in making sure that resources are available to all in an equitable manner.

Your school or school district probably already has a staff person or whole office devoted to accessibility and meeting the Americans with Disabilities Act, the Individuals with Disabilities Education Improvement Act of 2004, Section 508, and other regulations and standards. There is also likely to be another person or office who handles issues related to students with limited English proficiency and their families. If you incorporate people in these roles in your Web planning team, you will make a better, more useful Web site for everyone.

Joomla! can be used to create sites that meet accessibility guidelines if you understand and implement the basic principles of accessible design. Joomla! can also be used to create multilingual sites if you want to present information in several languages.

## Accessible Template Design

The most important element in producing a Joomla! Web site that is accessible to all users is the design of its template. Fortunately, the Joomla! distribution includes Beez, which is a template designed to meet accessibility standards. You can work with Beez in two ways. One is to modify it in order to produce the desired design while remaining accessible. The other is to take the files from the */templates/beez/html* folder and copy them to the template you are using. If you are purchasing a stock template, accessibility is an issue that you should ask the seller about. Asking whether a template is Section 508 compliant is a good way to get specific information. If you are having a custom template designed, you should include Section 508 compliance as part of the project description.

## Multilingual Sites

Creating a multilingual site is similar to creating two Web sites in that you need to manage parallel content in two or more languages. If your school is already producing multilingual materials, you can incorporate them into your site by using a translation management system, or you can do it in a more limited way simply by having copies of already available multilingual documents presented in an organized fashion. The following are some multilanguage extensions to consider.

### Joom!Fish

Joom!Fish is a noncommercial extension that allows users to select a specific language for their content. This extension does not translate your site but will help you manage translations.

### Automatic Translations

The Joomla! Extensions Directory offers a number of automatic translation tools. However, for a school site, we recommend not using such a system because they can easily produce confusing and inaccurate translations. This is especially important for any documents that are official policy, legal forms, or legal in nature.

## Learning Extensions

Joomla! is not designed as a full-featured learning management system, but there are several extensions that are useful for implementing some aspects of Web-based learning. For example, they may be useful for professional development and other staff training or for delivering some materials to students.

### Joomlearn LMS

Joomlearn LMS is an extension that has both commercial and noncommercial versions that can be useful for learning management. However, if you want a full-fledged LMS, you may want to investigate using a separate application that can be integrated with your site. Moodle is the perhaps the most popular open source learning management system. It has a large number of users including tens of thousands of teachers who are active community contributors. If you want to investigate a learning management system, it is well worth investigating. Two free Joomla! extensions, Joomdle and Jfusion, integrate Joomla! and Moodle and allow for single sign-on (instead of users needing two passwords and having to log in twice). Although they require some technical proficiency to implement, the results for users are very powerful.

Although this book is about using Joomla!, there are other applications that are not Joomla! extensions but stand-alone products that you may want to consider for enhancing Web use in your school. Many of them can be integrated with your Joomla! site if desired.

### Moodle

Moodle is open source course management software that could also be referred to as a virtual learning environment application. Applications like this are very flexible in terms of creating online courses, tests, and team collaborations on work projects. Moodle is a very well-known open source project with a well-developed community supporting it. A number of instructional books are available on how to implement and use Moodle.

### Google Apps

Google Apps is a suite of online applications, including documents, spreadsheets, presentations, e-mail, and calendar applications among other items. K–12 schools can receive a free enterprise version. The advantage of this is that they display with your domain rather than the Google domain to restrict access to people with accounts on your domain. It is also a relatively easy way to provide e-mail accounts to students, teachers, or parents if that is something you want to do. Although anyone can also create individual Google accounts and access these services, having an official installation can provide a number of advantages including better access control.

Many Joomla! extensions integrate specific elements of Google Apps with your site. You can also create a single sign-on system to integrate your Joomla! site and Google Apps.

## Blogging Applications

There may be teachers who want to have students publish their work on the Web. Although it is possible to do this within your Joomla! site, it is also possible using Web services that provide free, easy-to-create, easy-to-close accounts in a hosted environment. Two such services are Blogger.com and WordPress.com. For example, on Blogger.com, a teacher can set up a blog and have up to 100 authors contribute. Access to the blog can also be restricted. We suggest that you provide a set of policies for use of such systems, especially by students younger than 13.

## Social Networking Sites

It may be useful for your school or district to have a presence on Facebook, Twitter, and other social sites. The most important purpose of this presence is to provide an easy way to notify users of these sites about important news coming from your site. For example, if you post a news item saying that school is going to be closed because of a weather-related issue, you can use a Joomla! extension to send notices of this to your Facebook friends or Twitter followers. We do not recommend that schools enable unmoderated two-way communication through these sites, since there is much potential for mischief with postings. Some useful extensions for these purposes are discussed in Chapter 8.

# School Web Site Demo

Just like schools, school Web sites vary widely. For this example, we are creating a site for a high school. Some of the audiences for the school are parents, teachers, students, and the public.

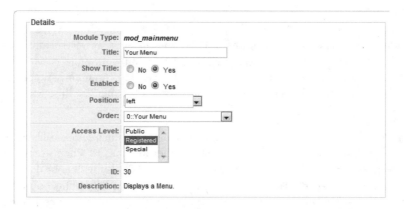

Figure 10.1  Creating a menu item that is seen only after someone logs
into the Web site

It is tempting to over-complicate a site, but in this case we decided that parents and students would not need to log in to find classroom information and news. It is important to consider that managing passwords for a large number of parents and students would add greatly to the complexity of site management. This means that members of the public will also be able to see the pages and use contact information.

In this model, all school staff will have accounts on the site. Each department will have a section and staff members from that department that will be able to write articles for publication in that section. In addition, each staff member will have a contact page on which they will be able to post information items and images. What these are will be up to the staff member in line with school and department policies.

Navigation will consist of one main menu and submenus using the techniques described in Chapter 7.

We added sections for each department. We made a news category for each department, but a department could add more categories if desired.

In the main menu, add a Departments link. Then we added a submenu link to each department's section page. This will serve as the home page for the department.

We expect that all the staff members who are content creators will add content using the front end of the Web site. Therefore, we created a new menu, User Menu (with the title Your Menu), with an article submission menu link. This menu will be displayed only to registered users. This is done by selecting the access level, as shown in Figure 10.1.

## JCE

We installed the JCE content editor because it allows us to manage editing more simply and makes training users easier. Among other things, it has the useful feature that allows image files to be uploaded without using the Joomla! Media Manager interface, and many people find this less confusing. Files can also be assigned to specific folders for spe-

Figure 10.2  JCE administration screen

cific content creators, which makes management easier. There are a number of plugins
for JCE that can extend its functionality.

The basic JCE installation includes both a plugin and a component. The plugin is the
editor, and the component controls configuration. Once you have installed both, navigate
to the JCE Administration Control Panel on the Components menu. Figure 10.2 shows
the Control Panel.

JCE has a large number of plugins as part of its basic installation, as shown in Figure
10.3. These control the icons on the top of the editing screen. You can enable and disable
the buttons as you desire. We suggest experimenting and coming to a reasonable balance
of functionality and ease of use. Some of the most useful additions, compared to
TinyMCE, are the Spell Checker, the Media Manager, the Image Manager, the Advanced
Link (which makes it easy to create links to other parts of your site from within articles),
and the File Manager.

Figure 10.4 shows the default arrangement of icons in JCE.

| 47 | ☐ | Print | ✓ | 3 | 6 | plugin | print | | 41 |
| 48 | ☐ | Spell Checker | ✓ | 4 | 7 | plugin | spellchecker | | 54 |
| 49 | ☐ | Layers | ✓ | 4 | 8 | plugin | layer | | 55 |
| 50 | ☐ | Advanced Code Editor | ✓ | 4 | 9 | plugin | advcode | | 56 |
| 51 | ☐ | Article Breaks | ✓ | 4 | 10 | plugin | article | | 57 |
| 52 | ☐ | Styles | ✓ | 4 | 1 | plugin | style | | 48 |
| 53 | ☐ | Non-Breaking | ✓ | 4 | 2 | plugin | nonbreaking | | 49 |
| 54 | ☐ | Visual Characters | ✓ | 4 | 3 | plugin | visualchars | | 50 |
| 55 | ☐ | XHTML Xtras | ✓ | 4 | 4 | plugin | xhtmlxtras | | 51 |
| 56 | ☐ | Image Manager | ✓ | 4 | 5 | plugin | imgmanager | | 52 |
| 57 | ☐ | Advanced Link | ✓ | 4 | 6 | plugin | advlink | | 53 |

Display # 20   Start  Prev  1  2  3  Next  End   Page 3 of 3

Figure 10.3  JCE plugins screen

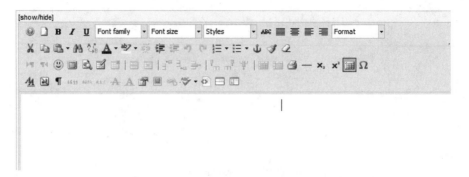

Figure 10.4  The default editor screen for JCE showing the arrangement
of icons

Because we expect that most content will be created in the front end of the site, we
went to the Groups screen and chose to enable the Front End group by clicking the
icon in the Enabled column, as shown in Figure 10.5. This is very useful because we may
want to limit the options available to front-end users in order to prevent problems and
to make the editor less overwhelming to them.

To further customize JCE, you can edit the settings of the Front End editor group by
editing the parameters for the group. If you click the group Front End, you will open
the group for editing. The first tab of information on the Setup tab is used to set the
user groups or people who are assigned to the group and what they are allowed to edit.
The second tab is Editor Parameters, as shown in Figure 10.6. To ensure that all front-
end editors in the Front End group are restricted to their own directories, set the Plugin
Options File Directory Path setting to images/stories/$group/$username.

If you install JCE, we recommend changing the site settings in Global Configuration
to make JCE the default editor (as shown in Figure 10.7) and changing the user settings
on the System tab to require all users to use it (as Shown in Figure 10.8). This will
decrease confusion as you train and support users.

Figure 10.5  JCE Editor Groups screen

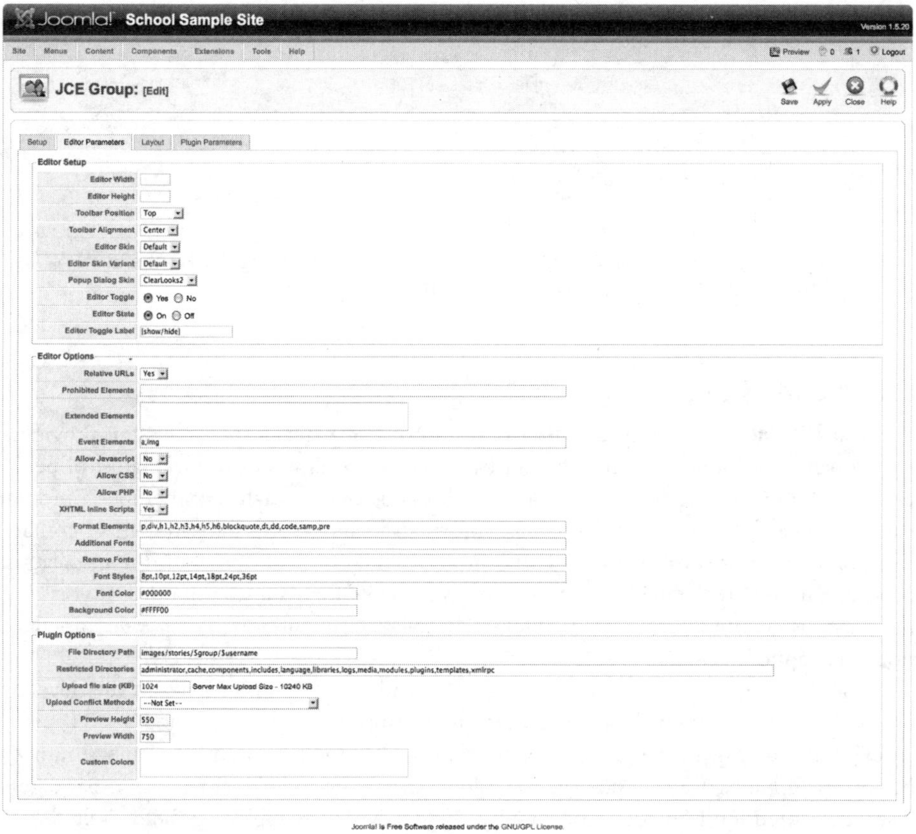

Figure 10.6  Setting the Plugin Options File Directory Path setting to
restrict an editor to uploading to a specific directory

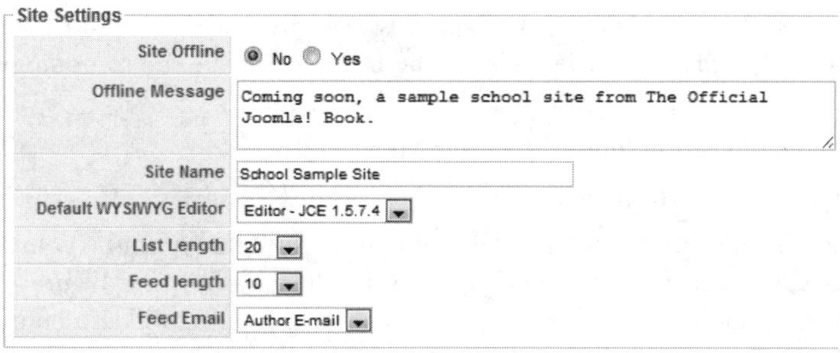

Figure 10.7  Global Configuration's site settings showing JCE as the
default WYSIWYG editor

Figure 10.8  Global Configuration's user settings showing the Front-end
User Parameters option set to Hide

## Community Builder

We installed the Community Builder extension for two main purposes. First, it provides functionality for listing users in different categories. This allows us to make a list of people in each department, for example. It also allows us to give each staff member a profile page. This makes it easy for them to post information and also to have individual contact forms. Basic instructions for use of Community Builder are available with the installation package, and highly detailed documentation is available for a subscription fee. If you decide to use Community Builder extensively, we recommend purchasing a documentation subscription.

To install Community Builder, we first downloaded the component from the developer's site. In the download package, there are a component and three modules. This is an extension that you have to unzip after you download it, because it combines a number of installable packages inside the download. Install the individual extension packages using the Extension Manager. Community Builder works by replacing the default Joomla! User Manager. To make the component work correctly, you need to follow these steps:

1. Disable the default front-end login module if you have it enabled.

2. Create a menu link to the Community Builder user profile. This is mandatory, as shown in Figure 10.9. We put this on the menu we created earlier, User Menu. One thing to note is this menu item must have the access level of Public if you want user profiles to be viewable on the front end of the site to nonregistered users.

3. Add a logout action link to the User Menu menu.

4. Add a login link to the main menu.

5. Sync the registered users with the Community Builder system by going to the Tools tab and clicking the Synchronize Users link, as shown in Figure 10.10. This will make sure that any users you have created in Joomla! will also be incorporated in the Community Builder user system.

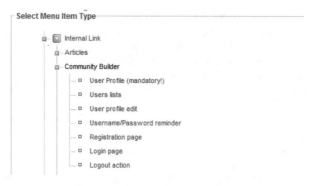

Figure 10.9  Community Builder menu item type choices

Figure 10.10  CB Tools Manager page

## Community Builder Profile Pages

One of the features of Community Builder is the user profile. A profile is a central page about the user and can be seen when clicking the user's name. Users can see their own profiles by clicking the menu's Profile link. Figure 10.11 shows a basic Community Builder user profile. The basic information displays an image, contact information, and a linked list of articles that the person has on the site.

If Jane Smith is logged in and she visits the profile, there will be an additional Edit link. By clicking Edit, she can change the image or her contact information. Community Builder includes some basic images that can be substituted for the default one, but users can also upload their own, as shown in Figure 10.12. When training users, it is often easiest to have them practice by changing to one of the built-in images.

After changing images, the display will change to that shown in Figure 10.13.

This profile can be expanded in a number of ways:

- Adding new fields (pieces of information such as mailing address) in the Community Builder Fields Manager
- Adding new tabs (in addition to profile/contact information and articles) in the Community Builder Tabs Manager

■ Adding plugins that extend the functionality in the Community Builder Plugin Manager

These three features work together. For example, new fields or plugins can be displayed in new or existing tabs or elsewhere in the profile.

Jane Smith Profile Page

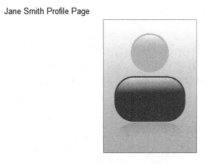

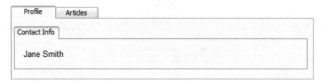

Figure 10.11  Basic CB profile page

Update Your Image

Submit a new image for upload
Your image will be resized if needed to a maximum dimension of 200 pixels width x 500 height automatically, but your image file should not exceed 2000 KB.

Select file [ Choose File ] No file chosen          [Upload]
By clicking "Upload", you certify that you have the right to distribute this photo.

Choose one from the image gallery

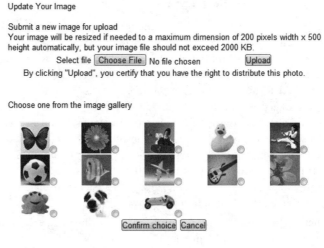

Confirm choice  Cancel

Figure 10.12  Default profile images that come installed with Community Builder

Figure 10.13  CB Profile with new profile image

We wanted to add these fields:

- Department, which is a drop-down list of the departments
- Role, which is a drop-down list with Teacher, Administrator, Professional Staff, and Other Staff items
- Job Title, which is a fill-in-the-blank field
- About Me, which is a space where users can write briefly about themselves

We want to display the first three on the Contact Info tab and the About Me field to the left of the image.

From the Community Builder Field Manager (shown in Figure 10.14), we created a drop-down field for departments, as shown in Figure 10.15. The Name field will automatically transform a simple name into the format that the database needs. Additional options can be added using the Add a View button. We followed the same procedure to create the role field. Some important things to remember are to set the Published field to Yes, Show on Profile to Yes on 1 Line, and Searchable in user-lists to Yes. Yes is indicated by a green check mark in the list view.

To create the Job Title field, we created a field with Type Text field, as shown in Figure 10.16.

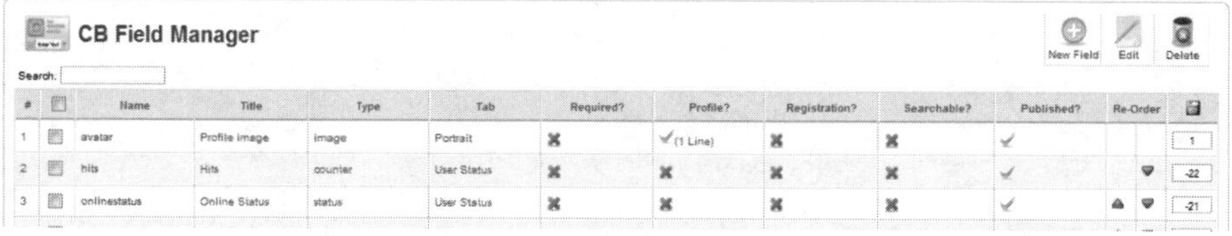

**CB Field Manager**

New Field    Edit    Delete

Search:

| # | | Name | Title | Type | Tab | Required? | Profile? | Registration? | Searchable? | Published? | Re-Order | |
|---|---|------|-------|------|-----|-----------|----------|---------------|-------------|------------|----------|---|
| 1 | | avatar | Profile Image | image | Portrait | ✖ | ✔ (1 Line) | ✖ | ✖ | ✔ | | 1 |
| 2 | | hits | Hits | counter | User Status | ✖ | ✖ | ✖ | ✖ | ✔ | ▼ | -22 |
| 3 | | onlinestatus | Online Status | status | User Status | ✖ | ✖ | ✖ | ✖ | ✔ | ▲ ▼ | -21 |

Figure 10.14  CB Field Manager screen

Figure 10.15  Creating a drop-down field for Department

| Type: | Text Field |
| Tab: | Contact Info |
| Name: | cb_jobtitle |
| Title: | Job Title |

Figure 10.16  Creating a field for the Job Title field

To create the About Me field, we used a type of text area. In this case, we want to display the field next to the image, so we changed the tab to Portrait, as shown in Figure 10.17.

Now when Jane Smith edits her profile, she will be able to update these fields. To other people, her profile now looks as in Figure 10.18.

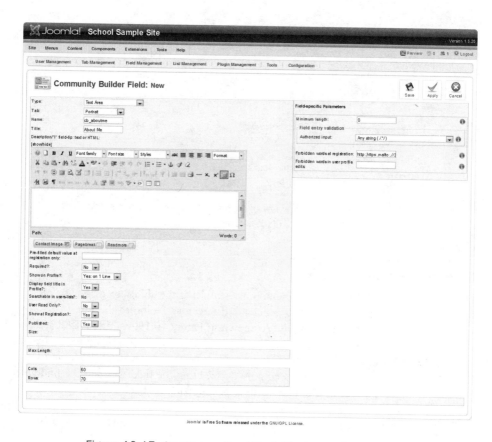

Figure 10.17  Creating an About Me field and assigning it to the Portrait tab

Figure 10.18  Front-end view of a profile page with newly created
fields showing

## Community Builder Lists

One of the most useful features of Community Builder is the ability to make lists of users. We used this feature to create a general staff directory. Going to the List Management tab, we created a new list. As shown in Figure 10.19, we titled it All and set Default to Yes. Community Builder lists have up to four columns. These are set in the lower half of the page. We enabled all four and chose Name, Department, Role, and Job Title as the fields. You put a field in a column by selecting the field name in the middle and then using the Add button to place it in a specific column. Each column must also have a title.

We then created a menu link from the main menu to the list. Figure 10.20 shows how the list appears on the front end.

We also wanted to create lists for each department, and for that we needed to use the Filter options in the list creation view. Initially, we set the field we want and the search criteria. This seems complex, but for most situations it is not hard. First, as shown in Figure 10.21, we set up the filter.

Then after clicking Add, the filter will be set as shown in Figure 10.22.

You also must make sure to include all user groups in the list, as shown in Figure 10.23.

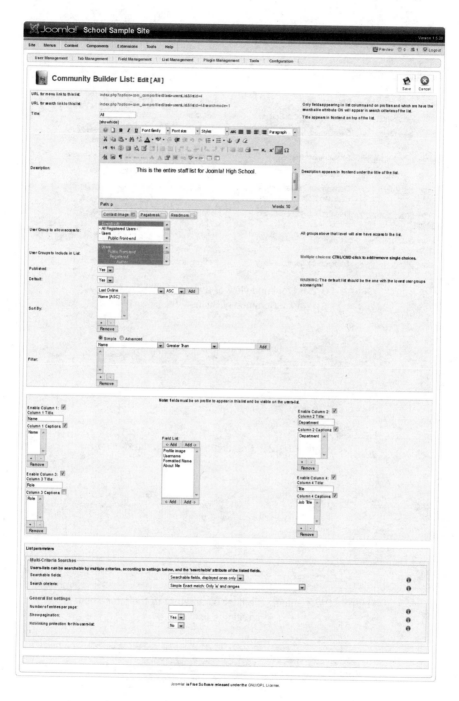

Figure 10.19  Creating a list in Community Builder

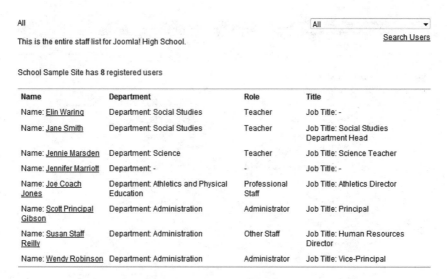

All

This is the entire staff list for Joomla! High School.

All ▼

Search Users

School Sample Site has 8 registered users

| Name | Department | Role | Title |
| --- | --- | --- | --- |
| Name: Elin Waring | Department: Social Studies | Teacher | Job Title: - |
| Name: Jane Smith | Department: Social Studies | Teacher | Job Title: Social Studies Department Head |
| Name: Jennie Marsden | Department: Science | Teacher | Job Title: Science Teacher |
| Name: Jennifer Marriott | Department: - | - | Job Title: - |
| Name: Joe Coach Jones | Department: Athletics and Physical Education | Professional Staff | Job Title: Athletics Director |
| Name: Scott Principal Gibson | Department: Administration | Administrator | Job Title: Principal |
| Name: Susan Staff Reilly | Department: Administration | Other Staff | Job Title: Human Resources Director |
| Name: Wendy Robinson | Department: Administration | Administrator | Job Title: Vice-Principal |

Figure 10.20  Front-end view of a member list created by
Community Builder

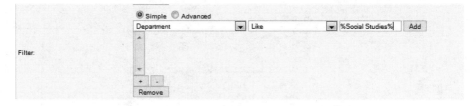

Figure 10.21  Creating a list with a filter

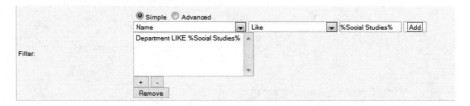

Figure 10.22  Adding the filter parameters to the filter when
creating a list

Figure 10.23  Selecting which groups to include in a Community Builder list

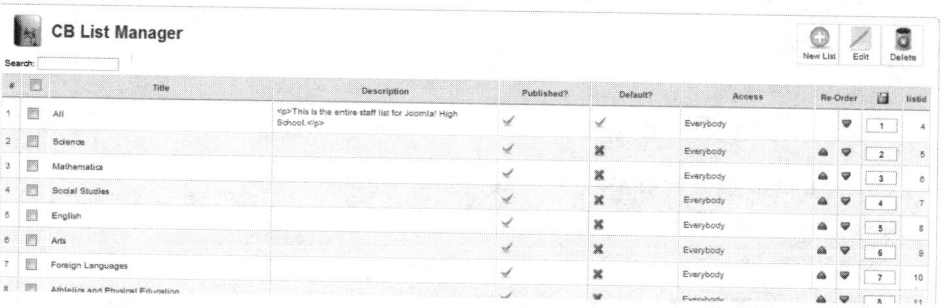

Figure 10.24  CB List Manager showing the list ID on the far-right side of the grid

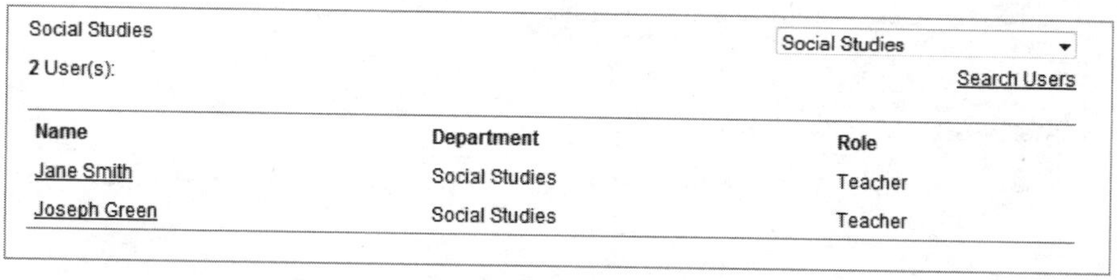

Figure 10.25  Front-end view of the Social Studies staff list

Each list has a list ID number that you can see in the List Manager on the far right, as shown in Figure 10.24. You need this number when creating a menu item linking to the list. We linked each list from the corresponding item in the department menu.

Linking to the Social Studies list produces the display shown in Figure 10.25.

## Community Builder Plugins

To implement the site, we used several Community Builder plugins that extend its functionality. Two are noncommercial, and two are commercial. Although an advantage of using Joomla! as your CMS is that it is free in cost, that does not mean that all open source software can or should be noncommercial. The time we would have spent writing a customized plugin compared to the cost of using a commercial plugin in our case favored using the commercial plugins. One advantage of Joomla! is that there are large numbers of commercial extensions at very reasonable prices, so you do not need to spend time or financial resources on custom development. The choice is up to you.

The installation procedure for a Community Builder Plugin is very similar to installing a Joomla! extension. As shown in Figure 10.26, go to the Plugin tab, and scroll to the bottom. There you have the usual installation options for installing from your computer, a directory, or a URL.

We used the following plugins:

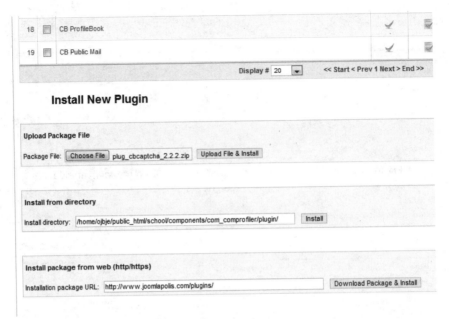

Figure 10.26  Installing a Community Builder plugin

## CB Public Mail

This enables there to be a contact form for each staff member but does not display the e-mail address of the staff member. This is important for preventing e-mail abuse.

## CB Captcha

This provides a security code for the contact form. This prevents spam.

## CB Profile Gallery

This allows users to upload images, PDFs, or other files. You can and should restrict the types of files that can be uploaded to prevent abuse, but the default list of file types that are allowed and blocked is appropriate for most sites. Because images will be publicly available, make sure that your school has a photo use policy for any images of children. Most likely you will want a signed photo release for each child. It's easiest to ask for these from all families rather than to do it on a case-by-case basis as images are uploaded.

## CB Profile Book

This provides a quick and easy way for staff members to post items of various kinds. We call the tab Classroom Updates, and it might include items for parents or students such as homework, deadlines, or announcements of field trips. We set it so that users can post on their own profiles but others cannot.

Figure 10.27  CB Tab Manager screen

For any plugins that you install, you will need to make sure that they are present in the Tab Manager and published as shown in Figure 10.27. Each plugin will have its own configuration option, and many can simply be left at their defaults. You will need to read the configuration instructions for any plugins you install.

### Tip

We used Jlord to generate some example users so that we could see how things looked as we were working. This can be very useful as you design a site. In making the site, we use dummy text from Lipsum.com. This text is traditionally used by designers in mocking up pages.

## More on Navigation

Now that there are staff lists for each department for each department, we added a new submenu by creating a link to the department's news category blog and one to their staff lists, as shown in Figure 10.28.

| # |  |  |  |  |  |  |  |  |
|---|---|---|---|---|---|---|---|---|
| 9 |  | └ English | ✓ |  | 2 | Public | Articles » Section | 7 |
| 10 |  | └ Staff List | ✓ | ▼ 1 | Public | Community Builder :: Userslist | 15 |
| 11 |  | └ English News | ✓ | ▲ 2 | Public | Articles » Category / Blog | 24 |
| 12 |  | └ Mathematics | ✓ |  | 3 | Public | Articles » Section | 8 |
| 13 |  | └ Staff List | ✓ | ▼ 1 | Public | Community Builder :: Userslist | 16 |
| 14 |  | └ Mathematics News | ✓ | ▲ 2 | Public | Articles » Category / Blog | 22 |
| 15 |  | └ Science | ✓ |  | 4 | Public | Articles » Section | 9 |
| 16 |  | └ Staff List | ✓ | ▼ 1 | Public | Community Builder :: Userslist | 17 |
| 17 |  | └ Science News | ✓ | ▲ 2 | Public | Articles » Category / Blog | 23 |
| 18 |  | └ Foreign Languages | ✓ |  | 5 | Public | Articles » Section | 10 |
| 19 |  | └ Staff List | ✓ | ▼ 1 | Public | Community Builder :: Userslist | 18 |
| 20 |  | └ Foreign Language News | ✓ | ▲ 2 | Public | Articles » Category / Blog | 29 |

Figure 10.28  Menu links created for navigation to staff lists and blogs

## Calendars

As discussed earlier in the chapter, we think that Google Calendar and the extension GCalendar is a good solution for many schools, so we installed that on the site. We explained in detail how to configure GCalendar on the sample site in Chapter 9.

One advantage of using Google Calendar is that we used it to create a separate calendar for just sports listings to be managed by the athletics and physical education department. We could easily create a new calendar for any other department or group if that was desired. Having separate calendars allows for more complete control of displaying, accessing, and posting of events. For example, perhaps student clubs could have a calendar, but you would not want students to have access to posting on the official school events calendar. Also, people can subscribe to specific calendars for integration into their own calendars apps and programs but not be overwhelmed with irrelevant events.

GCalendar comes with a number of separate modules. We used the loadposition plugin to display the sports calendar in an article in the Athletics and Physical Education section. This is a very useful technique that increases the flexibility of modules greatly. This plugin is enabled by default in Joomla!

First we made a new GCalendar_upcoming module, just as we made new modules in Chapter 9. However, in this instance, instead of using one of the positions listed in the drop-down list of positions, we made up a new name sports_calendar_load and typed it directly into the box, as shown in Figure 10.29. We also chose what specific pages we wanted it to display on, specifically those for the athletics and physical education department. We also changed the color of the highlights to one of our choice.

Next we created a new article in the Content Manager that contained the following code, as shown in Figure 10.30:

```
{loadposition sports_calendar_load}
```

This produced the front-end display that appears as in Figure 10.31.

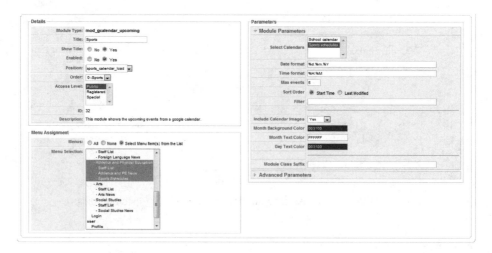

Figure 10.29  Creating a GCalendar module to show upcoming sports events

Figure 10.30  Inserting a module into a content item using loadposition

## Athletics News

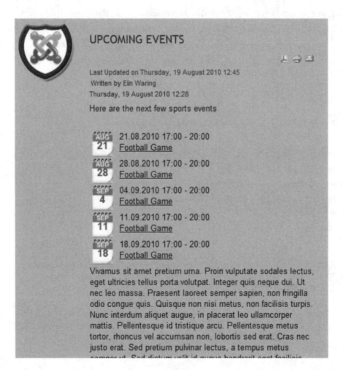

Figure 10.31  Front-end view showing the GCalendar module in a content
item with upcoming events

## Template Customization

As demonstrated in Chapter 8 and Chapter 9, follow the instructions to copy one of the default templates. We chose to copy the Beez template as an example for the school sample site. Again, an *override.css* file will need to be created and placed in the *css* folder of the template. This file is where you will override some of the default CSS and customize your template. Remember to rename your new template as previously instructed by editing the *templateDetails.xml* file and replacing the name with your new name. The name should match the folder name you gave to new template.

For our sample site, we also edited the icons that come in the *images* folder of the Beez template to further customize the look of our template to match our color scheme. Remember to name any replacement images with the same name and make them the same dimensions. Adobe Photoshop or the open source image editor GIMP are good choices for manipulating, editing, and creating images for your site.

We changed the color scheme to green using the same approach as in Chapter 5. Figure 10.32 shows a color chart with the hex codes (color represented by letters and numbers code) and the transformations that occur with each color. (If this image is being shown as a black-and-white image in your copy of this book, please go to *The Official Joomla! Book* Web site at *http://officialjoomlabook.com* to view the color version of this image.)

We also replaced the Beez logo with a new school crest image by replacing the default Beez logo in the template *images* folder and added a tag line in the *index.php* file. We also added an *override.css* file in the same way we did in Chapter 9.

The following are some of the CSS changes we made by adding CSS to the *overrides.css* file.

Specifically, this CSS changes the menu look:

```
/* ################ Main Menu ################ */
#left ul li ul {
        background: #fff;
        border: solid 1px #99B399;
        border-bottom: solid 0 #004000;
        border-left: solid 4px #004000;
        border-top: 0;
        margin: 0;
}


#left ul li ul li {
        border: solid 1px #fff;
}


#left ul li ul li {
        margin: 0;
}
```

```
#left ul li ul li a:hover,
#left ul li ul li a:active,
#left ul li ul li a:focus {
        background: #004000;
        color: #fff;
}

#left ul li ul li ul {
        border: solid 0 #99B399;
        padding: 10px 0 10px 5px;
}
```

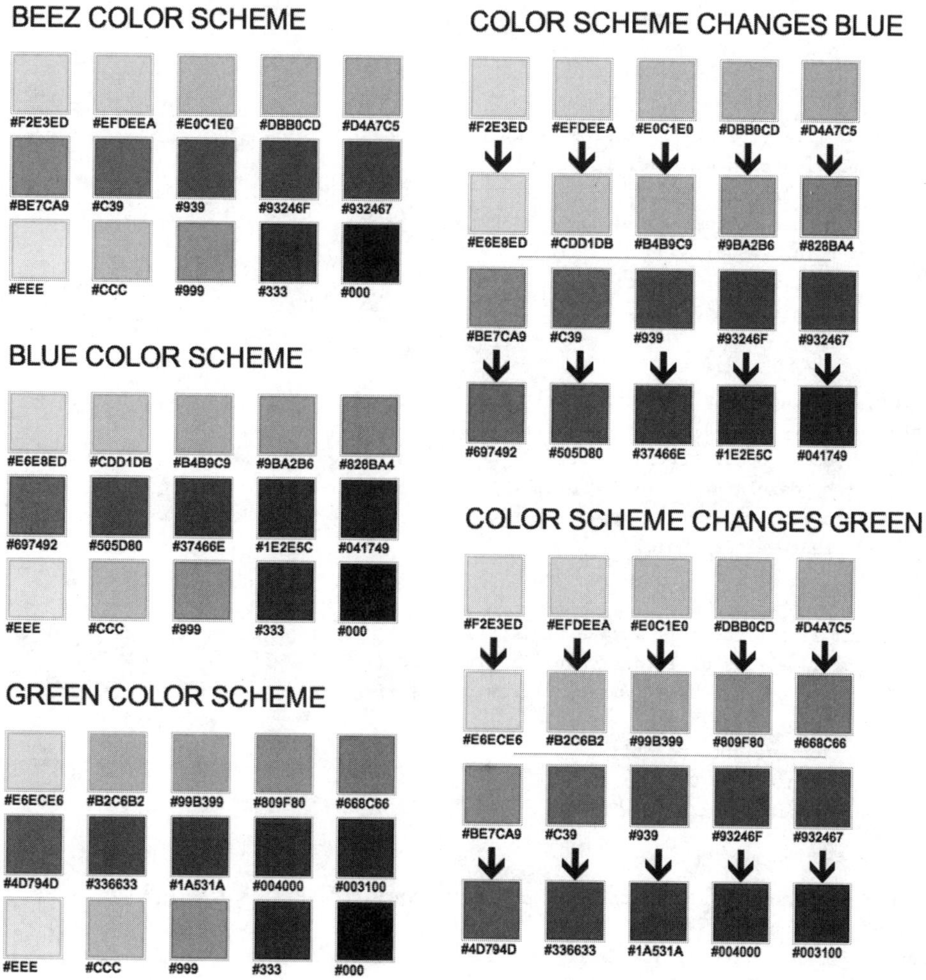

## BEEZ COLOR SCHEME

| #F2E3ED | #EFDEEA | #E0C1E0 | #DBB0CD | #D4A7C5 |
| #BE7CA9 | #C39 | #939 | #93246F | #932467 |
| #EEE | #CCC | #999 | #333 | #000 |

## BLUE COLOR SCHEME

| #E6E8ED | #CDD1DB | #B4B9C9 | #9BA2B6 | #828BA4 |
| #697492 | #505D80 | #37466E | #1E2E5C | #041749 |
| #EEE | #CCC | #999 | #333 | #000 |

## GREEN COLOR SCHEME

| #E6ECE6 | #B2C6B2 | #99B399 | #809F80 | #668C66 |
| #4D794D | #336633 | #1A531A | #004000 | #003100 |
| #EEE | #CCC | #999 | #333 | #000 |

## COLOR SCHEME CHANGES BLUE

| #F2E3ED | #EFDEEA | #E0C1E0 | #DBB0CD | #D4A7C5 |
| ↓ | ↓ | ↓ | ↓ | ↓ |
| #E6E8ED | #CDD1DB | #B4B9C9 | #9BA2B6 | #828BA4 |

| #BE7CA9 | #C39 | #939 | #93246F | #932467 |
| ↓ | ↓ | ↓ | ↓ | ↓ |
| #697492 | #505D80 | #37466E | #1E2E5C | #041749 |

## COLOR SCHEME CHANGES GREEN

| #F2E3ED | #EFDEEA | #E0C1E0 | #DBB0CD | #D4A7C5 |
| ↓ | ↓ | ↓ | ↓ | ↓ |
| #E6ECE6 | #B2C6B2 | #99B399 | #809F80 | #668C66 |

| #BE7CA9 | #C39 | #939 | #93246F | #932467 |
| ↓ | ↓ | ↓ | ↓ | ↓ |
| #4D794D | #336633 | #1A531A | #004000 | #003100 |

Figure 10.32  Beez template color scheme chart with transformations

```
#left ul li.active a:link,#left ul li.active a:visited {
        background: #004000;
        border-left: solid 4px #4D794D;
        color: #fff;
        border-bottom: solid 1px #004000;
        padding: 3px 0 3px 6px;
}

#left ul li.active ul li a:link,#left ul li.active ul li a:visited {
        background: #fff;
        border-bottom: solid 1px #99B399;
        border-left: solid 0 #DD75BB;
        color: #000;
        font-weight: normal;
        padding: 3px 4px 3px 20px;
}

#left ul li.active ul li ul li a:link,
#left ul li.active ul li ul li a:visited {
        background: #fff;
        border-bottom: solid 1px #99B399;
        color: #000;
        font-weight: normal;
        margin: 0 0 0 10px;
}

#left ul li.active ul li.active a:link,
#left ul li.active ul li.active a:visited {
        background: #fff;
        border-left: solid 0 #DD75BB;
        color: #000;
        font-weight: bold;
}

#left ul li.active ul li.active ul li a:link,
#left ul li.active ul li.active ul li a:visited {
        background: url(../images/arrow.gif) #fff no-repeat top left;
        color: #000;
        font-weight: normal;
        margin: 0 0 0 15px;
        padding: 3px 0 3px 15px;
}

#left ul li.active ul li.active ul li.active span.active_link {
        background:
url(../images/arrow.gif) #fff no-repeat top left;
        border-bottom: solid 1px #99B399;
```

```
        color: #000;
        font-weight: bold;
        margin: 0 0 0 15px;
        padding: 3px 0 3px 15px;
}

#left form a:hover,#left form a:active,
#left form a:focus {
        color: #fff;
}
```

This CSS changes the module styling for the GCalendar Upcoming Events module:

```
/*Module Styling*/

.moduletable-calupcoming {
        background-color: #E6ECE6;
        border: 1px solid #004000;
        margin: 10px;
        width: 195px;
}
```

A copy of each of the template modifications will be available for download and examination at *http://officialjoomlabook.com*.

# Conclusion

Joomla! is a strong solution for school Web sites. Starting with a basic informational site, you can progressively enhance the information offered and interactivity of the site. Developed effectively, your Joomla! Web site can help engage parents, teachers, students, and community members in learning and support of students.

# 11

# A Look at Joomla! 1.6 and the Future

This book focuses on the use of Joomla! 1.5 for making Web sites, but just like all software, Joomla! will have new releases that add major new features and make other changes. These are different from the maintenance releases for 1.5 that are regularly distributed that fix bugs and deal with any security issues. Although you should always keep your 1.5 site up to date with the current release of Joomla! 1.5, whether you should move your site to Joomla! 1.6 or a newer release is a more complicated issue.

Eventually, you will want your site to be on the most up-to-date version of Joomla!, but for many 1.5 users who are happy with the functionality of their sites, there is no reason to rush to move your site to Joomla! 1.6. Although each new release includes new features and improvements, if your site doesn't need those features and you don't want to move it, there is no reason for you to hurry to do so. Joomla! 1.5 will be supported for one year after the release of Joomla! 1.6, so you have lots of time to make the transition to a new version and may even decide to wait until the release of 1.7 or 1.8 to actually move your site.

On the other hand, if you think you need the new features or are adding new extensions, you may decide to move to the new release since many extension developers will be turning their main attention to Joomla! 1.6. Inexperienced users should not create a site with any new Joomla! release until the release is labeled General Availability or Stable. Many users will want to wait until after the first maintenance release, which will be Joomla! 1.6.1. That release will resolve any issues that emerge soon after the initial release.

This chapter will review some of the key changes between Joomla! 1.5 and 1.6 in order to help you make the decision about moving an existing site to Joomla! 1.6. For those developing a new site, the decision of whether to develop it with Joomla! 1.5 or 1.6 will also be discussed. At the time of writing, 1.6 was in heavy development. This chapter includes examples of what has changed between 1.5 and 1.6, but the exact procedures and appearances may be different at the release of 1.6 GA or Stable.

## Changes in Minimum Requirements

Joomla! 1.5 requires that your site be on a server that has PHP with a minimum version number of 5.2 and MySQL of 5.0.4. If you have an existing Joomla! site, you can visit the phpinfo tab, which you can find by clicking Help on the top menu and then selecting System Info to find the PHP versions you are currently using. If they do not meet these requirements, ask your host whether a newer version is available. Some hosts will upgrade software only if they are sure you are not using any applications that require older versions. Submit a support ticket to your host requesting an upgrade or upgrade instructions. If an upgrade is not available, you will not be able to migrate to 1.6 and remain on the same host.

# User Interface Changes

There are a number of places where Joomla! 1.6 makes minor changes that will take some getting used to for Joomla! 1.5 users. These are called *changes* in the user interface.

## Administrator Menu

Some items have been moved around in the administrator as follows.

- The Media Manager is now located in the Content submenu.
- Cache management and the check-in of items are now on the Site menu (far left) in the Site Maintenance submenu.
- The User Manager is now in the Users menu along with the links for managing access control and mass e-mail.
- The Help menu now consists entirely of links to external resources.
- The Help system linked from the toolbars on each page has been simplified so that the links relate more directly to the specific context from which you click the Help icon.

Content items are called *articles*. This reflects the reality that articles are just one kind of content, along with contacts, Web links, newfeeds, and items created by other extensions.

## Modules

Modules have four new fields. Although useful for some sites, if you do not need these features, you can ignore them.

Publish and unpublish dates allow you to display modules for specific time periods.

Note is a place for you to put notations that only people with access to the module-editing screen can see. This is useful if you have many items with the same or similar names or some other reason to make notations; otherwise, it can be ignored.

Language lets you designate a specific language for a module and is used in combination with the language switcher module and the language filter plugin.

## Menu Manager

The Menu Manager has some usability improvements in Joomla! 1.6, although the functionality remains the same. The most obvious change is that choosing a new menu item is now done in a modal from the menu item–editing screen, but there are much more useful refinements.

The biggest change is the ability to assign modules to menu items directly in the menu interface. Similarly, you can assign template styles directly when creating or editing the menu item. If alternative layouts are available for a given menu item type, they can be assigned in this screen. Figure 11.1 demonstrates the new edit screen for creating a menu item, showing the extensive functionality of selecting module assignments in the right column of options. Figure 11.2 demonstrates the modal or overlay window that opens, allowing you to select options for module assignment.

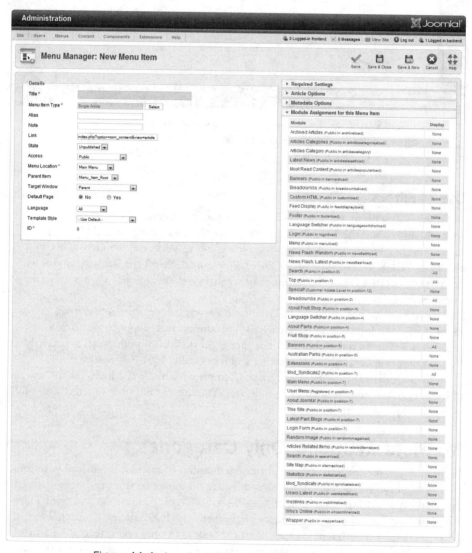

Figure 11.1  Joomla! 1.6 new menu item–editing screen

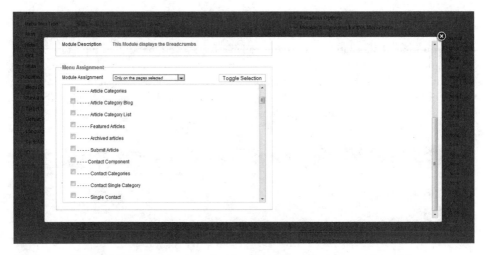

Figure 11.2  Modal overlay that is shown when module assignment is clicked in the main menu–editing screen. This modal shows the selections for assigning the menu item to a page's module.

## Use of Filters

In Joomla! 1.6 trash management is handled in the interfaces for each component, the Menu Manager, and the Module Manager. To see the items that are in the trash, go to the appropriate location, and then use the state filter to select trashed items. This will change the Trash icon in the toolbar into a Delete icon. Select the items you want to delete, and click the Delete icon. You can also change trashed items to the published, unpublished, or archived states.

All components now offer an archived state. As was true in for content items in Joomla! 1.5, Web links, contacts, newsfeeds, and banners now allow you to archive specific items. This means that they will not appear on the lists of items, such as category lists, but they will be available for linking and (optionally) in search results.

In the Joomla! 1.6 Module Manager and Template Manager, the items for the site and the administrator are presented in a single view. You use the filter bar to select site-only or administrator-only modules or templates.

# No More Sections, Only Categories

In Joomla! 1.6, the sections and categories organization of content is replaced with infinitely nested categories. That means that there are no longer sections and categories. In 1.6, categories nest inside each other, with the nesting going as deep as you need. (The same structure is used in all the content components, such as Articles, Contact, Web Links, Newsfeeds, and Banners.) Each item can still be in only one category. All articles, newsfeeds, banners, Web links, and contacts must be placed into a category, but this was also true for all except articles in Joomla! 1.5. Articles in 1.5 could be placed in the

Figure 11.3  The new Category Manager in 1.6 demonstrating
nested categories

included Uncategorized section and category, which had specific properties. Figure 11.3 shows the Category Manager.

If you use the migration script that is available for moving to Joomla! 1.6, your sections will become the top-level categories, and each category that was within that section will be nested within it. You will then be able to move all the categories around however you like.

Migrated content that was uncategorized in Joomla! 1.5 will be moved to a category called Uncategorized with the migration script. In addition, each of the content components will now have a category labeled Uncategorized. You can delete these if they are not helpful to you.

The categories system is very powerful, but it has the potential to create unnecessary complexity. As always, your site and users will benefit if you plan carefully before implementing.

Categories are integrated into the new language-handling system managed by the language switcher module and language filter plugin. If you want to use this feature, you will need to designate a language for each category. There is no automatic copying or translation management for categories.

# Templates

Joomla! 1.5 templates must be modified to work with Joomla! 1.6. How complex this process is depends on the template itself. If your template is relatively simple, it will not be hard to migrate it. If you purchased it from a template firm, you may want to check with them to see whether they have a 1.6 version. If you created a template or modified one of the core templates, you will find instructions on migrating to 1.6 on the *http://docs.joomla.org* Web site, but it may be best to wait until you are ready for a site redesign to migrate.

## Included New Front-End Templates

Joomla! 1.6 includes two new front-end templates, Beez2 and Beez5. Both templates feature designs that meet stringent standards for accessibility for all people as well as standards for HTML and CSS. Beez5 uses the HTML5 standard; HTML5 is a newer standard that is being rapidly adopted.

The new Beez templates are somewhat easier to use because a replacement header image can be uploaded using the Media Manager. To exactly replace the header image in Beez2, you need an image that is 1060 pixels wide and 288 pixels high. To replace the image in Beez5, you will need an image that is 1050 pixels wide and 180 pixels in high. However, most images should work well with either template. You can also not use an image and put your site name there instead.

Joomla! 1.6 also includes the Atomic template, which has no styling and is designed to be used as a skeleton for creating new templates.

Also, Milkyway is included as a 1.5 to 1.6 template for those who are migrating and need to utilize old templating options.

## Administrator Templates

Joomla! 1.6 has a new basic administrator template called Blue Stork and a second called Hathor. Hathor features full accessibility for people who use screen readers and other assistive devices. For the first time, the ability to manage a Joomla! site is truly open to everyone. If you have users with disabilities that may impair their ability to work with Joomla! or if you have to comply with accessibility regulations, these improvements may make migration to Joomla! 1.6 attractive.

## Template Styles

The most important new feature for site design is the addition of template styles. In Joomla! 1.5, you were able to select a specific set of options for your template. For example, in Milkyway, you could select the background and trim colors. However, if you wanted to vary these options such as having one section of your site have a red background and another section a blue one, you have to copy the whole template. In 1.6, this is handled using template styles.

Each template style represents a specific set of options chosen for a template. For example, in Beez2, those options might be as follows.

- *Logo:* Select or upload a specific logo image.
- *Position of Navigation:* Before content.
- *Template Color:* Black.

Then you might have a second style.

- *Logo:* Select or upload a different specific logo image.
- *Position of Navigation:* After content.
- *Template Color:* Personal.

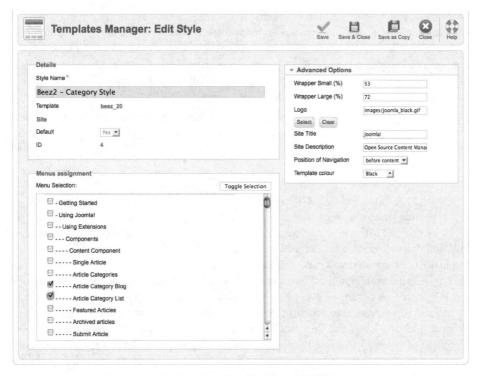

Figure 11.4  New Template Manager: Edit Style screen

Each menu link has an option to apply a specific template style to the linked content. Figure 11.4 shows the new Template Manager: Edit Style screen and options. To see examples of how template styles are applied, the sample data shows Beez2 – Default and a template style that is called Beez2 – Parks Site.

# Access Control (ACL)

The largest and most anticipated addition to Joomla! 1.6 is the flexible access control system, called ACL (for *access control lists*). ACL allows you to control who sees what and who can do what on your site. This has long been the most-requested feature for Joomla!

In Joomla! 1.5, you are already working with a basic access control model. There are three access levels controlling what a user can see (Guest, Registered, and Special) and eight access groups controlling what a user can do (Guest, Registered, Author, Editor, Publisher, Manager, Administrator, and Super Administrator). For the many Web sites, these groupings are adequate, and for many they may even be too complicated (for example, you may not want to distinguish between authors, editors, and publishers). When you install Joomla! 1.6, the Joomla! 1.5 access control system is re-created for you.

From there you have the option of leaving the settings as they are or modifying them. Migrating your site will leave your users with the same access rights they have now.

Some Web sites will, however, be strengthened by taking advantage of the new flexibility of this system in Joomla! 1.6. However, you should plan carefully about the needs of your site before implementing any changes. The following are some situations where you might want to create more detailed access control.

- You want a group of users only to be able to create articles in one specific category.
- You want to hide something from a group of users.
- You want someone to help you administer some parts of your site but not other parts.

Figure 11.5 shows the new Global Configuration page's Permissions tab where you set up permissions for user groups.

In Joomla! 1.5, each item of content from a component, each module, each menu link, and each plugin can be assigned to exactly one access level. This is still true in Joomla! 1.6, except that you can create more levels.

Those levels are hierarchical. So, special users can see everything registered users can see. Registered users can see everything the public can see.

In Joomla! 1.6, you have much more flexibility, but it is also much more complex. You can add new levels and groups. Groups can be assigned to more than one level. Users can be assigned to more than one group. Both groups and levels may inherit permissions from each other. You can also modify the privileges given to the existing groups from Joomla! 1.5 that are present when you install. Because of this complexity, you should plan any changes in detail before implementing.

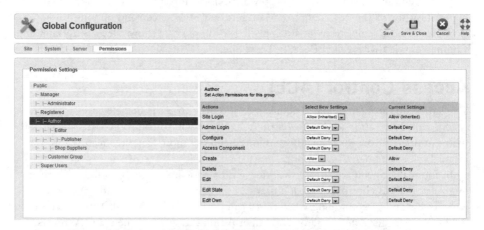

Figure 11.5  Joomla! 1.6 Global Configuration page's Permissions tab
showing group permissions

Access levels allow you to control what users *see*. Much more powerful are the access groups that control what users can do. The access groups can manage nine actions.

- Site login, which controls logging into the front end of your site.

- Administrator login, which controls logging into the administrator.

- Create, which controls the creation of content such as articles, Web links, contacts, and categories.

- Edit, which controls whether the user can modify existing content.

- Edit State, which controls whether the use can publish, unpublish, archive, or trash content.

- Delete, which controls deletion of trashed content items.

- Manage, which allows access to the administrator for a component, but by itself only allows the user to view, not create, edit, edit state, or delete.

- Admin, which allows the user to configure component options. When set globally, the admin controls whether a user can set global configurations and a user with global admin access can always see everything on a site. You will always want to have the chief administrator of your site to have this access.

- Edit Own, which allows the user to edit content they created (as indicated in the created by field in the editor).

All of these privileges can be set at the global level, at the component level, and at the category level within each component. They can also be set for individual articles. Figure 11.6 demonstrates the ACL settings for a category.

Detailed documentation about the new access control system will be available on the Joomla.org sites. Appendix C of this book gives an example of setting ACL rules for the sample site that is detailed in Chapter 10.

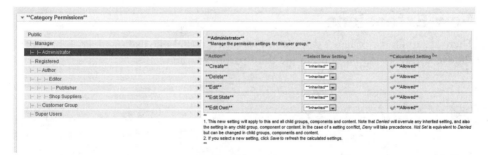

Figure 11.6  Joomla! 1.6 category access rules (ACLs are located on the bottom of the editing screen)

## Languages

As mentioned in the discussion of changes to the user interface, in Joomla! 1.6 you can select a specific language for your content, categories, modules, and menu links. This feature is not a substitute for an extension that manages a full multilingual site with translated content, but it is effective if you have a small site with content in two or more languages. If you want to use this feature, you will need to enable the language switcher module and the language filter plugin. Full use of this feature also requires you to install the language pack for each included language and to designate a home page for each language. Unless you have a site that has content in more than one language, you can ignore this feature.

## Extension Manager

The Extension Manager in Joomla! 1.6 has important new functionality. Extensions may still be installed in the same manner as in Joomla! 1.5. However, a new Discover option allows you to use your File Manager or FTP to move files into the correct location; just click Discover, and then click Install. This is especially useful if you have large extensions on hosting with memory limitations.

If the developers of any extensions you have installed have implemented it, you will be able to search for and install extension updates with one click. Figure 11.7 shows the new Update capability in the Extension Manager for Joomla! 1.6.

## Updating Joomla!

Updating your Joomla! installation is easier in Joomla! 1.6 than in Joomla! 1.5 thanks to the Update Manager. When a new maintenance release of Joomla! is announced, simply go to the Updates tab and check for updates. If Joomla! appears on the list of updated items, selecting the box by its name, and then click the Update icon.

## New Extensions

There are a number of new extensions in Joomla! 1.6, and one extension, Polls, has been removed. To replace polls, you can use third-party extensions.

Figure 11.7  Extension Manager Update screen showing that there are no
updates available for any of the extensions installed on the test site

## Components

The new Redirect component allows you to seamlessly point one URL to a new one. This is especially important when you are migrating a site because your URLs may change. By redirecting the old URLs to new URLs, existing links and search engine results will not return broken links. After moving your site, you should use the redirect component to move URLs that you are aware of but also monitor the component for at least a week to identify and redirect other paths users are taking to your site.

## Modules

There are five new modules.

- *Weblinks module:* Presents a list of Web links in a given category.
- *Latest users module:* Shows a list of the most recently registered users.
- *Language Switcher module:* Allows users to select content in a specific language as tagged in content, modules, and menus.
- *Article Categories:* Shows a linked list of all the categories within a given category. This is similar to the sections module in Joomla! 1.5 but takes advantage of the new nested categories structure.
- *Article Category:* Shows a linked list of articles within a given category.

A number of modules have been renamed to make it clearer that they are used only for articles.

## Plugins

Five new plugins have been added to Joomla! 1.6.

- The Profile plugin provides a method to add new fields to the registration screen and/or the profile screen. This plugin is an example, with the idea that users who are comfortable with coding can make their own versions. In this example, each field can be required, optional, or hidden. It is disabled by default.
- The Contact Creator will automatically create a linked contact for each new user who is created. It is disabled by default.
- The Language Filter is used in combination with the creation of content in more than one language and the language switcher module. It allows the creation of a home page for each language and the filtering of content by language. It is disabled by default. It should be used only in combination with the language switcher module.
- Article Link allows you to make a link to articles from within an editor in a modal screen. It is enabled by default.
- The Code Mirror Editor has been added and replaces xStandardlite. It is especially useful for editing HTML and templates because it provides code highlighting. It is enabled by default.

This chapter was written based on the beta 10 release of Joomla! 1.6 and is based on our knowledge of the goals for 1.6 as participants in the Joomla! Bug Squad. It is possible that some details may change between the time of writing and the release of 1.6 Stable.

## Conclusion

Joomla! 1.6 is a major advance for the Joomla! content management system, with important and exciting new features. However, it is not necessary for all sites to be moved quickly to the new version or even moved at all in the immediate future. Instead, Webmasters should carefully consider the new features and whether they will be useful for their sites. If you do choose to migrate your site, you should plan carefully and avoid creating unnecessary complexity that will not help your users have a better experience. Carefully consider the amount of time it will take, the availability of 1.6 versions of the extensions you use, and the importance of new features in making your decision.

# 12

# Interviews with Experts

The Joomla! project is filled with people with expertise in all kinds of areas. Both we and Joomla! have benefited greatly from their knowledge and experiences. Getting to know them and working with them on various tasks have enriched our knowledge and understanding of many of the issues touched in this book. We can't introduce you personally, but we have brought together participants in the Joomlasphere to talk personally about the project, their involvement, and their experiences working with Joomla!

## Expert Q&A with Andrew Eddie: Owner of NewLifeInIT and Lead Developer of Joomla!

*I'm an IT consultant based out of Toowoomba, Australia, and have some ten years of professional experience in Web-based software application development though I've been programming since the early 80s. I'm known mostly for my involvement in the Mambo and Joomla! projects, which started very early in 2003, and since then, I've worn many official and unofficial hats within both projects. I've also made past contributions to other open source projects such as dotProject and phpDocumentor and a few other smaller ones. I was very privileged to win the 2009 Software Queensland Medal for outstanding contribution to the Queensland Software Industry and also a High Commendation from the Pearcy Foundation.*

Q: What prompted your interest, and/or how did you learn about Joomla?

A: Well, my involvement predates Joomla! I became involved in Mambo (the project from which Joomla! forked) in February 2003. At the time, I was working for Toowoomba City Council, and we were looking for replacement systems for our 300 static-page Web site. Prior to this, I'd been learning the open source ropes in a project called dotProject, which I believe is still around. I had been trialling a number of CMSs (there weren't actually that many to choose from back then, and even fewer would install reliably) and, after a few failures, found that Mambo 4.0 had the makings of what we needed for Council's Web site. I knew I'd be putting a lot of company time into the system based on what I was allowed to do customising dotProject for Council's use. So, I sent an e-mail to the guy running the forum to put my hand up to help, and things took off from there.

Q: Do you regularly use open source software, and why?

A: It depends. I always look for an open source solution first for desktop applications, even though I don't really need the "source." It's usually a case of it's "free," as in "free beer." But for Web-based applications, I go exclusively with open source systems, mainly so I can fix it when I find bugs (and I usually do). For other platforms such as my iPhone, I'm obviously restricted to what I can use.

Q: Joomla! has a large community with a lot of active contributors. In your opinion, what is the most exciting part of being involved, and how do you contribute to the community?

A: The most exciting part is meeting people who are talking about what they've done to create something that they could not have done without Joomla! Seeing people enabled to produce Web content without having to know all the technical Web stuff is fantastic. I also have some quite emotional moments when people have rallied around to get a site up quickly when there is a great need. I remember the time I went to Byron Bay and that local user group helped a women get a site up quickly to keep everyone informed about her husband (a popular footballer) who was badly injured one day. It really tugs at your heart strings when you know you've been part of making a difference in that person's life. There's obviously some personal excitement when you produce a really cool feature or something, but ultimately it is seeing ordinary people do extraordinary things with the software that keeps me going.

Q: Given your history with the project as someone who has been involved in development since the inception of Joomla! and before that with Mambo, what sort of changes have you seen in the CMS market? How have these changes helped end users?

A: Mambo was born out of the frustration with the "Nuke" years (phpNuke, postNuke, and a heap of others that just copied the same formula). It was really the first CMS to my mind that was catering for the business sites, and this also meant that it would be suitable for "normal" people as well. Mambo was really on the cusp of that period where the CMS could be used by people who weren't programmers or geeks. Mambo and Joomla! have certainly been criticized for concentrating on eye candy and what looks good for the regular person, but that's kind of the point of what a CMS is supposed to do. So, the major changes I've seen are the CMSs are constantly trying to look better and be easier and more intuitive to use. I thinking Joomla! and Mambo have also been ahead of the pack in terms of making the CMS easier to style and extend. I really feel the others are only now starting to catch up with that philosophy.

Changes in Web standards, hardware, and browser capabilities also allows for natural improvements that make things easier on the user, and we've certainly seen that in the Web 2.0 space.

Q: As an independent developer, you have given lectures on some of the solutions you have developed using Joomla! You also offer training and documentation. What are some of the most interesting challenges you have been able to solve using Joomla!

A: I certainly seem to attract "interesting challenges" from various people. There are a couple of notable projects that come to mind.

For *www.is4profit.com*, they have a lot of data that comes from an XML-based Web server that they subscribe to. This data needed to be converted from XML markup into something suitable for a Joomla! article. Not only that, but these articles were multipage, had links to other pages in the article, and also had links to other articles from the Web service. I devised a command-line version of Joomla! that sucked the XML information from the Web service and converted that into the Joomla! articles, doing differential checks so that only new articles are added and modified articles updated. Then we had to coax the Joomla! router to get all the interpage links to work properly. On top of that, it was a Joomla! 1.0 to 1.5 migration, so all up, it was probably the most complex traditional Joomla! site I've done.

The other big site I've worked with is PeopleBrowsr.com. The company building it had decided to use Joomla! as a base, and I was called in to guide the initial architectural development of the Joomla! site. The client-side site was nothing like you'd ever seen in a typical Joomla! site. It's basically a JavaScript framework that's running everything through Ajax calls. The challenge here was to give their developers a good framework to allow that Ajax system to work, on top of all the other idiosyncrasies that accompanied that site.

Certainly these systems could have been done via bespoke methods, but the Joomla! framework is capable of handling a 12-page brochure site as much as it can really complex animals like the previous two I mentioned. Without the discipline of working within a framework, I would be reinventing the wheel on nearly every project.

Q: As one of the lead developers for Joomla!, how has the development process changed since Joomla! 1.0 came out? Can you give a bit of history behind the main releases and how the project has evolved to 1.6?

A: Joomla! 1.0 had a very quick birth. It was born out of the salvaged wreckage of Mambo 4.5.3 that was nearing alpha release. Back then, the Core Team was almost entirely developers, and you had to be on the Core Team to actually commit code. It was an extremely exclusive club. We also generally had one or two people who were able to devote massive blocks of hours to the project, and that kept the pace up. After our first Joomla! Core Team Summit in 2005, there was a tepid plan for the features that were to be released in the next few versions. But as the months rolled on, problems arose that delayed some areas of the code, which meant that we really just started playing with other interesting things.

Unfortunately, that's all we ended up doing, and the changes that were happening on a daily basis meant that reaching a point of stability was just not going to happen.

By this time, we had so many new things in the stack that the release was rebadged from 1.1 to 1.5. The Joomla! Bug Squad was formed in an effort to stop the playing in the sandpit and begin the process of stabilizing the core code for release. The effectiveness of the JBS was unparalleled to anything we'd seen in Joomla!'s or Mambo's history. It worked really well—almost too well. Our most fatal mistake during the period up to release of 1.5 was that we did not encourage new development that could continue and slot in after its release. Also, after 1.5 was released, most people were so burned out that nobody had time to really think about the next version. Couple that with lack of planning and experienced leadership (for which I take some of that blame), and the development side of the project began to flounder.

Anyway, to cut a long story short, the way we were doing development wasn't going to ship 1.6 or any future version in a hurry, so we've made quite a few changes over the last year. We've opened up the development lists to the public, and anyone can apply to get a branch to work on new features, which has meant that a lot more people have been getting involved dealing with the real problems and issues to move development forward.

Q:  What is coming on the horizon for Joomla! development as the project looks to 1.7 and beyond?

A:  Well, that's an interesting question. Joomla! 1.7 is as much a new process as it is a new version of the software. Not all the details are finalized yet, but we are looking at a number of initiatives that will improve the reliability and credibility of the Joomla! release cycle. We'll be introducing operational changes such as a calendar-based release cycle. The idea here is that we release what we call a minor version (1.7, 1.8, and so on) every six months more or less to the day. This gives site owners and developers alike the ability to adjust their own internal maintenance cycles to the Joomla! cycle allowing for much better planning on host of fronts. This short time frame (in comparison to between two and three years between releases) also allows us to inject innovation back into the software at a much faster pace because the incremental steps are smaller. It also means that larger features can be worked that could possibly span two versions if the team working on it thinks it will take a year to develop. There is nothing stopping that kind of flexibility.

The second initiative is to give the both the user and the developer community a greater voice in what features are actually in the "next" version. What will probably happen is that the Production Leadership Team (PLT) will pick a "theme" for the next version, and there will be a system for processing ideas. Those ideas that reach a certain level of maturity and that align with the "theme" will be given a priority for the next version. Conceptually we either want to see a maturing of a concept, more or less like have the specification for a new feature, or actually have a coded proof of concept. In this way, both nondevelopers and developers can play an important role in the production of the software.

Of course, the last step is to try to marry people with the great ideas to people with the capacity to deliver them. Unfortunately, that is the part of the process that is least under our control.

So, in summary, I actually don't know what 1.7 will be, but I'm very keen to see how it works out because it's a massive paradigm shift compared to the culture we have worked in for many years now.

# Expert Q&A with Mark Dexter and Sam Moffatt: The Joomla! Bug Squad

*Mark Dexter: I started and ran a successful commercial software company for 28 years, before retiring in 2007. I am mostly self-taught as a software developer. My formal education was in liberal arts and business. As I thought about retiring, I decided that I would like to retire from business but continue working on software. I started learning about and working on open source software. My first project was to learn Java and Eclipse and create some video tutorials called* Eclipse and Java for Total Beginners. *Two years ago I became the Webmaster of a local community group and started learning Joomla! I found the community to be very welcoming and have gotten more and more involved with the project over the past two years. As of now, my Joomla! roles include development coordinator, a member of the Production Work Group, a member of the Leadership Team, and a coordinator of the Joomla! Bug Squad. Last year I also served as the Google Summer of Code Administrator.*

*Sam Moffatt: Sam Moffatt is quite possibly a geek and almost certainly a developer. Vicious rumors of anything more won't be entertained. As a narcissistic hobby, he maintains a collection of biographies he's written (or have been written) over the years, and strangely they seem to get read (or maybe it's just the bots):* http://www.pasamio.id.au/content/category/3/80/49/. *At one point he is considering writing a proper bio for this book but figured it would be too hard and then he realized it was supposed to be done first person, not third person, all too confusing. And yes, he did write the 1.0 to 1.5 migrator, and yes he still has a 1.0 site.*

Q: What prompted your interest, and/or how did you learn about Joomla?

A: **Mark:** I volunteered to take over as Webmaster for a local community group. I had no experience with Web site administration or content management systems. At the time, the Web site was a static HTML site. Someone suggested using a CMS and suggested looking at Joomla! I downloaded it and started learning it and eventually deployed it for the site.

**Sam:** I was working at Toowoomba Regional Council (previously Toowoomba City Council) as a school-based apprentice. As a part of that I was actually located in the Strategic Planning department (almost an oxymoron for local government, but it existed) and was working on a "Safer Communities" Web site and forum. The forum used phpBB2 and didn't particularly pick up, but I ran into a fellow called Andrew Eddie who was from the Information Management Branch. After a while, I shifted from working within Strategic Planning to working with Andrew within IMB, and from there I started working with Mambo and the various items. From here I participated in Summer of Code for Mambo in 2005, which turned into Joomla!, and the rest, as they say, is history.

Q:  Do you regularly use open source software, and why?

A:  **Mark:** Yes. I like the philosophy of open source, and I like the software. I use open source software for as much of my work as I can.

**Sam:** In addition to Joomla!, I strongly promote a wide variety of open source projects. To me it represents the ability to pick up high-quality software that meets a need and deploy it for the purposes that I need. I feel with open source software you get the choice of picking the best option out there. My present employer, the University of Southern Queensland, uses a significant amount of open source. In my time there, I have worked with Moodle (the PHP learning management system), ePrints (a Perl-based institutional repository tool), VuFind (a PHP/Solr-powered discovery layer and search tool), and Mahara (portfolio software). My desktop at one stage ran Ubuntu, and Eclipse is my primary IDE for work either at home or in the office regardless of platform. Personally I run a wiki powered by MediaWiki, my blog actually runs WordPress, and of course I have Joomla! for my main Web sites. The advantage I find is that when I find a bug or an issue with any of these systems, I have the source code to fix or improve it. Typically these systems predominantly support a plugin infrastructure, which means adding improvements is a lot easier and better supported than other proprietary platforms. At the moment, I'm running up some new software a division of my university has produced that is open source and provides a different way of searching and sharing information.

Q:  Joomla! has a large community with a lot of active contributors. In your opinion, what is the most exciting part of being involved, and how do you contribute to the community?

A:  **Mark:** I enjoy the fact that the Joomla! community is so international. I regularly work with people from all over the world. The community is also very friendly and welcoming, which is why I started to volunteer in the first place. I wear a number of hats in the community, including development coordinator, being on the Leadership Team, and being coordinator of the Bug Squad. Most of my time the past few months has been on finishing version 1.6.

**Sam:** For the longest time, and perhaps even now, I have a hard time believing just how popular and widespread Joomla! has become. I came from a different perspective where I missed a lot of the news about Joomla! because in some respects I was already there. I came to Joomla! with a completely different route than I believe anyone has ever done or perhaps will ever do again. So for me, the most exciting part is actually discovering all of these people not only using Joomla! but also using my extensions and seeing just how global the community is. Seeing how big the world has grown around Joomla! and seeing just how awesome everyone else is. In my way, I contribute in the little things that are out of sight and out of mind; it's how I prefer to work. I have a few extensions that I've developed since 1.0 that I keep on working on, mostly stuff I find useful that I feel the rest of the world might find useful as well. Nothing earth-shattering, just useful.

Q: What prompted the creation of the Joomla! Bug Squad?

A: **Mark:** The Bug Squad was created before I started with Joomla!, but my understanding is that it was created with two goals in mind: first, to have a group whose only focus is to fix bugs and improve the overall quality of the code; second, to lower the barrier to entry for new contributors to the project. For example, you don't need to be an expert in Joomla! or in programming to join and be a great contributor to the Bug Squad. Working on the Bug Squad is also a fantastic way to learn more about Joomla! and programming. Several of our bug squad members are now contributing to the 1.6 project.

**Sam:** A lack of pies. The Dutch don't have pies like the Australians do, and Wilco Jansen needed an excuse to visit Australia. I think it may have nearly killed him (something about having a pie at 3 a.m. in the morning; personally I find that's exactly when you want a pie after you've drunk too much), but one of the first things I did when Wilco came to visit Australia was to get him a pie at a pie shop on the side of a highway in almost the middle of nowhere.

In all seriousness, Wilco was the driving force behind the Bug Squad. JBS was his drive to create an entity within Joomla! that effectively and efficiently handled bugs within the system, handled the stabilization of the product, and was open and accessible.

Q: How do you think the Joomla! Bug Squad has benefited the project?

A: **Mark:** By allowing less experienced people to contribute to the project. This has expanded the number of people working on the project. Some of these people have gone on to contribute in very significant ways.

**Sam:** JBS is a place where almost any skill set is required: it needs people to test things, not only the bugs themselves to confirm them but also the fixes that are developed, and it needs the people to make those fixes and the changes to the system that make them work. As such, the Joomla! Bug Squad is a great entry point for the project. It is a place where it doesn't matter if you can't put in much time because every little bit works, and the infrastructure is designed that way. Find a bug, do what you can do on it (confirm it, fix it, or test a patch), and contribute your thoughts. This has led to a lot of squished bugs and perhaps some of the most stable software around.

Q: Outside of maintaining the stable releases, has the Joomla! Bug Squad affected other areas of the project such as in core development?

A: **Mark:** Yes. For example, several people who started out in the Bug Squad have contributed significantly to version 1.6.

**Sam:** Bug Squad is a good entry point for the project to help people grow into different roles. For some, Bug Squad has meant that they've risen all the way to development coordinators (yes, I'm looking at you, Mark and Ian). Bug Squad is a great place to get to know the environment, is a great place to learn the code, and can be a great launching pad into the different areas of the project. This has meant we've picked up developers for the core of the product who have improved it and work on different aspects (particularly unit testing) that help us make great software quicker.

Q: What is bug squishing, and why does the Joomla! project organize Bug Squashing Events such as the Pizza, Bugs, and Fun (PBF)?

A: **Mark:** We try to create fun events. Fixing bugs is hard work, and some people find it more fun to do it as part of an organized event. It is also a way for people to see how much fun it is to do meaningful work.

**Sam:** Bug squishing is what JBS exists to do. We have bugs, like all software, and they need to be fixed. The process is rather aptly called squashing bugs. We try to do collaborative bug squashing because getting people together is a great way to be productive and get instant feedback and something you can aim to set time aside for. Pizza is involved because you can't have a software event without pizza; it has to be some form of geek rule. But pizza is also there so that we can get people to be sociable; I've never met a geek who will turn down a free pizza, and talking over pizza is always an interesting thing. The fun bit is rather obvious. You need to enjoy what you're doing; otherwise, it becomes like work. Bugs, fortunately for us and unfortunately for them, are the losing party in the whole equation: not only do they not get pizza or fun, but they hopefully don't exist by the end of the event.

Q: What is the tracker, and how do people report bugs?

A: **Mark:** The tracker is a software program that anyone can use to report on and follow the progress of bugs or issues with Joomla! When a user first reports an issue, someone needs to look at it to determine whether it is really a bug and whether it has already been reported or fixed. Many times there are questions or comments that go back and forth. Eventually, the issue is either closed because it is not a bug or because it is fixed and tested and the fix is added to the next software release.

**Sam:** The tracker lives on JoomlaCode.org at this big ugly URL (*http://joomla-code.org/gf/project/joomla/tracker/*), and basically it has this equally as ugly form where you have options you have absolutely no idea about; if you click them in the right order, you get a magical prize. Nobody has yet worked out the right combination, not even me, and I'm the JoomlaCode administrator! So, the tracker is where Joomla! stores its bugs, feature requests, and all sorts of other things we should keep track of in the long term. There is a tracker for each release of Joomla! (1.0, 1.5, 1.6), and this is where bugs are reported for each release. Reporting a bug is a matter of working through the submission screen; it really is scarier than it looks. You don't need to get it all right the first time. Just answer as best you can (and no you won't be examined on it later) and describe with as much detail as possible the steps to replicate the problem. The hardest thing about bug squashing is trying to replicate the bug (particularly the tricky one), so the little details of what you clicked in what order can make the difference. There is obviously a bit more too it, but check out *http://docs.joomla.org/Filing_bugs_and_issues*, and there are some more details on how to report new bugs.

Q: What is the criteria for joining the Joomla! Bug Squad?

A: **Mark:** The Bug Squad can use people with a variety of skills and experience. Most people need to have a good understanding of how to install and use Joomla! You do *not* need to be a programmer. The three main jobs that Bug Squad members do are: (1) monitor the tracker and determine whether newly reported issues are really bugs, (2) write code to fix bugs, and (3) test proposed bug fixes to make sure they really fix the bug and don't cause any new problems. If you notice, only 2 requires programming skills. Nontechnical people can do 1 and 3. A new and exciting development for the Bug Squad is the introduction of automated testing. For version 1.6, we are hoping to incorporate automated software testing into the daily work of the Bug Squad. For example, when a bug is fixed, the tester might write an automated test for that bug that gets added to the list of tests that are run each day. That way, if a future change accidentally breaks that fix, we will know about it right away and can fix it before it gets released in a production version.

**Sam:** There is really no major criteria for joining the JBS; you just rock up, put in some time, follow the procedures, and have fun. Anyone can join the JBS, and there is no particular limitation. JBS welcomes people who are starting with Joomla! who perhaps want a place they can explore issues, and believe me, replicating bugs is always a great way to learn how a system works. Anyone can be a tester and either confirm issues or test patches and give feedback; no special programming skill required. Of course, the people with those coder skills who perhaps aren't all that familiar with Joomla! can jump into JBS and for the same reasons as before: nothing teaches you a system more than trying to dig through a system to find a bug. And sometimes you need a hand, and that's where the experience in the JBS comes in. JBS is a friendly place to ask the questions and get them answered so that you can improve your knowledge of Joomla! even more.

# Expert Q&A with Ian MacLennan: Joomla! Production Leadership Team and Joomla! Security Strike Team

*I have been involved with the Joomla! project in a variety of capacities, most recently as a member of the Production Leadership Team.*

Q:  What prompted your interest, and/or how did you learn about Joomla?

A:  I first discovered Joomla! while working on a Web site for a nonprofit for which my wife was the executive director. As I was building the site, there was one thing of which I was quite certain: I didn't want to have to be doing all the updates for the content. So, I took my knowledge of PHP and began to write a simple application that would make it easy for her and her staff to make the edits themselves.

I invested a good deal of effort into this pursuit and ended up with a feature-poor rudimentary solution. Somewhere around the time I was beginning to build on and develop new features, I stumbled across an application called Mambo. As I investigated, I discovered that it did just about everything I was hoping to do right out of the box, and there were extensions available to make it easy to do the rest. It seemed like a no-brainer decision. About six or seven years later, here I am.

Q:  Do you regularly use open source software, and why?

A:  Open source software is a part of my daily life. I have some flavor of Linux installed on every computer I own. I use Linux because in my experience it is at the point where it just works. Also, as a Web application developer, it makes sense because the Internet runs on Linux. It is what the majority of Web sites (and especially Joomla!) are running on.

Q:  Joomla! has a large community with a lot of active contributors. In your opinion, what is the most exciting part of being involved, and how do you contribute to the community?

A:  I find being part of the Joomla! community exciting for a number of reasons. First, it is exciting to be a part of producing software that is used by a significant number of people. I take pride in doing the best I can to help create something that is stable and useful to many people.

I have also thoroughly enjoyed the opportunity to work alongside very talented people. I have learned far more than I have contributed.

During my time with Joomla! I have contributed in a variety of ways. My first area of significant involvement was with the developer documentation team. This was an incredible opportunity for me to really dig into the Joomla! code and to understand the framework.

I moved on from there to become a member of the Joomla! Bug Squad. I transitioned through there to become a member of the Development Working

Group and was then invited to become a member of the Production Leadership Team.

Q: You are part of the Joomla! Security Strike Team. What are some of the main security issues that you are concerned about?

A: The JSST works hard to ensure that Joomla! is secure. We take all reported vulnerabilities seriously. Obviously, vulnerabilities that are more severe in their impact or are particularly easy to exploit are considered most urgent.

Q: What is the right way for someone to respond if their site is attacked?

A: The best way to proceed is to follow the security checklist that is hosted on *http://docs.joomla.org*. If a site administrator does not feel that they have the necessary qualifications to ensure their site is safe, it is recommended that they find a professional who is able to do this.

Q: What should someone do if they discover a Joomla! security problem?

A: If somebody discovers a vulnerability in Joomla!, they should report it to the JSST. Once you have reported the vulnerability, we will investigate it and ensure it is valid and decide the best path forward for solving it.

Q: Do you have any other tips for keeping a Joomla! site safe?

A: In my experience, the two most important things in keeping a Joomla! site safe are a trustworthy, knowledgeable host and using extensions from reputable vendors.

Q: As the Developer Documentation lead and then as the lead for the Joomla! Bug Squad, you've taught a lot of us how to code. What do you think is the best way for someone who wants to learn more about Joomla! development to learn?

A: The answer to this question really depends on what somebody wants to achieve and what their background is. That being said, one of the best ways to learn how to code is to find a good tutorial that introduces you to the basics of computer programming (that is, control structures, conditionals, data types, and so on). It's also important to learn the basic principles of object-oriented programming.

From there, the best way to learn how to code is often to study good code. There is a great deal to learn by inspecting the core code and by inspecting the code of third-party extensions.

# Expert Q&A with Elin Waring: Professor, Author, and Joomla! Contributor—Trademark and Licensing

*In my work life I am a professor of sociology at Lehman College, City University of New York. I teach sociology and do research on white-collar crime, organized crime, and social networks. I have also been president of the board of Open Source Matters, the nonprofit organization that handles legal, financial, and organizational matters for the Joomla! project, as well as a board member. I am an active community and code contributor.*

Q: What prompted your interest, and/or how did you learn about Joomla?

A: I was actually part of the Mambo community, so I have been with Joomla! since the beginning. I was someone who hand-built Web sites for a long time. As long as I was doing it myself and the sites were small, that was fine, and I learned a lot of HTML and then CSS (yes, there was a time before CSS). But at some point, some of the sites started to get bigger and more complex, and I also wanted to turn over the day-to-day management of them to other people. I really found that the way most of the systems for implementing site templates and WYSIWYG Web page creation produced unsatisfactory code, and there was no way my users were going to understand them or be able to afford the software. Then someone told me about this thing called a content management system, and I was off and running. I looked at all the major open source ones available at that time (this was probably late 2004 or early 2005) and ended up with Mambo. It was the easiest to set up and had by far the friendliest and most active community.

Q: Do you regularly use open source software, and why?

A: I use open source software as much as I can, but I'm not always going to reject a closed product just on that basis. For Web applications, I have always been able to find good open source solutions; on the desktop, I think it is a lot harder to do that, although the situation is getting better. I think that open source produces better code. All of those thousands of people looking at the code pushes it to be better, and that means there is continuous improvement. With closed code, you really have no idea what the quality of the code is. You also have to wait for releases to get the changes you want. With open source, you have the ability to open up the files and make changes. And if you come up with a good solution, you can contribute it to the community so your solution becomes the standard, or you can just keep it to yourself.

Q: Joomla! has a large community with a lot of active contributors. In your opinion, what is the most exciting part of being involved, and how do you contribute to the community?

A: Well, I've been active in most parts of the project at one time or another. I started off as an active forum user and answering lots of questions. Because of that, I was asked to work on the creation of Frequently Asked Questions, so that was documentation plus I got to join the forum moderator community. Later I got involved in OSM, so I spent a fair amount of time working in areas like licensing and trademark as well as financial management. And somehow or other along the way, I was one of the people who helped start the Joomla! Bug Squad, so I've done some development too.

To me the Joomla! community is absolutely amazing. It's people from all over the world, of all different ages and backgrounds all helping out just because they can, really. Right from the beginning I was amazed at how people would help me do the things I wanted to do with my sites. I still feel that way. The Bug Squad has been amazing with how it works as a team to solve issues. The camaraderie is fantastic. I've also been lucky enough to go to a bunch of in-person Joomla! events, and they always are a lot of fun because the people are a lot of fun.

Q: Joomla! is an open source project licensed under the GPL v2 or later. Can you explain what the GPL license is and how it is beneficial for users of Joomla! to have this license?

A: First, let's say what a license is. A license tells you terms under which you may use a copyrighted work, in this case a piece of software called Joomla! The official name is the GNU GPL, and it has three basic versions plus some variations; Joomla! uses version 2, which allows it to be changed to version 3 or later.

The most important things about the GNU GPL are the four freedoms that the copyright owners (in this case the developers of the software) give you—the freedom to run the program, to study it, to modify it, and to share it. But those freedoms come with a major condition, which is that if you do share, you have to pass the exact same right onto the people you share with. That is, they have the rights to run, study, modify, and share as long as they pass on the same rights to others. And so on into infinity.

This is a great license for software, because it encourages users to improve the code. It allows them to open up the files and fix bugs or improve them and to share their improvements with other people. It lets thousands of people build extensions for Joomla! to do all kinds of interesting and useful things and to distribute those extensions. It lets other people make specialized distributions. They don't need to ask permission; as long as they follow the license, they can do whatever they want. It lets Joomla! exist, because it was what allowed the fork from Mambo back in 2005. If something ever happened to the Joomla! project, the GPL will let other people pick up the application and continue to develop it.

Q: There is a significant third-party developer community involved with the Joomla! project. How has the Joomla! ecosystem been influenced by their contributions?

A: Joomla! would not be the world's most popular content management system without the third-party developer community. Joomla! is unique among content management systems in terms of the sheer size of its retail economy of plug-and-play extensions. Some of them are simple (I have released simple extensions, although for no cost), and some are incredibly complex.

Q: What are some of the most common incorrect assumptions people make about GPL-licensed software?

A: Probably the biggest misunderstanding is that "free" software has to be given away for no cost. Freedom in software means that you have the ability to run, examine, modify, and share code, not that people have to give away their work for free. Free software would not be the powerful force that it is if developers were not able to earn a living out of it. So, even though Joomla! is free of cost, we're happy that there is a commercial GPL community around it that consists of people building new and exciting extensions to the Joomla! core.

People also sometimes think that they have to keep the "Powered by Joomla!" message visible on their sites. While we appreciate that, it's not required. What you can't do is remove the copyright or licensing information from the source files (all those PHP and other files that make up the Joomla! application) if you share them with someone else.

People are always sending me e-mails because they have seen Joomla! being rebranded under another name. That's perfectly fine with GPL software as long as you don't remove the copyright and licensing information from the source code. Again, as a project, we appreciate it when people credit the work, but it is not required.

Q: Can you explain what the Free Software Foundation is and how it assists open source projects?

A: The Free Software Foundation is a nonprofit organization in Boston that was founded by Richard Stallman, the author of the original GNU GPL. Today the FSF is centrally involved in the continued development of the GPL (such as writing GPL v3) and related licenses and with general software advocacy. Their Web site is a good place to learn more about free software issues in general. They also have a really strong compliance staff that works with software projects and copyright holders to ensure compliance with the GPL. They also answer a lot of questions from developers and the public.

Q: What are some of the most important things someone should take into account when trademarking their logo or brand?

A: The most important things are to come up with a unique name and image that create a good impression for potential customers around the world. It is vital that it that does not infringe on anyone else's trademark. This is actually a lot harder than people think, because you have to check not just the name itself but for similar names and compounds. If you are just starting out and can't afford professional help, at least do some searching in the U.S. and European Union trademark databases, although that still leaves a lot of the world uncovered.

One thing I'd recommend against is using the Joomla! name in a product, business, or site name. OSM will most likely give you permission to do that, but you will never be able to register the trademark for the name because it would conflict with the Joomla! trademark. And OSM does not guarantee that your name will be unique.

Q:  What steps can people take to protect their logo, license, or brand?

A:  In terms of licensing, there are two areas people using Joomla! need to think about.

First, think about your site content. If you are writing it or doing art, you have the copyright. Let's assume you're doing all the creative work. Make sure you have a clear statement of what you do and do not want to allow people to do with your content. If you want to let people use your content, do that with a license such as one of the ones from Creative Commons, which will protect your rights. Do not just say, "Do whatever you want with it." That will come back to haunt you in the future when someone starts claiming your work is actually theirs. If your site is really successful, you may want to reuse it or publish a book based on it or do something else. Definitely know your rights under the Digital Millennium Copyright Act and enforce them. If other people are contributing, you need to make it clear what the copyright terms are. For example, are you allowed to reuse their work? Are other people? It's best to make things clear up front.

If you are building a Joomla! extension, you should of course use the GPL license, and you should make sure you understand what people can and cannot do with your code. Also, make sure that you work to build a strong brand identity so the people will want to come to you for the extension, not another site. Also, know your rights in case anyone takes your code and incorporates it in a proprietary application. The Free Software Foundation and Software Freedom Law Center may be able to help you if that happens.

Also, if you do choose to use a non GPL application, make sure you also understand your rights there. For example, if a product violates the Joomla! terms, that does not give you the right to violate the license terms under which it was distributed. That is because you are (most likely) not a copyright holder in the Joomla! code base. They are the ones whose rights are violated when people violate the Joomla! license.

In terms of trademark, I think this is an extremely important area that people neglect early on. If you are providing any kind of trade or service, it is important to build a strong brand identity. That means have a clear, well-chosen, and unique name and also probably a logo.

I definitely recommend filing for at least basic trademark protection in one class in your home country and the country where your largest group of customers is as soon as you are sure you have a brand or logo that you will stick with. It's an investment, but if you are successful at building a good brand, you will be glad you took care of that early. Even if you don't register the trademark, make sure that you use the trademark symbol and put a trademark notice somewhere on your site. Also, publish rules for the use of your trademark, because if you don't protect the mark, you will lose it. Make sure that anyone who uses your trademark has your permission even if it is just filling out a simple form.

One powerful thing about a trademark is that it is a basis for filing a complaint with a host if someone is distributing copies of your software using your trademark. Since most warez sites operate by providing copies of software people are looking for, having to use a different name makes them much less effective.

# Expert Q&A with Wendy Robinson: Rochen Ltd.—Creating Your Brand

*I've been a Web designer and graphic artist for the past five years and an artist in various forms for as long as I can recall. I think my interest in branding and logo design began in the 80s when my parents owned a local print shop. I'd spend hours pouring over clip art books and designing my own notepads and cards on the floor of the shop. This spawned in me an obsession with aesthetics from colours to spacing to patterns. From there, it's just something that never left me and has proven quite useful in my Web/graphic career. I have volunteered for the Joomla! project for the past five years, currently as a member of the Community Leadership Team.*

Q: What prompted your interest, and/or how did you learn about Joomla?

A: I had just a little bit of experience with HTML/CSS when I wanted to build my first Web site for my photography. Because coding something like a photo gallery was way beyond my experience level at the time, I began to research software solutions. I tried out a few different free CMSs before finding Joomla! In the end, it was simply the best solution for my needs at the time. Four years later it is something that I use daily.

Q: Do you regularly use open source software, and why?

A: Yes. Most of what I use is open source including my operating system and the majority of my photo and graphics software. The reason why is mostly that it allows me the freedom of choice. With OS software, if you want to contribute or build upon something to suit your needs or make it better, you're free to do so as long as you abide by the license. That is not an option with proprietary software. Affordability is also a factor for me. I'm happier to pay a modest amount of money or make a donation to be able to use something that has potential to evolve than I am to shell out a large amount of money for something I have no say in or way of contributing to. The way I see it, open source is just more flexible. I don't understand how anyone could not want a choice.

Q: Joomla! has a large community with a lot of active contributors. In your opinion, what is the most exciting part of being involved, and how do you contribute to the community?

A: I think the Joomla! community is diverse both in its culture and its levels of user/developer experience. That is what I feel makes it so great. I've held a number of positions in the past four years as a community member. Most recently I have served on the Open Source Matters board, have been a forum global moderator and administrator, and have helped launch the Joomla! Resources Directory as an editor.

Q: Can you guide us through the thought process you go through when you are creating a brand for a client?

A: I usually start with asking people what their aim is for their Web site/product and who their target audience is. I also request a list of logos/brands or Web sites they identify with as a consumer as well as whether they have any strong dislikes. From there I create three or four concepts for them to review, usually from completely different visual takes (for example, corporate vs. minimalist). Once we find a comfortable ground, I do another three or four concepts of their preferred style and reduce from there with the client's feedback until we find a winner.

Q: What is the top piece of advice you would give to someone trying to design their own logo/brand?

A: Keep it simple, use clean lines, and make sure it's a design that will look clear in black-and-white print.

Q: What are the three most common mistakes people can make in regard to their logo or brand identity?

A: Sometimes people make their design too personal. A brand should reach out to an intended target group, and you need something that creates an instant visual to obtain a buy-in from your audience. Your logo for your new Web site about running shoes should not be a sketch of your childhood dog because you used to take it for runs in the park. Nobody can relate to that but you.

I see way too many cliches in branding. I feel it is paramount in building a strong brand to make sure that your design is clean and classic. You shouldn't have to update it in a year. For example, one branding concept that I am really bored with is the [company name] trend (your name in square brackets). I think it is great to stay current with trends, and it is wise to implement them in your colours and shading and the more subtle aspects of the design. I do not think that trends should be applied too literally, though, and because they change so often these days, you can be sure your logo will be outdated in no time.

Not only as a designer but also as a person with an astigmatism, I have a real problem with logos or brands that use too much colour or pattern, especially on the Web. A design should be readable without having to blink a few times to focus on it.

Q: A Web site is usually just a piece of branding strategy. What are the top three ways a person can leverage their Web site and brand in other areas?

A: Social networks are a rising trend in advertising. Make the best use of sites like Facebook and LinkedIn for promoting yourself. Also, start using Twitter if you haven't already. It is a very convenient way to get your name out there as well as help bring in page impressions to your Web site.

Blog. Pick topics that you are well informed about and write about them. Tweet (Twitter) your blogs, and tweet the comments to your blogs. Respond to comments quickly and respectfully. Gain interest and trust from your visitors to ensure they return to your Web site.

Get involved locally. Research organizations or clubs in your region that you feel would be a good fit for your company. Attend events and hand out your business cards. If you can, sponsor some events either financially or with services that you offer.

# Expert Q&A with Brad Baker: Rochen Ltd.— Joomla! Hosting

*I have been a member of the Rochen team since early 2003, and I am a founding member of the Joomla! open source project. I am currently part of the Joomla! Leadership Team and regularly speak at JoomlaDays around the world on the subject of Joomla! Hosting and Security. I run and maintain www.joomlatutorials.com as well as my own local Web hosting business, www.xyzulu.com.*

Q: What prompted your interest, and/or how did you learn about Joomla?

A: Being on the team that supported Mambo (the project that Joomla! grew from), I was one of the founding members of the Joomla! project.

Q: Do you regularly use open source software, and why?

A: I find the open development often encourages high-quality products due to the ease at which developers can contribute/change code. Often too, open source software has a much faster release cycle, leading to new features at a much quicker rate than other differently licensed projects.

Q: Joomla! has a large community with a lot of active contributors. In your opinion, what is the most exciting part of being involved, and how do you contribute to the community?

A: The sheer size and scope of the community is exciting to me. As one of the founding members of the project, my contributions are in the infrastructure and hosting support of the Joomla! project. You'll usually find me on the Joomla! Community Forum trying to help and educate people.

Q: Rochen is a host that specializes in Joomla! Can you tell us what procedures and setup you have implemented that assists your clients who are using Joomla?

A: As the host of all the official Joomla! Web sites, we've gained a large amount of experience hosting Joomla! sites of all sizes, from small-business sites to enterprise sites receiving tens of millions of page views. We configure all our servers with the optimal security and performance settings for Joomla!, allowing Joomla! to run securely while not limiting functionality. Some security technologies we have deployed include running PHP in CGI mode with *su_php*, *open_basedir*, and Apache's *mod_security* application firewall. No longer do you need to worry about using the Joomla! FTP layer because our server takes care of your file and folder permissions for you. We have also invested in a revolutionary managed backup system, called Rochen Vault, that allows customers to easily roll their account (including Joomla! install) back to points in time over the past 30 days.

Q: What are some of the most important things someone should take into account when searching for a host?

A: Are their plans realistically priced? Does their server setup provide a balance between ease of use and performance and security for your Web site?

Q: What are some of the most common mistakes people can make when choosing a host?

A: They often choose the cheapest (or free) host they can find, with little regard to site security, backup procedures, and performance.

Q: What is the first piece of advice you can give to people who are completely new to running a Web site in regard to hosting?

A: Do your research. If you want to be equipped to choose a good host, you'll first need to make yourself aware of some of the technical aspects of a Web hosting environment. Once you've gained a basic understanding, you'll be able to see through the marketing hype of many hosts and be able to make the right choice.

# Expert Q&A with Chris Davenport: Joomla! Production Leadership Team—Finding and Editing Templates

*I come from the town of Shrewsbury in the very rural county of Shropshire, one of the most sparsely populated counties in England. Although I started out as a mathematician, I've been a software developer on and off for most of the past 30 years. Only in the past decade or so, I have been focusing on open source software. Before that, I was working on proprietary platforms. Today I'm on the Joomla! Production Leadership Team with particular responsibility for documentation. For my day job I work as a developer for Clickingmad, a local Web design and development company in the picturesque town of Bridgnorth.*

Q: What prompted your interest, and/or how did you learn about Joomla?

A: I first came across Mambo (the predecessor to Joomla) in 2003 while looking for a content management system for an intranet project I was working on at the time. I was impressed by the ease with which I could build a working system, and I particularly liked the way in which extensions could be quickly packaged and installed using a Web interface.

   After using it for some time, I really wanted to contribute something back to the project and perhaps even help with its development. I noticed that there was almost no developer documentation available, so I started writing notes as I was learning about different parts of the code. Pretty soon I was invited to join the Documentation Team, which I eventually went on to lead, and in November 2006 I was invited to join the Joomla! Core Team.

Q:  Do you regularly use open source software, and why?

A:  My preference is always to use open source software whenever possible. Of course, sometimes I'm forced to use a proprietary product, but nowadays that's mainly just to do testing to make sure that what I develop works with it. I think there will always be a place for proprietary software, but for the vast majority of software projects, particularly large-scale projects, there is no better way to create software than to use the open source model.

"Open source" is probably the wrong term to use, though. I should be talking about "free" software, or perhaps "free and open source" software. What makes this kind of software so important and useful is the guarantee of freedom that comes along with it. Being able to look at the source code is just one aspect of that freedom. Free software gives you the freedom to run, copy, and modify the code. You can also pass it on to someone else if you want to, but only if you grant to that person the same freedoms that you were given when you got a copy of the code. I think it encourages everyone to behave more altruistically, but the fun thing is that actually everyone benefits!

I'm constantly surprised to see free software popping up in places I didn't expect to see it. For example, I recently bought a television from a major Japanese manufacturer and only when I started delving into its menus did I discover that it was running on the Linux operating system. How cool is that? Free software has become part of the fabric of our daily lives without us really noticing it.

Q:  Joomla! has a large community with a lot of active contributors. In your opinion, what is the most exciting part of being involved, and how do you contribute to the community?

A:  The great thing about a large, active open source project like Joomla! is that people are constantly pushing the software in new directions, and I find myself learning new ideas and techniques all the time. I've learned far more about PHP, SQL, HTML/CSS, design patterns, and so on, because I'm involved with the project than ever I could from more conventional sources.

I enjoy contributing to the project whenever I can, and it's exciting to see the work that I've done being used by so many people around the world. It's also fun to see how other people are using Joomla!, and I still enjoy answering the odd question on the forum if I have a spare few minutes. Actually getting to meet Joomla! users and developers in person is even better, and I love going to Joomla! events whenever I can.

Q:  What advice would you give someone new to Joomla! regarding finding templates to use on their site?

A:  Firstly you need to be aware of your own level of skill, your willingness to learn, and the amount of time you have available.

If you have few HTML/CSS skills but you're willing to put some time into learning about templates, then you can consider modifying an existing template, either one of the ones included in the Joomla! distribution or a template purchased from one of the reputable template clubs. But if you don't have the time to spend on customising a template yourself, then you should be looking to hire a professional to do it for you.

When looking for an off-the-shelf template, you should first and foremost look for something that has the layout you are looking for. Colour schemes are relatively easy to change, and images are relatively easy to replace, but layouts can be really hard to change, even for experienced designers. So, look for a template that has the right arrangement and sizes of images and blocks of text, and ignore the colour scheme to begin with.

Q:  What tools would a novice user need to edit their template?

A:  There are actually many ways in which you can edit a template, and different people use different methods, so it all depends on finding something that is comfortable for you. It is possible to edit a template using just the Template Manager, and that is probably a good way to get started, although you should be very careful about doing that on a live site. I recommend using a text editor that has an undo feature because you will usually need to try things out and revert changes that don't work the way you want them to. Sadly, developing in HTML and CSS is more craft than engineering, and you need to be prepared to experiment and learn as you go.

When working with templates, you should always work in the first instance with the Firefox browser and then test against the others, notably Internet Explorer. With time and experience, you will get better at writing CSS that works across browsers with the fewest possible workarounds for the problems with Internet Explorer.

With Firefox you can install some really useful plugins that help enormously when working with HTML and CSS. In particular, Firebug is absolutely indispensable, and I use Chris Pederick's Web Developer Toolbar quite often too. These are professional tools, and there is a learning curve to using them, but modern Web sites would be almost impossible to build without them.

Q:  Is it really true that you don't have to know coding, HTML, or CSS to use Joomla? Is it true for editing and creating templates?

A:  It's certainly true that you don't need to know coding, HTML, or CSS to start and run a successful Joomla! Web site. It's also true that you can make some types of basic changes to templates with just a little guidance. For example, you should be able to change a logo or an image as long as you keep the image dimensions the same. Creating a template from scratch is definitely a skilled task, though.

Building a template that will work across browsers takes time and experience and considerable attention to detail. But that's down to the fact that CSS is a difficult standard to work with; it has nothing to do with Joomla!

Q:  What are some of the common pitfalls people run across when editing their templates?

A:  One of the most common mistakes that newcomers make is to start modifying one of the templates included in the Joomla! distribution without even making a backup first. Joomla! is updated periodically, and you're in danger of losing your changes if you don't take precautions. If you want to use one of the templates included in the Joomla! distribution, then it is best to make a copy of it and then customise the copy. Leave the original template untouched. In Joomla! 1.6 there is a Duplicate button on the toolbar in the Template Manager that makes this a one-click operation.

Another common problem for novices occurs when swapping an image in a template, for example changing the logo to your own company logo. It's really important to ensure that the new image has exactly the same dimensions as the one you are replacing. If it doesn't have the same dimensions, then it is highly likely that the layout will break, and fixing layouts is not something that novices are likely to find easy.

Q:  Where is the Template Documentation located, and are there other resources that will help me learn how to create a template or edit my template files?

A:  There is an ever-increasing amount of documentation on Joomla! templates in the Joomla! documentation wiki. In particular, start here: *http://docs.joomla.org/Joomla!_1.5_Template_Tutorial*.

There is also a forum dedicated to helping people with template problems here: *http://forum.joomla.org/viewforum.php?f=466*.

I'm also in the process of writing a book on Joomla! templates, the bulk of the content of which will also be available for free from the documentation wiki. So, keep checking back there from time to time.

# Expert Q&A with Vic Drover: Owner of Anything Digital—Extending Joomla!

*I am a professor of medicine and biochemistry by training and got interested in Web site development during graduate school circa 1997. I began hacking content management systems shortly thereafter. After much error-based learning, I started building Joomla! applications and now manage an extension and Web development shop at http://dev.anything-digital.com. In 2008, I joined the editorial team at the Joomla! Extensions Directory where I focus on policy making, extension evaluation, and directory maintenance. I am also a member of the Trademark Team. When not online, my primary hobby is the sport of rugby. I have spent about two decades on the pitch and now primarily contribute to my rugby club as an administrator and Web/PR coordinator. Our Web site, the Milwaukee Harlequins Rugby Football Club, is of course based on Joomla! and is one of the top club rugby sites in America.*

Q: What prompted your interest, and/or how did you learn about Joomla!?

A: I stumbled on another PHP-based CMS (phpWebSite) when starting a Web site for a sports club I belong to. The club quickly outgrew this CMS, and with the experience from using phpWebSite, I did a proper search and evaluation of the leading open source CMSs at the time. Mambo was at the top of the list, and then of course Joomla! followed shortly (*http://phpwebsite.appstate.edu/*).

Q: Do you regularly use open source software, and why?

A: It is essentially the only thing I use, though WordPress is very attractive for many of my sites these days; 80% Joomla! and 20% WordPress is a good estimate for my work.

    The initial reason I started using open source was the cost advantage. Even with the advent of commercial GPL extensions in the J!sphere, sites are still much less expensive than proprietary systems. In addition, I've met some great folks in the Joomla! community, because the barrier to entry is really low (just answer a few threads in the forum, for example). Finally, I think open source apps are inherently more secure than proprietary ones because the baddies can see all the exploits, as can every coder who is interested. Thus, these tend to get fixed quite publicly and usually quickly.

Q: Joomla! has a large community with a lot of active contributors. In your opinion, what is the most exciting part of being involved, and how do you contribute to the community?

A: I think the J!Days and other Joomla! conferences are the most exciting parts. I talk sometimes at these meetings or help moderate group discussions.

    Outside of these venues. I contribute primarily in two ways: I'm an editor on the Joomla! Extensions Directory, and I cofounded and comanage the Joomla! User Group Milwaukee. I've really enjoyed meeting the other Joomla! users in my community and made some good friends.

Q: What are some of the most popular types of functionality that people look for to extend Joomla!?

A: Almost anything that involves user input, such as forms for collecting data or registering for an event, for example. Social networking is very hot right now and arguably has been for some time. I am finding more interest in the ability to add custom fields to forms (which is not new) but also to content. Thus, most applications are trending to having some sort of CC (content construction) functionality, most notably the full-fledged content constructors like K2, ZOO, and FLEXIContent. However, you even see this on smaller apps.

Q:  What is the best way for a new user to go about deciding which extensions they
    need and which ones to choose? How does a user use the JED to get the best
    results when looking for an extension for their site?

A:  The JED is a great resource, but it can be daunting. The search feature on the
    JED can be a bit unproductive also, so navigating using the categories is the best
    place to start (after some initial Googling, of course).

    Selecting and evaluating extensions is really one of the most important tasks
    when building a Joomla! Web site, and the JED can help tremendously in this, of
    course. There is not enough space in this interview to do it justice, but I would
    say having a clear list of features is critical before you start. Once you have a
    short list of extensions to compare, evaluate the reviews (not so much the votes),
    evaluate the developer and their reputation, solicit some input on the Joomla!
    forums, and ask any experts you know (in other words, maybe you have a local
    JUG to attend). Once you download the application that best suits your needs,
    there are also some good ways to evaluate them for basic security. Again, this is
    for another interview.

Q:  Being an editor for the Joomla! Extension Directory allows you a lot of interac-
    tion with the third-party developer community. Can you explain what a third-
    party developer (3PD) is and their role in the Joomlasphere?

A:  I love parties! The first party is the Joomla! project. The second party is the
    users/consumers of Joomla! 3PDs generally write application add-ons (we call
    them *extensions*) that install within the Joomla! framework and add new function-
    ality. For example, a photo gallery for Joomla! would be a third-party add-on.

    I truly believe that a large part of the success of Joomla! has come from the
    active 3PD community. This has only improved since most developers ditched
    encryption and adopted GPL-compatible business models (see the next answer). I
    think many developers rightly benefit (that is, commercially) from this important
    role in Joomla!'s evolution, but it has also bred fierce competition. This is a good
    motivator for application development but can also make interacting with 3PDs
    on the JED challenging because people's livelihoods are affected by JED policy
    and decision making.

    Since traffic generated by the JED is so abundant and valuable, the JED is also
    a place for fraud and mischief as some devs jockey for top honors in their cate-
    gories. When we detect this, we often give short bans, and this can be difficult at
    times to deal with.

Q:  Software licensing can be confusing to new users. Can you explain what com-
    mercial and noncommercial GPL means and the differences between them both?

A:  There is no difference in the license per se. In each case, it is a nonproprietary
    license that guarantees that any changes made to the source code *and distributed to
    the community* are available to anyone who requests it. This is the essence of the
    GPL.

Importantly, if I make a change to a GPL-licensed application on my PC, the GPL doesn't apply. The guarantees and freedoms of the GPL come into effect when I distribute my changes (in other words, post the edited application on a Web site for download).

That said, the only difference between commercial and noncommercial GPL is really a business decision; it is not a different license. Historically, GPL-licensed extensions are distributed at a cost of $0 (noncommercial). A commercial GPL business model is one where the distribution cost is greater than $0 (commercial). Note that we avoid using the term *free* when describing GPL extensions because many people confuse this with "zero money." This is the most common source of confusion in regards to GPL-licensed applications. The *free* part of the GPL license is the freedom to make and distribute changes to the code.

To help explain this concept to users, you will often hear the phrase "Free as in freedom, not free as in beer." I have used this on occasion, but I think novices also find this confusing. To be direct and concise, the GPL guarantees creative freedom but not freedom from cost.

Q:  If someone becomes interested in developing an extension for Joomla!, where is a good place for them to get information and documentation on how to begin?

A:  Before someone jumps into Joomla! extension development, it is best to take a course in PHP. This is the bare minimum prerequisite. Once that's done, I think the best tool is to download some popular extensions, examine the code, and thus learn by example from Joomla! experts. I also highly recommend Joseph LeBlanc's book entitled *Learning Joomla! 1.5 Extension Development* (Packt).

# Expert Q&A with Gary Brooks: President of CloudAccess.net—Benefits of Joomla! for Business

*I am the founder and CEO of CloudAccess.net, a firm that specializes in offering software as a service (SaaS) based on the Joomla! platform. I love working with people and believe that good business is based on personal and attentive interaction with your clientele. My firm is the backbone behind the Official Joomla! Demo site, and it has been an incredible experience to be part of the recent exponential growth of the project. When I am not busy overseeing operations for my firm, I enjoy music and spending time outdoors with my family. Previously I was the founder of NMO.net. NMO.net was a dial-up ISP that was built when 28.8 modems came out. Our team managed a network of 4,000+ dialup and wireless broadband users. I got started in technology when my dad sat with me one day and showed me how to build a computer from the ground up. I can remember the first computer we built was a 386 turbo-powered AMD. It even had the little turbo button on the front. When I am not busy overseeing operations for my firm, I love spending time with my family, studying, fishing, playing basketball, and playing frisbee golf.*

Q:  What prompted your interest, and/or how did you learn about Joomla?

A:  I had a client who wanted to have control over his own Web content. He wanted a suite of applications to be included in the architecture. At the time I was working with WordPress. I quickly found out that WordPress was not the tool for the job. I had a limited budget of around $10,000 dollars, so I needed to find an application that was almost ready for the job. I could not make this deal happen if I had to code from scratch. I started my search, and one magical day I was sent a link to Joomla! I built the client's site in Joomla!, and everything went smoothly. I had a front-end coder, back-end coder, and artist put together the project with perfection. After doing the implementation work in Joomla!, the client asked me to change parts of the calendar system, user profile management, and other moving parts of the code that I had downloaded from the extensions directory. I had to do a little research, but I quickly found out that the software in the directory is free to modify to fit the needs of your business. What I found even more interesting is that many of the developers would help you for a consulting fee. Joomla! had an amazing pool of talent all in one place. The project was a great success, and it led me to many larger Web applications using Joomla! I continue to have success with Joomla! and love the large talented community of developers around the project.

Q:  Do you regularly use open source software, and why?

A:  I had not heard of open source software until I found Joomla! Joomla! made it possible for me to understand open source. I later learned that many cell phones (Android), micro chip software, and Linux servers are open source as well. I feel the trend of open source is taking market. It's hard to compete with the passion of community-based projects. Nobody can take the code away from you. When you download open source software. it's yours to have and change as you see fit. If you want to put open source software on your local computer, you can do it. If you want to make open source software work on a large cluster of servers, no problem. If you have the talent and time, you can make open source do what you need. Joomla! is a perfect example of why open source is better. How can you compete against a community with hundreds of thousands of users and developers?

Q:  Joomla! has a large community with a lot of active contributors. In your opinion, what is the most exciting part of being involved, and how do you contribute to the community?

A:  Honestly I love everything about Joomla!, but the best things are the people and the code. The community is very alive, and they all have a passion to make Joomla! better. That passion transcends to a energy you can't find in many places. The community has this fantastic belief to improve and innovate. You can't pay for the passion you see from the Joomla! community and the quality of work you get.

I'm personally involved in the resources directory, trademark team, and our CloudAccess.net team runs the Joomla! Demo site. In exchange for running the

Joomla! Demo site, we donate money to the organization and share a percentage of the revenue from each hosting account.

Q: What is one of the main talking points you use to convince your business clients to move to Joomla! as a Web solution? Are there specific issues you have to address on a regular basis when it comes to talking to clients about open source software?

A: I tell clients that if you were to write Joomla! from start to finish, you would be looking at a $6 million investment. I tell them that Joomla! is used by millions of sites with thousands of premade applications you can install just like the iPhone app store. The system has the ability to alter the look and feel of each area on the site. I offer them security in that they own the code at the end of the day and that they can add and subtract from the code as they please. The data can be backed up to a local disk. Once a business owner knows that they can keep a copy of the site local, they feel better.

I also tell them that Joomla! is all about usability. It has the capabilities to run a simple brochure site or multimillion-dollar Web application initiative.

Here are a few more points I make when talking to clients.

- Draw any design or GUI, and you can code it to the Joomla! CMS.
- You can build applications inside Joomla! using the built-in framework.
- It's secure and easy to set up on dedicated servers.
- It scales to any level required.
- It's supported by thousands of people.

Q: What are some of the edge case uses for Joomla! you have been involved with in terms of business sites?

A: 
- Large intranets
- LDAP integration
- Google SSO integration
- Full applications with Facebook-like JavaScript actions
- Fulfillment processing and tracking
- Search engine optimization
- Search portals
- Directory sites
- Learning management applications
- Large-scale shared hosting arrangements (30,000 plus domains per month)
- Running a single Joomla! instance in a 25-node cluster
- Cloud Web services integration
- API connections to external CRM applications

Q:  Can you outline some of the training protocols you have set up to help your corporate client's workforce learn Joomla! and how their Web site works?

A:  Joomla! training is readily available from many credible third-party sources. The Joomla.org Web site is full of resources, too. In fact, I know of a college that specifically instructs Web applications using Joomla! as the basis and structure. Typically we offer training with our service packages. The clients get remote training through live online meetings. The live meetings teach clients exactly what task they need to accomplish. Most larger cities have an active Joomla! user group that meets on a regular basis.

Q:  The Joomla! Demo site is an initiative that is managed by CloudAccess.net. What are some of the most common questions business owners ask regarding Web sites and Joomla! in the interaction you have with them as Joomla! Demo site users?

A:  Demo users are coming from all angles. We have small church sites and governments to large Fortune 500 companies interested in the Joomla! CMS. We see all angles and all questions. Some of the more common are questions about getting started, such as finding and installing a template and installing and configuring third-party components. CloudAccess.net is unique in that we provide standard Joomla! support for all users, even demo users. We want to make sure that these new users are able to get going quickly and easily with Joomla! It's a big comfort to users knowing they have a team of Joomla! engineers that they can go to with any questions they might have about Joomla!

Q:  When you were developing *http://demo.joomla.org*, what were some of the functionalities that you had to plan in advance for, and what sort of structure did you have to put in place to handle the load of the Joomla! community, which seems to be growing exponentially as each year passes?

A:  We had to add and train new staff to help support and process tens of thousands of new Joomla! instances per month. Each staff member had to know Joomla!, Internet protocols, customer service, hosting, and much more. It was a very large task. On the technology side, it was not any easier. When you start talking terabytes instead of gigabytes, things get a little more complicated. Our studies led us to enterprise high-performance computing. The Joomla! demo system needs to scale to 1,000+ domains per day, and the only affordable way to handle the job was to build a cluster of servers to deliver the service. Every day is a learning experience for our team. It was much more than anticipated, and we continue to be surprised each day. The Joomla! Demo site is very popular, and it's only growing.

Q:  Cloud computing seems to be a big buzzword right now. What is the cloud, how does it relate to scalability, and why is it beneficial to business clients? Also, how does a cloud-based system benefit running a site like the Joomla! Demo site with thousands of users at any given time?

A: Defining *cloud* can be hard. I don't see one definition for *cloud*. It has been defined by many companies and individuals and is usually specific to the case in study. I see the extreme of cloud as the convergence of software becoming data center and rack aware. It's much like Google Apps and how it's provided as a service and can be delivered to you from many data centers without failure. Some people think of cloud as software service or a utility you purchase online. The cloud typically offers you flexibility in resources. Resources can come in the form of hardware, software, capacity, and even API services. The cloud comes in all shapes and flavors. The term might sound cloudy, but it's how it works in this industry.

Q: What is the next big thing you predict in terms of hosting, software, and CMS software solutions? As an expert working with Joomla!, how do you see the future of the project, Joomla! 1.6, and the new technologies that are being developed?

A: On the hosting side I'm excited to see the possibilities of future versions of Joomla! working with cloud-enabled file systems and new-style NoSQL data-bases. I envision a Joomla! platform for developers building SaaS products. Joomla! could become data center and rack aware just like Google Apps.

   Joomla! 1.6 will be a pinnacle step for the Joomla! CMS. I do see Joomla! going enterprise with 1.6, and it's pretty exciting. The new Joomla! 1.6 features are going to make the community really come alive. I can see the third-party developer community really getting financially stronger and growing large serv-ice-based companies. The future of the Joomla! project is bright. The people, the culture, and the system are what is driving this project.

# Expert Q&A with Ryan Ozimek: President of Open Source Matters, and CEO and Founder of PICnet Inc.—Joomla! in the NPO/NGO Sector

*I'm the president of Open Source Matters (OSM), the nonprofit organization that helps manage the Joomla! project. I've had the great opportunity to be an officer on OSM's board of directors since 2007, and I've provided stewardship and guidance most specifically in the project's fund-raising and event management. I'm also the founder and CEO of PICnet, Inc. In the nine years since the founding of the PICnet, the company has grown from a graduate school concept into one of the most recognized and trusted names in the open source nonprofit technology field. We've been able to forge strong relationships with open source software communities, most obviously Joomla!, in our efforts to provide organizations with the sophisticated and affordable services they need to be success-ful in meeting their missions. Through the years, I've been able to learn and guide PICnet through the natural evolution found in many open source business models, including custom development, support services, and most recently a SaaS model. This business experience, coupled with my work as the recently elected president of OSM, provides me with a great opportunity to bring my skills to*

*the table to help contribute to the success of the growing socially responsible business and organiza-*
*tion communities. I have a master's degree in public policy from the University of California, Los*
*Angeles (UCLA), as well as an bachelor of arts degree in communications from UCLA.*

Q:   What prompted your interest, and/or how did you learn about Joomla!?

A:   Throughout the history of our company (PICnet), we have been strongly
     focused on increasing efficiencies within organizations. One way we sought to do
     this was by delivering technology tools that made life easier for organizations by
     enabling them to more effectively spread the word about their great work. Back
     in 2003, we used a variety of open source Web publishing tools, but none of
     them were as well accepted by our organizations as Mambo (Joomla!'s predeces-
     sor). After seeing the reaction by our community in using Mambo, and then
     Joomla!, I was extremely interested in getting more involved to help this great
     software grow more successful in our nonprofit.

Q:   Do you regularly use open source software, and why?

A:   When it comes to software usage, I consider myself a pragmatic person: find the
     right job for the tool. Whenever possible and appropriate for my needs, I prefer
     using open source software. I believe that open source software often provides the
     control, privacy, and features that I need to get my work done. That's not all,
     though. I use open source software because I think that by doing so I can
     encourage and contribute to the next generation of brilliant developers and soft-
     ware designers. Investing and supporting open source software provides support
     of some of the most democratizing tools in the world today, and using open
     source software is my small way of being part of a very large world of open
     source contributors.

Q:   Joomla! has a large community with a lot of active contributors. In your opinion,
     what is the most exciting part of being involved, and how do you contribute to
     the community?

A:   I enjoy meeting people in person, and for me, the most exciting part of being
     involved in the Joomla! community is attending events. From Joomla! User
     Group meetings to Joomla!Days, the opportunity to meet people in-person helps
     me better understand and see the spirit of the Joomla! community. With so many
     active contributors in the community, we rarely all have a chance to meet in-per-
     son, so having an opportunity to attend events gives us a chance to tear down the
     technology wall that can stand between two individuals and enable us to better
     understand the true person behind the online avatar.

Q:   How does Joomla! help you serve the nonprofit and nongovernmental agencies
     that you work with through PICnet?

A:   We use Joomla! in nearly all our solutions for nonprofit organizations. At the
     core, we use Joomla! as the pivot point around which we can provide a highly

usable interface to a variety of Web services. In today's online world, organizations are looking to bring together a variety of affordable and powerful Web services into one user-friendly system. I don't believe that our Non-Profit Soapbox service (*www.nonprofitsoapbox.com*) would be nearly as successful if it weren't built on a powerful and inviting platform like Joomla! Using Joomla! enables us to focus on building powerful solutions that target the core needs of our organizations instead of spending time on technology problems. Joomla! provides us with the tools we need to help organizations be successful in their online publishing, social networking, fund-raising, and activism.

Q: What are some of the edge case uses for Joomla! you have experienced in the NPO field? What are the impacts you have seen in your work that make Joomla! the right fit in this sector as a solution?

A: We've seen Joomla! used in a variety of interesting ways, mostly based on the customizations needed by our organizations. We've built project management and collaboration solutions, created humanitarian relief data systems, and designed some effective integrations with third-party services (like constituent relationship management systems) with Joomla! Watching the impact of Joomla! within organizations is quite exciting. Joomla! shortens the distance between constituencies and organization leadership, by providing software tools that allow organizations to more easily communicate effectively and easily with their communities. Additionally, since organizations are highly attracted to low-cost Web services (such as photo, video, documents, and so on), Joomla! provides the flexible platform they need to connect all these services together.

Q: Joomla! is well known for its ability to be expanded and extended. What are some of the specific needs of NPOs and NGOs, and how are you able to extend to meet those needs? Do you have any specific extensions that are a "go to" for this sector?

A: The key functional requirements of nonprofits are not that much different from their for-profit friends: spread a message, bring in money, and execute on tasks to achieve a mission. Our company has spent the last ten years learning and investing in tools that help organizations do all three of these more successfully. We built Non-Profit Soapbox to bring together the tools we believed organizations needed to have a strong Web presence that also provided the services it needed to have a trusted partner in its online efforts. The kinds of add-ons we most often integrate for our organizations include an easy-to-use WYSIWYG editor, commenting system, integration services with Salesforce.com, and other CRM tools, donation processing extensions, and more. There is a huge variety of options to choose from, and we take the approach of finding the right tool for the job.

Q: As a long-standing board member of Open Source Matters, as well as being such an advocate for NPOs, how did your previous experiences in the sector aid you in defining and refining the processes and workflow of the OSM board?

A: I believe that all organizations should constantly be in a period of self-reflection and bar-raising. I've had an opportunity to see this done successfully, as well as dismally, in the past, and I'm bringing all my lessons learned from the nonprofit sector to the table to be a better leader on our OSM board. During the past 10 years, I've seen the growth of the earned income nonprofit model, as well as organizations that have focused strongly on improving efficiency and clarifying organizational structures. Having worked with leaders in more than 300 non-profit organizations, I've had a firsthand look at what works and what doesn't, and I've had a chance to build relationships with folks on the front lines of the new generation of social entrepreneurs that have shown that the most successful purpose-driven organizations are those with clear communication channels, strong leaders, and effective workflows that keep the engine running smoothly.

Q: Joomla! as software and as a community has exponentially grown over the years since it started. How have you as an OSM board member and as a community member viewed that growth, and what are some of your predictions for the future regarding Joomla! 1.6 and beyond?

A: It's been awe-inspiring to see the growth of the Joomla! community since it started. The growth in users, designers, developers, contributors, third-party devel-opers, and more have all contributed to the powerful success of the project. I believe that access control lists (ACLs) were one of the key features that Joomla! was missing in the eyes of many organizations and companies, so the release of Joomla! 1.6 will help the project continue to grow. Additionally, I believe that some of most exciting times in the project are during beta periods. That's when I've seen a lot of developers come out in strong support of the project by report-ing issues, squashing bugs, and contributing directly to the core system. With the focus on smaller and more timely releases of the software, I believe that our future will be even more exciting and engaging. Finally, I think that a number of successful businesses in our community are beginning to successfully grasp the power of the underlying framework. By doing so, I have a feeling that we're going to see some great new Web solutions built on the framework that might not use the CMS application but will definitely be powered by Joomla!

# Expert Q&A with Jennifer Marriott: Owner of Marpo Multimedia and Joomla! Contributor— Sites for Education

*I have a fascination with everything technology related stemming from using a Teletype for the first time as a young child. That experience set the stage for my current obsession with computers. I stud-ied broadcasting and communications in school, and combined with the emerging Web as a commu-nication tool, Web design and development became my passion. I am also a professional musician, an author, and a firm believer that FOSS and music can save the world.*

Q: What prompted your interest, and/or how did you learn about Joomla?

A: I was looking for a new host in 2004 and came across Rochen through the Webhosting Talk Forum. Connecting with Rochen as a hosting provider gave me the opportunity to talk with Brad Baker about Web technologies and content management systems, and he introduced me to Mambo. I really loved the concept and how it worked. I came over to Joomla! right at the beginning and was asked to be a forum moderator in the template forum. From that as the years have progressed, I have contributed in many aspects of the Joomla! project.

Q: Do you regularly use open source software, and why?

A: I use open source software every chance I can. I enjoy the aspect of contributing to open source to provide software solutions for others. If a client has a need for a software solution, I can usually find an open source version that does the job and does it well. The great aspect of open source for me is the community of user to user help and support that helps me in turn support my clients and gives my clients the ability get support and self-help themselves. I think open source software empowers people.

Q: Joomla! has a large community with a lot of active contributors. In your opinion, what is the most exciting part of being involved, and how do you contribute to the community?

A: For me the most exciting part of Joomla! is the people and the community they represent. From the least experienced person to the most adept experienced coder, all of the people contribute to make Joomla! a better project and better software. The collaborative environment has been very rewarding to me in terms of furthering my skills as a Web developer and designer.

   I started contributing to Joomla! as a Forum Moderator for the template forum. At that time, I had very little to no experience with PHP, but I was very experienced in HTML, CSS, and JavaScript. Being a Moderator on the template forum gave me an outlet to contribute by helping others with their sites, and I would say of my 4,000+ posts on the forum, the majority are in the template forum helping users and helping users help each other. From there I joined up with the Joomla! Bug Squad and started the process of learning PHP and understanding the code base. I also became a mentor for the Google Summer of Code, and coadministrator of our GSoC program. It was incredibly rewarding to see young students from all over the world working so hard to create software for others. I also was lead of the Trademark and Licensing Team until mid-2010, helping the community understand and use the marks of the project in a responsible way. In mid-2010 I stepped down from all official project duties, but I still dabble a bit on the template forum helping users and squishing bugs with the Joomla! Bug Squad.

Q:  You've been a consultant on a number of educational site projects as well as created a complex site for an entire school district. What is the scope of that site,
and how is it organized?

A:  The school district site was a distinct challenge. The district had the need of a site
that was more readily edited by nontechnical users. At the time, the site was
strictly a static HTML site that required all changes to go through the IT department, and with ten campus locations and administrative and other user groups, it
was time-consuming and not very efficient. I proposed to create one district-
wide site using Joomla!

One of the main challenges of the site was enabling an access control system
to be able to assign editors to their campus or administrative sections and creating an editing environment that was easy for the least technical user to understand. This was accomplished in the first inception of the Web site with JACL as
access control and using JCE Editor, which is a very easy editor for both Web site
administrators to configure, as well as for users to use for editing content.
Community Builder was the basis for our staff profiles and made it very easy-to-
create staff lists based on location and departments.

When the site was redesigned in 2009, it was updated from Joomla! 1.0 to
Joomla! 1.5. Using Joomla! made it easy to roll over content that was imperative
to the Web site. It was also important to maintain a certain level of familiarity
with the processes for end users and content editors to keep retraining to a minimum. There was also a need to add more functionality and information processes
to our staff profile pages, while still keeping the interfaces for staff easy to use for
nontechnical users. New access control was brought on board with the Art of
Joomla!'s Control and Content Manager. The combination of both extensions
made it very easy to create editor groups. JCE was used again, and also with its
extensive configurability, it was very easy to create user groups that allowed front-
end editors to easily edit content and protect their images and documents in
confined directories. Community Builder is a great choice for extended user profiles, and with the update we added the functionality of easy to use tools for
teachers and staff such as the ability to post lesson plans and announcements as
well as pictures of their classrooms and student works, without having to be
highly technical. An e-mail form was enabled on each teacher profile to allow
parents and students to easily contact teachers. As with any site that serves a
broad spectrum of users with differing levels of technical knowledge, every aspect
has to be efficient and easy to use for end users.

Q:  Who creates the content on the site? How do you plan for and train content
creators?

A:  The structure of the site followed a set form that was duplicated for each cam-
pus/administrative group. Each campus/administrative group was set up as a section, and within their section were categories that were common to all groups
and campus locations. Setting the structure of the site in this manner created a

consistent and understandable navigation across the site. This consistency was utilized to make the site easy to navigate and understand for the users and content contributors to the site, but also for parents, students, and the community. Using Control and Content Manager for access control allowed each section/campus to have control over their own content.

From the initial planning of the site, it was decided that a set group of people from each campus would be responsible for the content on their respective sections of the site. Each administrative group would also have an editor assigned to their sections and categories. Choosing set, small groups of motivated people allowed training to be done in phases. Once this initial group was trained, they were able to spread that training to the rest of the staff and faculty at their campus. Also, some online tutorials were posted for some of the more common tasks, and individual support was able to be given by the IT staff through the network to demonstrate editing techniques using screen sharing.

Q: What are some of the main challenges you faced in building the site?

A: I think the main challenge was balancing the requested functionality with the overall needs and experience level of the district staff and faculty. The beginning of the process had to start with the people who would be putting in content and making sure entering content was as easy as possible. Once that process was completed, the site structure and navigation worked into a form that facilitated the information that the district as a whole wanted to communicate to the community it serves.

Q: How is ongoing maintenance handled?

A: The IT staff for the district has handled ongoing maintenance. The basic maintenance of updating the site was made easier by using multipurpose extensions and keeping the total number of extensions used to a minimum. Extensions are monitored for updates and security issues. Akeeba Backup is being used to regularly back up the site, and a backup policy was put in place. Also, regular server maintenance is performed by the IT staff because the site is self-hosted on district servers. One of the greatest advantages of Joomla! is the ability for administrators of a site to do self-maintenance. I do consult and provide support on an as-needed basis.

Q: What are some of the main lessons you learned in building the site?

A: I learned that when a large number of people are involved in the planning process of a large Web site, it is important as a developer/designer to keep the group as a whole focused on the main purpose of the Web site. It is easy for the "want" of a person or specific portion of the group to overshadow the actual "need" that the site is trying to fulfill. Every person will have a different opinion as to what is essential and what is not. You also really do have to think in terms of what your least technically knowledgeable user is going to experience in their interaction with the site in performing any duties they may have and try to balance their need for ease of use with the more complex functionality that more experienced users may request.

I also learned that the initial planning of a site is most likely the most important part of the whole process. Good planning will ensure a smooth production phase, and that will make for a good site rollout. As a final thought, it is always wise to be aware of "creep" in scope as you are developing. It is better to roll out a site in phases, implementing additions in functionality, because this will allow you to analyze the adoption of usage and whether the additions are meeting the assessed needs of the site and the users.

# Expert Q&A with Louis Landry: Lead Architect of Joomla! and Joomla! Professional

*I am a development coordinator and architect for Joomla! I am and in the past have been a principal of a number of small businesses in the Joomla! space that specialize in Joomla! custom development and Joomla! extensions. Among the extensions I have worked on are the feed aggregator that powers Joomla! Connect on the Joomla.org sites and Finder and Comments distributed by JXtended. I have also worked on large-scale implementations that use the Joomla! framework such at the quizilla.com site. Currently I spend most of my working time managing Joomla! development and developing the Joomla! framework.*

Q: What prompted your interest, and/or how did you learn about Joomla?

A: I discovered Mambo when it was somewhere around 4.0.4 because I was building a site for a friend and, like many people, looking to get away from static sites. I started submitting feature requests and patches, and then when the fork happened, I went along with the Core Team to Joomla! A few months later, I was asked to join the Core Team, and I've been with the project ever since in various capacities.

Q: Do you regularly use open source software, and why?

A: I do use open source software whenever I can, but I am a firm believer in using the right tool for the job. I would not pass up a best-of-breed application to get the job done in a given situation to prove a point. I do think that for Web-based applications open source ones are almost always superior.

Q: Joomla! has a large community with a lot of active contributors. In your opinion, what is the most exciting part of being involved, and how do you contribute to the community?

A: I've been involved in so many different parts of the Joomla! project. My main role right now is working with leadership team members and senior developers to manage development for the project and keep the project wheels spinning.

Part of that is monitoring and maintaining the integrity of the code base, part of it is strategic planning around how the software and the project will evolve, and yet another part of it is doing a lot of speaking and education about Joomla! development both in person and online. In my role I also find myself interacting quite a bit with developers from external projects such as MooTools, Eclipse, and so on. In the past, I have had many different roles ranging from project manager to communications team leader. They have all been both challenging and incredibly rewarding, and I am grateful to have been able to serve in all of them.

Q:  As an independent developer, you have worked on some very large and challenging projects. What are some of the most interesting challenges you have been able to solve using Joomla? Can you give a small case study on one of your more challenging projects?

A:  Well, the Quizilla site is probably the highest-traffic site on which I have worked. It has millions of users and at times will reach roughly 60 million page views in a week. The project was to rebuild the existing Web site, maintaining all the existing features as well as adding several new ones using the Joomla! framework. The legacy code base was a mix of PHP and Perl applications, and our goal was to have a consistent, easy-to-maintain platform on which to base the current site as well as future enhancements.

One of the biggest challenges we faced was data migration given the vast existing data set. We built command-line data conversion tools on the Joomla! framework so that conversion could be done in batches and then hooked that code into the application to allow for conversion on demand in some situations.

Q:  As one of the lead developers for Joomla!, can you explain the development process and release cycle? How has it evolved over the years?

A:  Historically Joomla! has had a very slow release cycle with releases about every two years or so. It has been a strongly feature-oriented release process. Starting with 1.7, we will be using a time-based release process with releases every six months and a strong commitment to backward compatibility. This has required a rethinking and reorganization of the development process including what is called the "stable trunk model" in which the trunk will only have code that is ready for release.

We will also be implementing more of a long-term support model so sites that want to can settle on a particular release and then wait until the next long-term support release to upgrade. For many users, our two-year release cycle has been pretty functional in that respect. Joomla! 1.0 and then Joomla! 1.5 are highly stable and reliable releases that received support for many years, and in the case of 1.5 will be supported for a year beyond the release of 1.6. We have spent a lot of time thinking about how to manage the balance between the need to move the software forward and the need for end users and extension developers to have a stable platform, and we think this approach will have the right balance.

Q:  What is coming on the horizon for Joomla! development as the project looks to 1.7 and beyond?

A:  With Joomla! 1.6, we will have solved two long-standing wishes, that for granular access control and nested categories. For 1.7 and beyond, the horizons are really open, but I think that the content model will be looked at closely. That means both simplifying it so that there aren't so many separate extensions and making it more flexible so that it's easy to make custom content types. Also, Web services and integration with other applications will be very important. Infrastructure for both of these is in 1.6. Although it's less visible to end users, we'll keep improving standardization to make it easier to build custom applications that are secure and flexible. Our new release cycle will allow us to be much more agile in adding new features and improving all aspects of Joomla! There are great things on the horizon!

# Common Problems and Solutions

If you follow the instructions in this book, you will avoid most common problems. However, sometimes things go wrong. Here are the most common issues we see and how to solve them.

## Lost Administrator Password

If you lose your own password, you can recover it with the "Forgot your password?" link that is typically shown in the login module on a site. The exact wording may depend on the site and any modifications that may have been done. However, the more serious issue is when for some reason the people or person who had super administration access are no longer available either to do the super administration tasks or to promote someone else to be a super administrator. If someone is no longer associated with a site, it is very important that their access be restricted or removed entirely.

There are several schools of thought on the best way to regain super administrator access in Joomla! 1.5. They all involve working with your database directly. Joomla! 1.6 introduces a new method, which requires editing your configuration file.

### Joomla! 1.5

To access your database, you will need to log into your hosting account's Cpanel or the hosting panel your host provides. If you are using Cpanel, find the icon for phpMyAdmin or use the Find in the top-left corner of Cpanel to search for the icon. Figure A.1 shows an example, but as always, your host may have a different hosting panel in use, and the screen may not look exactly the same.

After clicking the icon, you will see the administrative interface for your databases, as shown in Figure A.2. In many cases, you will just have one, which is the one for your Joomla! installation. However, if you have several and are not sure which is the Joomla! one, go back to your control panel and, using the File Manager (see Chapter 3), open the *configuration.php* file. At about line 18, you will see a line that starts with `var $db=`. The text (not including the quotes) to the right of the equal sign tell you the database name.

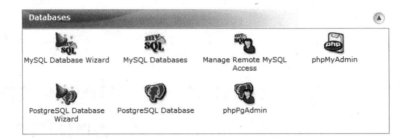

Figure A.1  phpMyAdmin icon in Cpanel

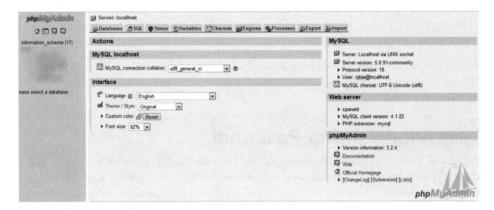

Figure A.2  Administration screen for phpMyAdmin

Click the name of your database. The top of your database will look as shown in Figure A.3.

Each line represents a database table. Find the jos_users table, which will be the second to last one on the list because it is arranged alphanumerically, unless you have installed extensions that add tables that are alphanumerically after jos_users. Click the

| Table ▲ | Action | | | | | | Records [1] | Type | Collation | Size | Overhead |
|---|---|---|---|---|---|---|---|---|---|---|---|
| jos_banner | | | | | | ✕ | 0 | MyISAM | utf8_general_ci | 1.0 KiB | – |
| jos_bannerclient | | | | | | ✕ | 0 | MyISAM | utf8_general_ci | 1.0 KiB | – |
| jos_bannertrack | | | | | | ✕ | 0 | MyISAM | utf8_general_ci | 1.0 KiB | – |
| jos_categories | | | | | | ✕ | 2 | MyISAM | utf8_general_ci | 5.6 KiB | – |
| jos_components | | | | | | ✕ | 38 | MyISAM | utf8_general_ci | 8.3 KiB | – |
| jos_contact_details | | | | | | ✕ | 1 | MyISAM | utf8_general_ci | 3.6 KiB | – |
| jos_content | | | | | | ✕ | 1 | MyISAM | utf8_general_ci | 9.2 KiB | – |
| jos_content_frontpage | | | | | | ✕ | 0 | MyISAM | utf8_general_ci | 1.0 KiB | – |
| jos_content_rating | | | | | | ✕ | 0 | MyISAM | utf8_general_ci | 1.0 KiB | – |

Figure A.3  Viewing the tables in your Joomla! database

Figure A.4  The data inside the jos_users database table

first button in the Action column, which is the Browse action. This will show you a group of rows and columns, as in Figure A.4.

Some of the important fields shown here include username, password, usertype, and gid. In this case, there are two super administrators, which you can tell by both the user-type text and the gid entry of 25. The gid is what actually controls this; the text is simply for display in the User Manager. The passwords do not look anything like a normal password. This is because they are encrypted as a security precaution. The simplest options are either to replace the e-mail with your e-mail address and then use the Forgot My Password feature on your site or to replace the password. To replace a password, you need a hashed version of a known word. Here's an example:

```
d2064d358136996bd22421584a7cb33e:trd7TvKHx6dMeoMmBVxYmg0vuXEA4199
```

This is the hash for the word *secret*. You can copy this string from *http://docs.joomla.org/ How_do_you_recover_your_admin_password* since typing it exactly is likely to be hard.

To edit the record, click the pencil icon on the left of the screen that is in the Administrator row. The screen will appear as in Figure A.5. Simply change the text in either the e-mail field or the password field. When you are ready, click the Go button on the bottom right of the screen.

Once it is saved, if you have changed the e-mail address, use the Forgot My Password link on your site. Your site will send you an e-mail with instructions to reset your password. Once you have completed the forgotten password process, you should be able to log in to your site. If you have changed the password to your site administrator in the database, go to the login of your Web site, either the front end if enabled or the back end, with the new password you entered in the database table.

At this point, it is imperative that you change the password to a secure password if you used a common hash like that given earlier for changing your password in the database. Also, in the User Manager, make sure that no one has super administrator access who should not. To block a super administrator, you must edit their user and change their user group to any other group, although Registered is best. After saving, you will be able to block the user in the User Manager, as shown in Figure A.6.

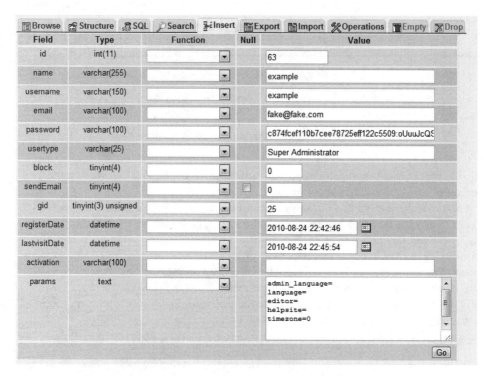

Figure A.5  Editing the database record for the administrator in the jos_users table of the database

Figure A.6  Blocking a Registered user in the Joomla! administrator back end

## Joomla! 1.6

In Joomla! 1.6, log into your hosting account, and, using the File Manager, find the file *configuration.php* located in the directory of your Joomla! site. Edit this file, and scroll to the bottom. Before the final bracket (}), put this line, replacing **myname** with the name of a registered user:

```
public $root_user='myname';
```

This will give that user superuser rights. You should immediately log into your site, change the password for the user, and make any other changes you need (such as resetting a password for the administrator or changing another account to have super user privileges). Then immediately delete the line from the *configuration.php* file, and save it in the original form. If you forget to do this and log in to your site administrator as a superuser, you will get a reminder to do so.

## File Permissions and Ownership Problems

If you followed the instructions for installation in Chapter 3, you should not have problems with your files. However, you might experience file problems over time, perhaps because you have FTPed files from an external client and uploaded some using the File Manager or because your server environment has changed. Some of the symptoms of this problem are an inability to save changes in a file that you edit and the inability to install extensions.

Each file on your site has an owner. Usually that owner is either your account or Apache. Joomla! is designed to work with one or the other, but not both at the same time. It is very important that you maintain consistency in your file ownership. For example, if you use the FTP layer in Joomla! for installing some extensions, then you should use it for all extensions. You must also make sure to use the same account consistently so that your files are not owned by different users. If you end up with mixed ownership, most likely you will have to submit a support ticket to your host who will then need to run a CHOWN utility (this is a Linux utility that all Linux-based hosting should have available).

Unfortunately, it can be difficult to determine what account owns your files. For example, the standard Cpanel File Manager does not show this. However, some FTP clients will show this.

File permissions are what different groups of users are allowed to do with your files and are usually represented by a three-digit number. Your Joomla! folders should be set to 755, and your files should be set to 644. At times you may receive advice to change file ownership to 777, but you should never do this if you are in a shared hosting environment (which most sites are) because it will make your files susceptible to attack from other sites on the same server. To change the permissions on a folder or file, select the box next to its name, and then click the Permissions icon in the top menu, as shown in Figure A.7. The configurations for 644 and 755 are shown in Figures A.8 and A.9.

Be sure to remember to click Change Permissions to complete the process.

Figure A.7  Change Permissions icon in Cpanel File Manager

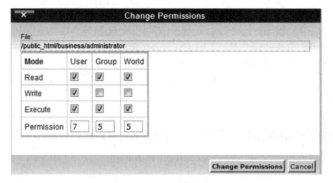

Figure A.8   Changing permissions for a folder to 755

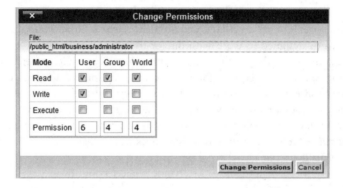

Figure A.9   Changing permissions for a file to 644

# "Location not found" When Using an Extension

If you install an extension and receive a "Location not found" message when attempting to use it, this usually means that the extension requires Legacy Mode. That means the extension was written for Joomla! 1.0 and not rewritten for Joomla! 1.5. You can use these extensions by enabling the Legacy plugin in the Plugin Manager. (See Chapter 6 for an explanation of plugins.) If an extension requires Legacy Mode to run, you may want to reconsider using that specific extension and research whether a similar extension exists that does not require Legacy Mode.

# Editor Background Has a Color or Looks Strange

If you install a template with a dark colored background, it can sometimes make the editor difficult to use because the editor attempts to use the template styles to make your content in the editor look more like that in your actual template. If this happens to you, the easiest solution is to create an *editor.css* file and add it to your template folder in the same way *override.css* was added in the sample sites in Chapters 8, 9, and 10. In the parameters of your editor (such as the default WYSIWYG editor that comes installed in Joomla! or if you are using JCE as your editor), you can then specify that you are using an *editor.css* file. Each editor has a specific place for this directive, so you may have to look in the documentation of the editor or review the parameter options in the editor you are using. You can make the *editor.css* file as simple or complex as you want, but be sure to use a light color for the background. For example, the following will produce a white background:

```
body { background: #ffffff; }
```

Some people make a copy of their *template.css* file or the CSS file that contains most of the CSS styling of elements in their template and add the above to the top of the file, replacing any body styling that may be present with the background directive of #FFFFFF (white).

## Template Disappears When Turning On SEF URLs

In some server environments, turning on SEF URLS, especially without using the `htaccess` option, causes all the pages except your home page to lose the template. In this case, you will just see black text and blue links on a white background. The solution to this problem is often to use the `$livesite` variable. To do this, access your file server by using File Manager via Cpanel as described in Chapter 3. Find the file *configuration.php* in the directory your site is installed in. Open that file to edit it, and find the following line at about line 21:

```
var $live_site = '';
```

Inside the quotation marks put the URL for your site (for example, *http:// mydomain.com*). Make sure to put *http://* at the beginning and do not put a slash at the end. If your site uses *www* as part of the domain name or if your site redirects all non-*www* traffic to *www*, you will need to include *www* in the URL (for example, *http://www.mydomain.com*).

## Site Displays Differently or Incorrectly in a Certain Browser

Cross-browser compatibility is one of the most difficult issues in Web design. Unfortunately, there are many browsers, and not all of them interpret the same code in the same way. This is why you will often see *ie.css* or *ie6.css* as part of your template. Those files make specific adjustments to the CSS styles for certain browsers. This is not a Joomla! issue but a Web standards issue.

When you have a problem with a particular browser, try to identify the CSS that is causing the issue. There are some useful tools for this, such as browser add-ons like Firebug for Firefox and Developer Tools in Internet Explorer 8. You can also find a great deal of advice and reference material about specific issues and browsers on the Web. Appendix B contains some useful links for this.

# B

# Resources

There are many resources for helping you make and improve your site. We have gathered a few of them that we have found useful here, but as you gain experience as a Web site administrator, you will find many more. The Joomla! community is always sharing links, advice, and information about various sites in the social networking sphere. Join Joomla! on Facebook, on Twitter, and on the People Site (*http://people.joomla.org*).

## Basic Joomla! Resources

The Joomla! project operates one of the largest families of Web sites in the world. Each of the sites serves a different purpose.

### http://joomla.org

The main site provides basic information about the Joomla! project and software. Major project announcements are posted here.

### http://forum.joomla.org

The Joomla! forums are the place to get (and give) support.

### http://docs.joomla.org

The documentation site includes detailed documentation for all aspects of Joomla!

### http://extensions.joomla.org

Known as the JED, the Joomla! Extensions Directory is the best central location for finding extensions for Joomla!

### http://resources.joomla.org

The Joomla! Resources Directory (JRD) is the best place to find Joomla! professionals ranging from hosts, designers, and template houses to consultants, trainers, and others.

## http://community.joomla.org

The community Web site is the center for information for people who are contributors to the Joomla! project. The team blogs that are posted here are important sources of information about what is happening in the project. The site also has information about Joomla! User Groups and translations.

## http://joomlacode.org

The code site is where the actual code that makes up Joomla! is stored and developed. It also hosts the issue tracker where bugs can be reported and is the development site for thousands of Joomla! extensions. If you ever develop an extension, you can use Joomlacode to manage it.

## http://api.joomla.org

This is the place where information for developers using the Joomla! framework is presented. If you want to understand the code behind Joomla!, this is an essential resource.

## http://people.joomla.org

People is the social networking site for users and people active in various parts of the Joomla! world. It is a fun resource where you can meet other people from around the world interested in similar topics.

The following are important specific pages that are on the family of Joomla.org sites.

### Vulnerable Extensions List

*http://docs.joomla.org/Vulnerable_Extensions_List*

The vulnerable extension list is the place to check an extension prior to installing it and also to monitor your extensions over time.

### Site Showcase

*http://community.joomla.org/showcase*

The Site Showcase features thousands of beautiful Joomla! Web sites that can inspire you. This is a great place to look for ideas.

### Download

*www.joomla.org/download.html*

This is the page to download Joomla! You can also check here to make sure you have the current version and sign up for the security notification mailing list.

# Tools for Webmasters and Site Developers

There are a large number of online tools that site developers can use to help build and manage their sites.

## Web-site-map

*www.web-site-map.com*

This site will help you produce a proper XML site map to submit to Google. These site maps work with Joomla! and a number of Joomla! extensions. The same site also offers a broken-link checker for your site. This is useful because broken links are annoying to your users and may hurt your search engine ranking.

## Lipsum.com

*www.lipsum.com*

This site generates the classic Lorem Ipsum dummy text that you can use to work on your site design before your content is completely ready.

## W3.org

*http://validator.w3.orgwww.w3.org*

There are established standards for Web site HTML and CSS. These are designed for accessibility and performance and to encourage browsers to work consistently in the ways that users and designers expect. You can test whether your site validates by entering a URL in the online validator. The *www.w3.org* site provides extensive information on Web standards.

# Search Engines

You want to make sure that people can find your Web site. These are the main places you should work on, as described in Chapter 6.

## Google

*www.google.com/analytics*
*https://www.google.com/webmasters/tools*

The best way to get results into Google is to integrate Google Analytics and Webmaster Tools. Follow the instructions on the sites.

## Ask

*www.ask.comabout/help/webmasters*

Ask.com requires a specific format for your site map. Make sure to follow the instructions exactly. The link will take you to a page with more information, but you should also review the material on submitting your site to Ask.com in Chapter 7.

## Bing

*www.bing.com/webmaster/SubmitSitePage.aspx*

Bing only requires you to submit your domain.

## dmoz

*www.dmoz.org/docs/en/add.html*

The Open Directory Project only requires a submission with a suggested category for your domain. Think carefully about what category makes the most sense for your domain.

# Learn HTML and CSS Skills

Joomla! is designed for easy content creation without the need to know the underlying languages of the Web, HTML and CSS. However, to take total control of your site and to be able to format exactly the way you want, you will need to learn basic HTML and CSS. If you have worked through the sample sites in Chapters 8, 9, and 10, you will have already seen the power of this.

## W3Schools

*www.w3schools.com/default.asp*

This site has one of the largest collections of reference materials and tutorials for Web site developers including extensive materials on CSS and HTML. It also contains tutorials for PHP and MySQL, which are useful if you want to understand the code in the files that make up the Joomla! software.

## Wikipedia

*http://en.wikipedia.org/wiki/HTML*
*http://en.wikipedia.org/wiki/CSS*

Wikipedia provides a wealth of information on HTML and CSS.

## CSS Play

*www.cssplay.co.uk*
*www.cssplay.com*

These sites contain a wealth of information that help you explore CSS in depth.

## HTML, CSS, and Color Cheat Sheets

There are many reference documents for HTML and CSS.

*www.webmonkey.com/2010/02/html_cheatsheet*
*www.w3schools.com/css/css_reference.asp*
*http://en.wikipedia.org/wiki/Web_colors*

If you look for reference materials on the Web, make sure to check the date published since in many instances old guidance will not work well with modern browsers or meet current Web standards.

# Improve the Design of Your Site

These sites can help you learn about design and improve the attractiveness of your site by showing inspirational examples or by supplying design elements such as images and media.

## Google Fonts

*http://code.google.com/webfonts*

Google provides access to a set of fonts you can use to move beyond the limited number of Web-safe fonts as described in Chapter 8.

## CSS Zen Garden

*www.csszengarden.com*

CSS Zen Garden is the best-known site for seeing examples of how to use CSS to radically change the way that Web content is presented.

## Color Pickers and Schemers

*www.colorschemer.com/online.html*
*www.colourlovers.com*
*http://kuler.adobe.com*

Color Schemer, Colour Lovers, and Kuler are all useful sites to try various color schemes and to produce color theory–informed schemes with a specific base color. All these sites have active communities that will give feedback and advice on schemes you develop and share schemes that they create.

## A List Apart

*www.alistapart.com*

This is a favorite Web site for Web site designers and developers because of its well-thought-out and useful articles.

## Smashing Magazine

*www.smashingmagazine.com*

This is a favorite online magazine for site designers and developers for its excellent articles, advice, and downloadable royalty-free graphics, icon sets, vectors, and other goodies.

## Stock.Xchng

*http://sxc.hu/*

This is a really useful source of royalty-free images. We got our images for the toy store example site from this site.

### Morgue File

*www.morguefile.com*
This is a great source for royalty-free photos.

### WikiMedia Commons

*http://commons.wikimedia.org*
This is a source for a variety of images and videos that are licensed for your use. In our nonprofit Web site, we obtained the image in the news article from WikiMedia Commons.

# Web Standards, Usability, and Accessibility

### Jakob Nielson

*www.useit.com*
Jakob Nielsen has a really ugly but highly usable site that features his research on Web usability.

### Usability.gov

*www.usability.gov*
A resource from the Department of Health and Human Services with detailed information on usability issues.

### Web Accessibility Initiative

*www.w3.org/WAI*
This group develops the guidelines regarded as the international standard for Web accessibility.

### Section 508

*www.section508.gov*
This is the official Web site for Section 508 of the U.S. Rehabilitation Act.

### Europa

*http://ec.europa.eu*
This is the official site of the European Commission. There are areas on this site that specifically detail initiatives taken in Europe regarding accessibility, usability, and Web standards.

# Underlying Software

Joomla! builds on a number of underlying applications. Although it is not necessary to master or even know much about these (because Joomla! takes care of that for you), you may want to learn more or increase your understanding.

## PHP

*http://php.net*
*http://us2.php.net/manual/en/index.php*

PHP is the language that most of Joomla! is written in. We love the PHP online manual, and it's really useful for things such as looking up how formatting dates work, which you need to know to customize calendars.

## MySql

*www.mysql.com/?bydis_dis_index=1*
*http://dev.mysql.com/doc*

MySQL and MySQLi are the databases that Joomla! uses to manage your content and other information. Manuals for different versions of MySQL are available on the MySQL sites.

## MooTools

*http://mootools.net*
*http://demos.mootools.net*

MooTools is the JavaScript framework that powers much of the Joomla! back end and provides many useful visual effects.

## Apache

*http://apache.org*
*www.apachefriends.org/en/index.html*

Your Joomla! site is hosted on a server. Apache is the most common server software used for Joomla! hosting. You can also download the application XAMPP from the Apache Web site, which will allow you to have Joomla! on your regular computer. Many experienced users like to have an installation on their own computers to test and experiment on before uploading to their host.

## IIS

*www.iis.net*
*www.microsoft.com/web/gallery/joomla.aspx*

IIS is an alternative to Apache and is a Microsoft Windows–based server. You can learn more about IIS at the main site, or you can download the Joomla! installation package to set up a local installation of Joomla! on a Windows computer.

# Other Resources for Business

There are thousands of resources for businesses, and of course many companies provide services for business Web sites.

## PayPal

*https://www.paypal.com*

As discussed in Chapter 8, PayPal is one of the simplest-to-use payment processors.

## Google Checkout

*http://checkout.google.com*

Google offers its own payment processor.

## U.S. Trademark Office

*www.uspto.gov*

The U.S. Trademark Office provides useful information about trademarks. If you are from another country, it will have its own office, but you may find the general information about trademarks at USPTO useful.

## World Intellectual Property Organization

*www.wipo.int*

The WIPO site contains information on trademarks for all countries that are signatories of the Madrid protocol.

## U.S. Library of Congress Copyright Office

*www.copyright.gov*

This Copyright Office provides information about copyright protection for your work in the United States.

# Other Resources for Nonprofits and Organizations

There are many organizations that provide support services of various kinds that can be integrated with your Joomla! site. Some of these are discussed in Chapter 9, although if you're managing a nonprofit Web site, you should watch for new opportunities.

## Techsoup

*http://techsoup.org*

This is a site where many nonprofit opportunities are announced and discussed by nonprofit professionals.

## Guidestar

*http://guidestar.org*

Guidestart lists information about all 501(c)3 organizations, and donors use the information there to learn about yours. Make sure that the information they report is accurate and up to date. Providing a link to your Guidestar listing is a good way of helping donors to be confident in your organization.

## Network for Good

*http://networkforgood.org*

Network for Good assists nonprofits with donation processing by managing some of the complex legal issues involved in soliciting donations on the Internet. They also provide important information about your organization to donors and volunteers.

## YourCause

*http://yourcause.com*

YourCause provides another way for your constituents to raise funds for your nonprofit.

## eBay and Related Sites That Tie into eBay for Charitable Giving

*http://missionfish.org*
*http://givingworks.ebay.com*

eBay provides several services specifically for nonprofits wanting to leverage eBay sites for fund-raising.

# Other Resources for Schools and Education

Schools have some special needs to consider, especially schools that are kindergarten through 12th grade. Frequently the network administrators of districts or schools that deal with minor children have to use specific Internet content filtering and other network security protocols. This can make finding resources that are usable in the classroom difficult. Resources that are child safe can be an important part of any school's curriculum. Check with your school's administrators for a list of online resources that are available to use in the content of your site, such as videos, streaming media, and images. You can also research what online chat and video software is available to connect your classroom to the world.

## Google Apps

*www.google.com/a/help/intl/en/edu/index.html*

Google provides a free special edition of its application suite to schools. Many of the elements of this can be integrated into your Joomla! site.

## Youth Voices

*http://youthvoices.net*

Youth Voices provides a safe environment for students and teachers to collaborate on the Web.

## TeacherTube

*www.teachertube.com*

Many schools have policies that prohibit the use of general video sites such as YouTube.

TeacherTube provides an alternative.

## National Geographic Online Education Resources

*http://education.nationalgeographic.com/education*

This is a child-friendly educational resource site.

## Discovery Education Classroom Resources

*http://school.discoveryeducation.com*

Discovery offers a number of classroom resources on a variety of subjects.

## Stanford University Center for Internet and Society

*http://fairuse.stanford.edu/Copyright_and_Fair_Use_Overview/chapter12/12-c.html*

The CIS at Stanford University provides a sample photo release form, including releases for people younger than 18, that schools can adapt for use when including images on their sites.

# A Look at Joomla! 1.6 ACL

The implementation of access control is the most important change in Joomla! 1.6. In this appendix, we will demonstrate how to implement a basic access control system for the school site example shown in Chapter 10. This example assumes you have installed Joomla! 1.6 without the sample data. Some images will differ if you have installed the sample data.

In our school site, we want to achieve the following:

- Limit the ability to create and edit articles in a department category to members of that department
- Give all member of the administration the ability to publish articles
- Limit the ability to see certain content to the school administration only

The first thing to notice is that the first two of the previous list involve limitations on the actions that users can take, specifically the actions of creating and publishing articles. The third item concerns the ability to view certain items.

In planning 1.6 access control, we need to clearly separate the ability to do actions and the ability to see things.

## Controlling What People Can Do

In a 1.6 implementation of the school site, the department sections will be replaced with categories, and the news categories that we created within each department's sections will now be subcategories within the main department categories. Figure C.1 shows the sections as categories in the 1.6 Category Manager. Figure C.2 shows the department news categories as subcategories.

Figure C.3 shows how to use the Parent parameter to make one category (Science News) a subcategory of another (Science).

When creating a new category, on the right there is a section called Category Access Rules. This is shown with the default values in Figure C.4. By default, as in Joomla! 1.5, editors have the right to create and edit in all categories, and authors have the right to

Figure C.1  Joomla! 1.6 Category Manager screen

Figure C.2  Joomla! 1.6 Category Manager screen showing subcategories

create in all categories. Neither authors nor editors can edit state, which means to change an article state to published, unpublished, trash, or archive. Only managers, administrators, and super administrators can delete completely.

Details

| | |
|---|---|
| Title * | Science News |
| Alias | |
| Parent | - Science |
| State | Published |
| Access | Public |
| Language | All |
| ID * | 0 |

Figure C.3  Joomla! 1.6 category-editing screen showing the
Details parameters

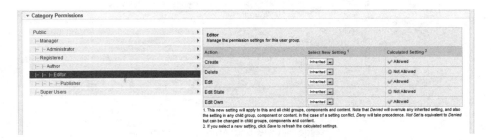

Figure C.4  Joomla! 1.6 Category Permissions section

Because we want each department to have its own separate content, the first step will be to make new user groups for each department. To do that, we go to the User Manager: User Group tab. Initially these groups are set as in Joomla! 1.5, as shown in Figure C.5. However, in 1.6, the Super Administrator group is called the Super User group and is in its own branch. This is just a difference of display. All of these groups have the same permissions that they had in Joomla! 1.5.

In the example site, we had most users in the Registered group. We will make the new user groups children of the Registered group. To make a new group, click New, and give the group a name and a parent, as shown in Figure C.6.

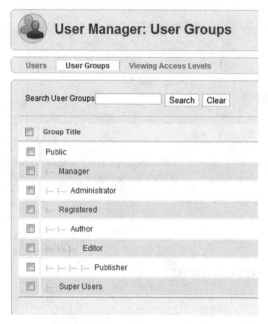

Figure C.5  Joomla! 1.6 User Manager: User Groups

Figure C.6  Joomla! 1.6 adding a new group

Once all the groups are defined, the Group tab will appear as in Figure C.7.

Now when we create or edit a user, we can assign that person to one of the groups by selecting the appropriate box in the Assigned Groups area of the User Manager, as shown in Figure C.8.

Now the user will appear with the new group in the list of users, as shown in Figure C.9.

Now we want to give users in the Social Studies group access to create and edit articles in the Social Studies category. To do this, return to the Content Category Manager, and click the Set Permission button to go to the Category Permissions area. Open the Social Studies slider. In the Category Permissions area, change Create, Edit, and Edit Own to Allowed, as shown in Figure C.10.

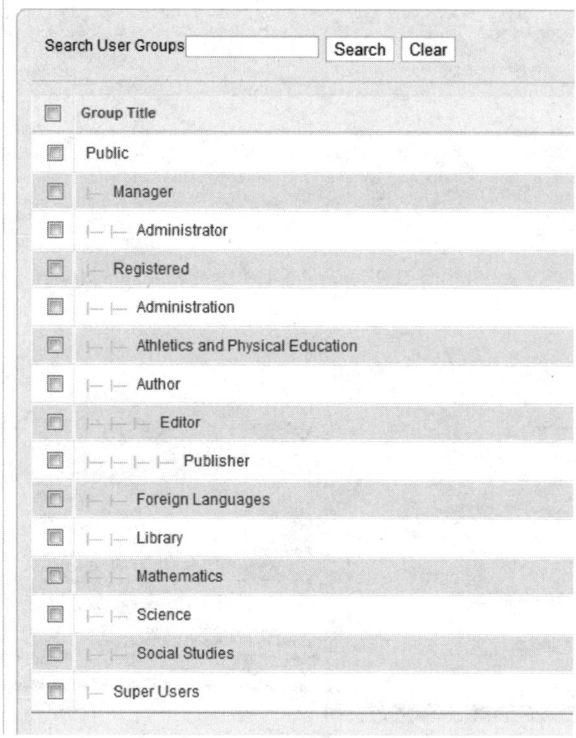

Figure C.7  User groups with new groups added

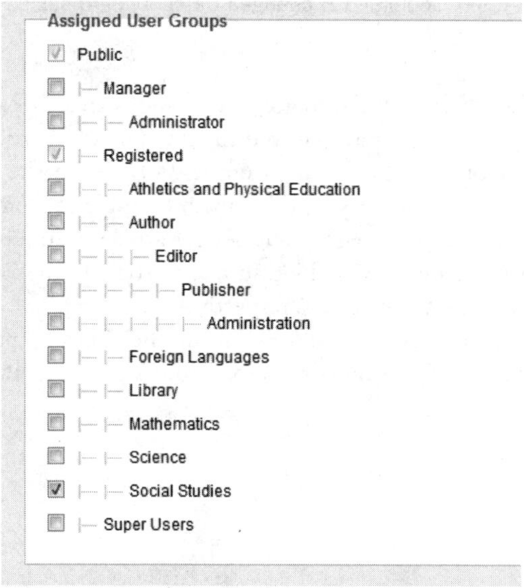

Figure C.8  Joomla! 1.6 user options showing Assigned Groups area

Figure C.9  Joomla! 1.6 User Manager: Users tab

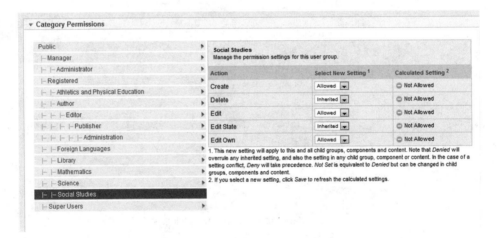

Figure C.10  Joomla! 1.6 changed Category Permssions prior to saving

After saving the category, the Category Permissions area will appear as in Figure C.11. Users in this group are now allowed to edit and create articles in this category.

Now when Jane Smith logs into the front end of the site, she can edit and create articles in the Social Studies category. This is shown by the edit icon that appears on the articles in the Social Studies category but not for articles in the other categories. This is shown in Figures C.12 and C.13, which show an article in the Social Studies category and one in the Mathematics category, respectively.

To give everyone in the Administration group the ability to publish articles, we change the Administration action permission group's parent to Publisher, as shown in Figure C.14.

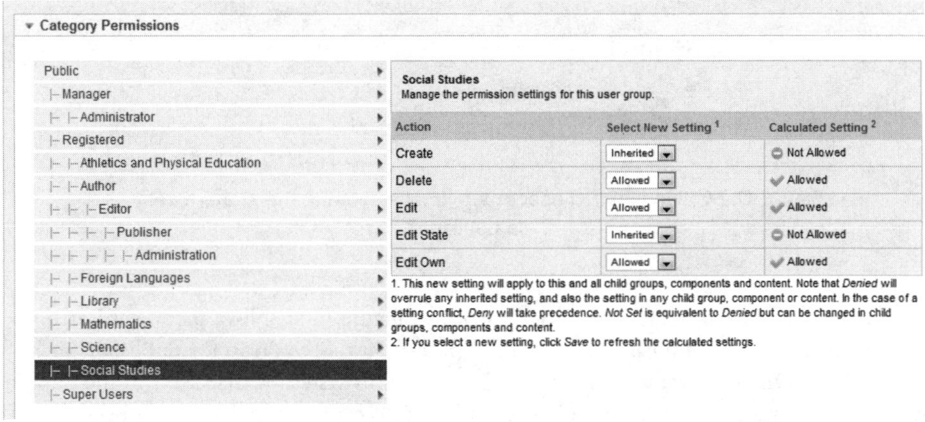

Figure C.11  Joomla! 1.6 changed Category Permissions after saving

Figure C.12  Joomla! 1.6 front-end view showing that the user has rights
to edit the article shown.

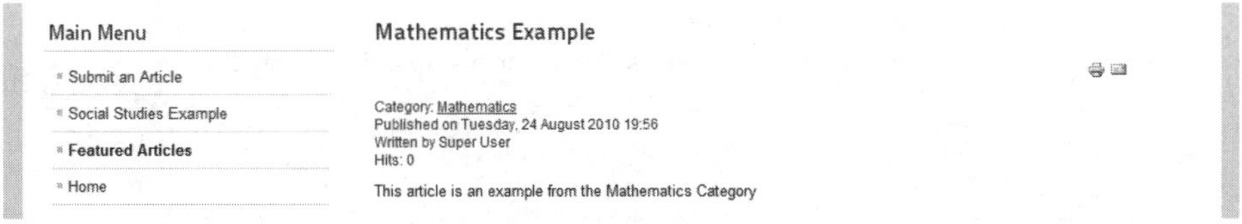

Figure C.13  Joomla! 1.6 front-end view showing that the user does not
have rights to edit the article shown

Figure C.14   Joomla! 1.6 user group details showing the group parent as
a publisher

So, our new group structure looks as shown in Figure C.15. Now anyone assigned to the Administration group can create, edit, or publish just as was true for publishers in Joomla! 1.5. One important element of the permissions system is that users in the Super User group (or any group with global administration) cannot ever have permission denied (shown in Figure C.16).

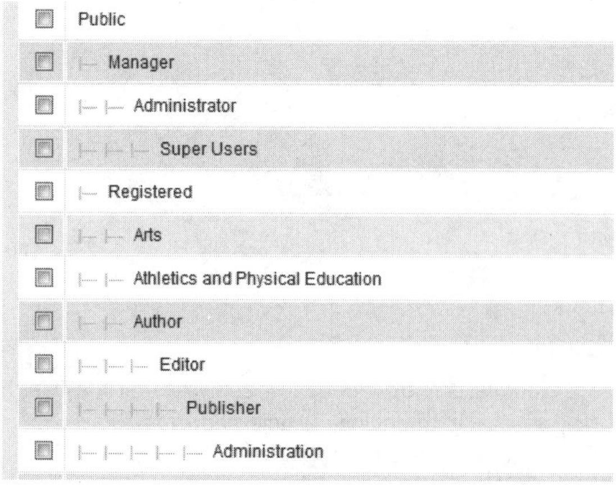

☐ Public
☐ |— Manager
☐ |— |— Administrator
☐ |— |— |— Super Users
☐ |— Registered
☐ |— |— Arts
☐ |— |— Athletics and Physical Education
☐ |— |— Author
☐ |— |— |— Editor
☐ |— |— |— Publisher
☐ |— |— |— |— |— Administration

Figure C.15   Joomla! 1.6 group screen showing the Administration group
as having the same permissions as Publisher because it is a child item
of Publisher

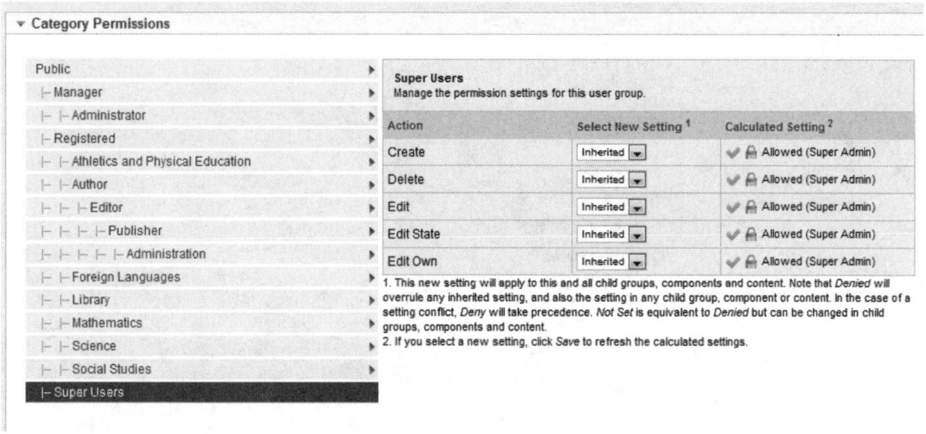

Figure C.16  Category Permissions screen showing that Super Users cannot have permissions denied

# Controlling What People Can See

Next we want to create a way to have some content that can only be seen by the Administration group. We will do this by creating a new view permissions access level.

In the User Manager, navigate to the View Permissions Level tab. It will show the three view permissions levels that are present in Joomla! 1.5: Public, Registered, and Special. Each level has groups assigned to it.

In the case of Public, all groups are automatically able to see what Public users are able to see. This is because all groups by definition have Public as a parent (or grandparent and so on), and they inherit right from it.

In the case of Registered, as shown in Figure C.17, because all the new groups that we created had Registered as a parent group (or in the case of Administration as a great, great grandparent group), they will all have access to any item that has its access set to Registered. This is because permission to view is inherited from parent groups to children groups. However, the public is not able to see items set to Registered because it does not inherit from the Registered or Manager group. This is exactly as it is in Joomla! 1.5 but with additional groups.

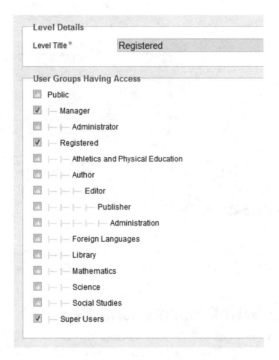

Figure C.17  Joomla! 1.6 User Manager: Edit Viewing Access Level

Next, by clicking New, we can create a new viewing access level, as shown in Figure C.18. This group is called Administration, and only the Administration group will have access to it.

As shown in Figure C.19, the new Administration group is now in the list of viewing access levels.

Now when an article is created, its access can be set to Administration, as shown in Figure C.20.

This appendix shows a simple implementation of access control. The access control in Joomla! 1.6 is extremely powerful and flexible and can be used in very complex ways. However, for most sites, we think that the examples shown here will be typical use cases. As discussed in Chapter 11, it is important that you think carefully about your access control needs before implementing. Think about your groups of users and what actions they should be able to do on what content. Think separately about what restrictions you really need to place on viewing published content for what groups. Then examine how the two structures relate to each other, and develop your groups and levels accordingly.

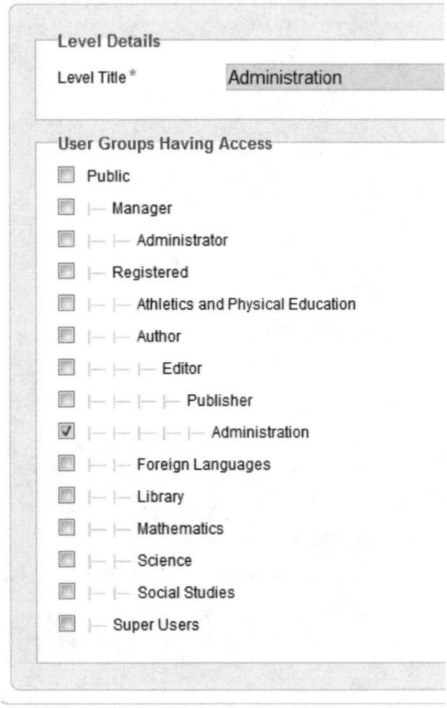

Figure C.18  Joomla! 1.6 User Manager: Add Viewing Access Level

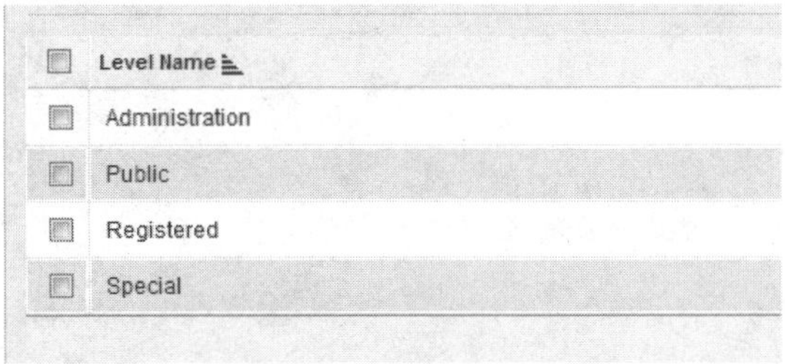

Figure C.19  Joomla! 1.6 new Administration group in Viewing Access
Levels tab

Note: The images in this appendix are based on the user interfaces for access control at the time of its writing. Although the concepts will remain the same, it is possible that the user interfaces (what you as a user will see on your site) will change. Please check *http://officialjoomlabook.com* for updated images and explanations of any changes.

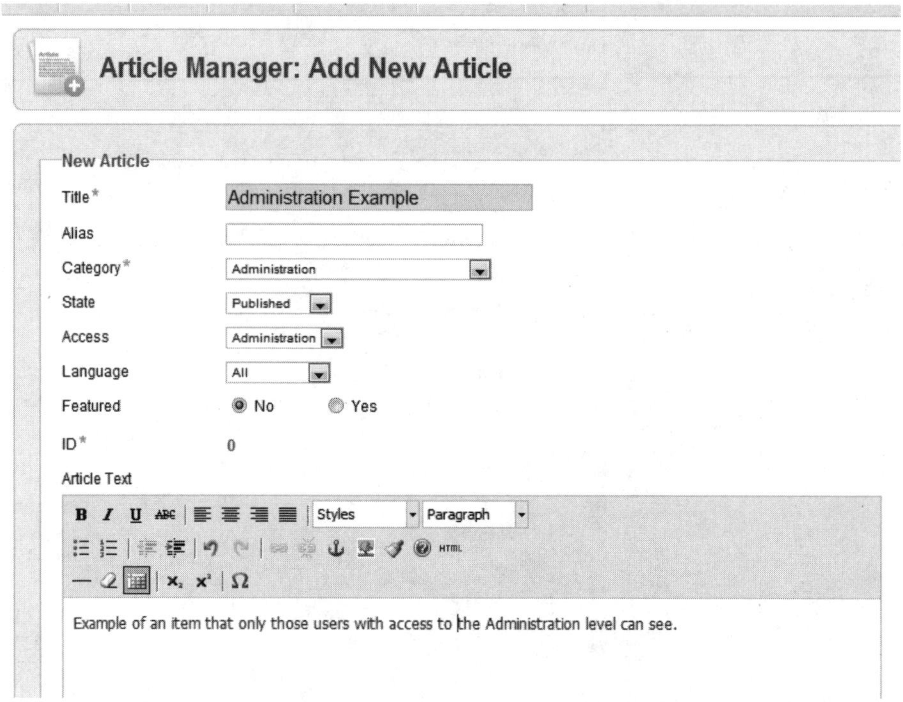

Figure C.20  Joomla! 1.6 Article Manager showing Access set to
Administration

# Glossary

These are terms that you will see people use when talking about Joomla!, whether in this book, on the Joomla! forums, at a JUG meeting, or during a Joomla! Day. This glossary should help you get a better understanding of what people mean when they talk about Joomla!

**3PD**  An acronym for "third-party developer," this is someone who makes extensions for Joomla!

**404 error**  A 404 error is what happens when a user attempts to navigate to a Web page that does not exist. There are a number of situations where site administrators can unintentionally cause 404 errors. For example, moving a page without setting up a redirect will cause this. Another common error is creating a public menu link to items that are restricted to logged-in users.

**accessibility**  Accessibility in a Web site refers to whether a site is usable for people with disabilities. For example, if someone is blind and using a screen reader, they will be able to use your site if it is accessible. Similarly, if someone is color-blind and can't distinguish certain colors (which is true for about 8 percent of all men), your site should still be accessible to them. Beez is a template designed to meet accessibility standards.

**ACL**  An acronym for "access control lists," this system controls who can see what and who can take which actions on your site. Joomla! 1.5 has a fixed list of user groups (Public, Registered, Author, Editor, Publisher, Manager, Administrator, and Super Administrator) and access levels (Public, Registered, and Special). Joomla! 1.6 has a flexible system that administrators can make as simple or complex as needed.

**Administrator**  Users in the Administrator user group can log into the back end and front end of Joomla! and perform all functions except for global configuration and can produce all kinds of content. For example, administrators can create new users, manage modules and plugins, and install and uninstall extensions. This applies in Joomla! 1.5 and is set by default in Joomla! 1.6.

**alpha release**  An alpha release is usually the first release of a new version of Joomla! to a wider network of developers and experienced testers of a new major version of software. Alpha releases are used for testing, acceptance, and stabilization of the basic functionality that has been implemented.

**API**  An acronym for "application programming interface," an API lets one software application interact with another. The Joomla! framework provides an API. Many Joomla!

extensions use APIs from other applications to include information from them in a Joomla! site.

**ASCII**   American Standard Code for Information Interchange is the set of 128 characters based on American English. These characters are generally considered safe to use, although the number of situations in which you are limited to them has decreased markedly.

**Author**   A user in the Author group can create a new article or Web link in the Joomla! front end and edit that article in the future. This applies in Joomla! 1.5 and is set by default in Joomla! 1.6.

**back end**   This is the administrator for a Joomla! site, found at your *http://domain.com/ administrator.* This is where your site is configured, menus are created, and other administrative functions are performed. You can also create content, install extensions, and carry out other site management tasks. The back end has a separate login from the front end, and only users who you designate can log in to it.

**below the fold**   Coming from the newspaper world, Web site content is below the fold if a user needs to scroll down to see it. Content above the fold refers to content that appears on the screen when a page is rendered.

**beta release**   Beta versions of software are usually feature complete, meaning that no major changes in features or functionality will be implemented during the remainder of the release cycle. This release is unstable and not suitable for live or production sites. However, as a community member, this is your time to participate by testing the software and identifying and helping to fix bugs.

**blog layout**   A blog layout is a multi-item layout that features only the introductory ("intro") text (that before the "Read more" line) for articles. These are arranged in rows and columns.

**brochure site**   This is a Web site that simulates a printed brochure in that the information is static, and the only interactive element is the provision of contact information.

**browser**   Browsers are the applications that are used to view Web pages or, as it is commonly phrased, browse the Internet. Some of the commonly used browsers are Internet Explorer, Firefox, Chrome, and Safari, but there are dozens of others including some specifically designed for mobile devices.

**category**   Content (articles, contacts, Web links, news feeds, and banners) is grouped into categories. In Joomla! 1.5, categories have only one level. In Joomla! 1.6, categories can have subcategories nested infinitely.

**component**   Components are essentially mini-applications that run within the Joomla! content management system. They are most commonly used to control the main part of your Web page.

**configuration.php**   The file that contains your site's basic configuration settings.

**content management system**   A software application that manages the creation and presentation of various types of contents on the Web.

**CSS**  Cascading Style Sheets are the modern way to control the style elements for HTML. For example, CSS can control the color of text, the bullets used in a list, or the width of a region of your Web page.

**database**  An organized collection of data. Joomla! 1.5 and Joomla! 1.6 use the MySQL or MySQLi relational database managers to store your data and manage the data behind your site.

**div**  A div is used in HTML to define an area of the page. Among other things, it is commonly used to apply styles such as background colors or images, font sizes, and width. Div tags are in the form `<div></div>`, and in troubleshooting, you may find that a div that is not closed, which is to say lacks an `</div>`, will be the cause of a problem.

**domain name**  A domain name is the name of your Web site. Joomla.org is the domain name for the Joomla! family of Web sites. Domain names are registered with a registrar. ICANN is the international organization that manages domain names.

**domain name server**  This is the computer system that translates your domain's human-readable name to an IP address.

**drill-down**  A drill-down is what happens when you move from one layout to another layout. For example, when you have a linked list of contacts in a category list layout and you click a specific contact name, you are drilling down. Similarly, if a contact name has a linked category name and you click it to go to the category list, you are drilling down.

**DTD**  An acronym for "document type definition," a DTD appears in a file to establish what set of rules the code in that file is following. For example, in the *index.php* file of the Beez template, you will see the following, which defines what set of standards the template is trying to meet:

```
<?php echo '<?xml version=1.0 encoding=utf-8?'.'>'; ?>
<!DOCTYPE html PUBLIC -//W3C//DTD XHTML 1.0 Transitional//EN
http://www.w3.org/TR/xhtml1/DTD/xhtml1-transitional.dtd>
<html xmlns=http://www.w3.org/1999/xhtml xml:lang=
<?php echo $this->language; ?>
 lang=<?php echo $this->language; ?>
 dir=<?php echo $this->direction; ?> >
```

Joomla! 1.5 general uses the XHTML 1 transitional standard.

**Editor**  A user in the Editor user group can edit any article in the Joomla! front end. This applies in Joomla! 1.5 and is set by default in Joomla! 1.6.

**environment**  This refers to the setup of your server. This includes PHP, MySQL, and server versions; the operating system; and the PHP extensions that are installed. For example, *mod_security*, SuPHP, and *mod_zip* are PHP extensions that can impact Joomla! performance in various ways. If you are asking for help on the Joomla! forums, you may be asked for your environment. Most of this information can be found in the System Information area (in Joomla! 1.5, find this in the Help menu; in Joomla! 1.6, it is linked from the Site menu).

**extension**    An extension is any software that you install that extends Joomla! extension types include components, modules, plugins, templates, and language packs.

**feature request**    A request for a new feature in Joomla! (or an extension). Most feature requests are decided upon in the pre–alpha stages of a release cycle. If you want to request a feature, you will need to present it and make a strong argument about why it is needed. Each release cycle for Joomla! has a period in which feature requests are made. Be aware that what you may think of as a bug may actually be a request for a new feature.

**featured**    Featured is the new name for the front page in Joomla! 1.6. The featured designation is also extended to contacts, Web links, and newsfeeds, although only contacts and content are provided with layouts.

**framework**    The Joomla! framework is a set of libraries that provide the infrastructure for building the Joomla! CMS and extensions. The framework files can be found in the *libraries/joomla* folder of your Joomla! installation.

**front end**    The front end of your site, found at *yourdomain.com*, is the site as it displays to the public and to other end users of your site.

**front page layout**    A blog-style layout of introductory text from a number of articles arranged in rows and columns. It includes those articles that have been designated Front Page in the Article Manager. This is renamed *featured* in Joomla! 1.6.

**GPL**    Joomla! is licensed using the GNU GPL. This is a free software license that allows you to use, study, modify, and share the software. The only restriction is that when you do share it, you must not remove the copyright and licensing information, and you must give the same rights to others.

**host**    A host is a company where the files for your site are actually located. Criteria for selecting a host are discussed in Chapter 2.

**HTML**    Hypertext Markup Language is the basic language for putting together the layout of Web pages. It consists of tags such as `<p></p>`. In this example, any text between the two tags would be defined as a single paragraph.

**intranet**    A Web site that is developed for use inside an organization instead of for use by the public.

**IP address**    The numerical representation of anything (including your domain) that is on the Internet. IP addresses are useful for a number of purposes. For example, if you identify a spammer, you can block the IP address the spam is originating from. IP addresses can also be used to give the geographic location of a computer in many cases, although this is not 100 percent accurate.

**issue tracker**    The issue tracker is the place where reports of problems in the Joomla! software are made. You should report an issue as a bug only if you are positive it is a bug. Before doing so, always seek help in the Joomla! forums.

**itemid**    An itemid is associated with each menu item in Joomla! It controls which modules and template are used on a page linked from a menu.

**JavaScript**    JavaScript is a scripting language used in Joomla! In the Joomla! core, it is largely used in the back end, but many extensions use it extensively for creating visual effects.

**JUGs**    Acronym for "Joomla! User Groups," JUGs are groups of users in the same physical location who meet in person to talk about topics related to Joomla! You can find a listing of JUGs on the *http://community.joomla.org* Web site, and many JUGs also have groups on *http://people.joomla.org.*

**LAMP stack**    This is shorthand for the combination of Linux operating system, Apache server, MySQL database, and PHP that the majority of Joomla! sites are found on. In reality, only the MySQL (or MySQLi) and PHP are actually required.

**language pack**    A language pack contains the common words from Joomla! (such as Save, Menu, or Article) that are used in the operation of Joomla! but not in content. The pack contains the terms in a specific language. You can install as many language packs as you would like in your site.

**layout**    A layout refers to how the content of a component or module is arranged on a page. These are typically controlled by the PHP and XML files found in the */tmpl* folders in a component. For example, the layout files for a content archive view can be found in this folder on your server: *components/com_content/views/archive.*

Core layouts can be overridden in the template, enabling you to make your Web pages display in a customized way.

**list layout**    This is a layout that features a linked list of content items in a category or category items in a section. When clicked, these links send the user to the specific item or the specific category list.

**loadposition**    A plugin that loads the modules in a specific position into a content item, such as an article.

**maintenance release**    This is a release of a stable software with minor changes or security fixes. Joomla! has maintenance releases approximately every eight weeks, although the schedule is not fixed.

**Manager**    Users in the Manager user group can log in to the Joomla! back end and perform a limited set of functions focused on creating, editing, and publishing content (including articles, Web links, newsfeeds, polls, contacts, categories, and sections) and menu items. This applies in Joomla! 1.5 and is set by default in Joomla! 1.6.

**module**    Modules are the boxes of content that are displayed in addition to the main body of the page. Usually these are around the edges, but they can also be put inside content items.

**MooTools**    This is the JavaScript framework used in the core of Joomla!

**MVC**    MVC stands for Model-View-Controller and is the architectural pattern used to create Joomla! components and modules.

**MySQL**    Joomla! uses a MySQL database to store your site's content and configuration options. Queries are used to retrieve, store, and modify the data. Data are stored in tables, which are each made up of rows and columns. For example, each article is stored in one row with columns such as title, alias, and intro text.

**navigation**    This is the system your site has that allows users to use from page to page in your site.

**Open Source Matters**    The nonprofit organization that provides legal, financial, and organizational support to the Joomla! project.

**override**    An override in Joomla! lets you replace code that is in the Joomla! core with other code. The most common type of overrides replace core layouts. You can see examples of these in the HTML folder of the Beez template.

**parameter**    A parameter is an option that you may set, though most parameters have default values. For example, you may use parameters in a blog layout to decide how many items to display on a single page.

**PHP**    PHP is the computer programming language that most of Joomla! is written in.

**phpMyAdmin**    phpMyAdmin is software that is commonly provided by hosts to manage MySQL databases.

**plugin**    A plugin is a relatively small piece of code that is executed when specific events, such as rendering a page or creating a user, take place. System plugins run every time a page is rendered. Search plugins run only when pages from com_search are rendered.

**position**    In Joomla!, positions are areas in your Web page defined by your template. Each position has a specific name. Modules are assigned to specific positions and will show in the named positions on selected pages.

**Public**    The user group and user level for site visitors who are not logged in.

**Publisher**    Users in the Publisher group can change an article to Published or Unpublished in the Joomla! front end. This applies in Joomla! 1.5 and is set by default in Joomla! 1.6.

**query**    Code that is used to act on a database. Commands such as SELECT, ORDERBY, and INSERT are used to retrieve information, sort record, and create new records in your database.

**redirect**    A redirect is when you send users who enter one URL into their browser to a different URL. An example of when you would need to do this is when you move content from one category to another category.

**registered**    A user in the registered group is one who can log in to the front end of a Joomla! site. Users in the Registered group can view content (such as article or contact) that is designated Registered. They can also view everything that a Public (non-logged-in) user can see. This applies in Joomla! 1.5 and is set by default in Joomla! 1.6.

**release candidate**    This is a version of the software that may be the stable or general availability version if no new problems are identified. It may be used on live sites but usually by so-called early adopters. We recommend that beginners do not install release candidates on their live sites, but as active community members, this is an important time for testing and reporting issues.

**render**   The process of a browser producing a page from HTML, CSS, images, and other pieces is called rendering. A page renders correctly when it appears as intended.

**RSS**   An acronym for "Really Simple Syndication," RSS applications send content from one site to other locations. For example, in Joomla! your site can have RSS feeds that send the most recent content items to a news reader that someone has set up in their Yahoo! or Google accounts. Or by using the Joomla! Newsfeeds component, you can display an RSS feed from another site on your site.

**section**   In the Content Manager of Joomla! 1.5, categories are nested in sections. Articles are nested in categories. Joomla! 1.6 does not have sections.

**security release**   This is a release that is similar to a maintenance release but focused on security issues. You should always upgrade when there is a security release.

**SEF URL**   An acronym for "search-engine-friendly URL," this is the type of URL that is believed to make it easier for search engines to search your site. Most commonly, this means using words in the URL and not dynamic URLs like *http://index.php?options= com_content&view=article&id=13*. You can enable SEF URLs in the Joomla! Global Configuration section.

**SEO**   SEO is an acronym for search engine optimization. This means developing your site with the conscious goal of making it appear among the top results when a user searches using words related to the content of your site. The techniques used in these approaches are known as SEO.

**server**   A Web server is both the computer on which your site is located and the software it uses. A shared server is a computer on which many Web sites are located. Server can also refer to the software used to take content and present it to the Web. Joomla! is most commonly found on Apache and IIS servers, both of which are officially supported. However, there are a number of server applications, such as lighttpd, nginx, and glassfish that can be used for Joomla!, but these other server applications are not officially supported.

**Special**   The Special access level include all users who are in the Author, Editor, Publisher, Manager, Administrator, and Super Administrator user groups. This applies in Joomla! 1.5 and is set by default in Joomla! 1.6 except that Super Administrator has been renamed Super Users.

**stable release**   Also known as a general availability release, this type of release is stable and suitable for use on live and production sites. All major issues have been resolved.

**string**   A string is a series of characters like *abcd*. The term *string* is used in many different ways in software, but most often when end users in Joomla! talk about strings, they are referring to the strings in code that need to be put into human-readable and translatable format. An untranslated string is a string that is not translated in the appropriate language file. If you come across one, it may not be readable or readable only in English.

**style sheet**    A style sheet is a file with the extension *.css* (such as *template.css*) that contains the instructions for the use of various style elements. These are usually found in the *template/templatename/css* folder, although they will sometimes also be found in the folder for a third-party extension.

**Super Administrator**    A user in the Super Administrator group can perform all functions in the Joomla! front end and back end including changing the Global Configuration. This applies in Joomla! 1.5 and is set by default in Joomla! 1.6.

**template**    A template controls the design of your site, including layout, colors, and typography. It may include other elements such as JavaScript and layout overrides.

**third-party developer**    A third-party developer is someone who creates extensions that can be added to Joomla! but are not part of the Joomla! core distribution. Most extensions made by third-party developers can be found in the Joomla! Extensions Directory.

**TinyMCE**    TinyMCE is the editor that installs with Joomla! and is used by default.

**uncategorized content**    Articles can be created with no category. All other content types (contacts, Web links, newsfeeds, banners) must be placed in a category.

**update**    The process of installing a maintenance or security release. There should be no visible changes in functionality except for a reduction in bugs, but it is important to read the release notes for an update to make sure that you make any necessary adjustments. For example, going from 1.5.20 to 1.5.21 would be an update, while moving from 1.5 to 1.6 would be an upgrade.

**upgrade**    This is what you do when you move from one release to another, such as from Joomla! 1.5 to Joomla! 1.6. This may involve database and other important changes (such as removing the Polls extensions in Joomla! 1.6) and is therefore potentially challenging. An upgrade path is the script or set of steps used to upgrade your site from one version to another.

**URL**    An acronym for "uniform resource locator," a URL is how a browser knows where to go to find a page. For example, *http://forum.community.org* is a URL.

**usability**    This refers to how hard or easy it is for visitors and users to navigate and use the features of your site. Usability testing is done to assess this.

**user interface**    The user interface (commonly called UI) is everything that your site presents to users, with a particular focus on the interactive elements, such as the use of forms, uploading files, and similar items.

**UTF-8**    UTF-8 is a set of characters that include all characters found in most of the world's languages. Joomla! is designed to work with UTF-8 in most contexts. An exception is that in Joomla! 1.5 only ASCII characters can be used in URLs, while in Joomla! 1.6 UTF-8 characters can also be used.

**validation**    Validation is a way of making sure that your site complies with established standards for Web design. The validator at *http://validator.w3.org/* is most commonly used for testing if you site validates.

**Vulnerable Extensions List**    This is a list of extensions for Joomla! that have unresolved reported security issues. You should always check this list before installing an extension and periodically review it for extensions you have installed. It is found at *http://docs.joomla.org/Vulnerable_Extensions_List.*

**WYSIWYG editor**    WYSIWYG is an acronym for "What You See Is What You Get" in an editor. TinyMCE is a WYSIWYG editor because it does not show you the HTML for your content but instead shows you how the content will display. This is in contrast to a text editor.

**XML**    Extensible Markup Language is used in Joomla! to store certain kinds of information, for example the definitions of parameters in extensions.

# Index

# C

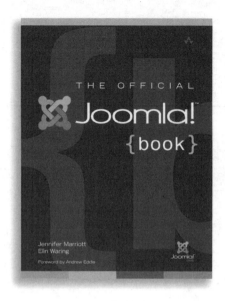

# FREE Online Edition

Your purchase of **The Official Joomla! Book** includes access to a free online edition for 45 days through the Safari Books Online subscription service. Nearly every Addison-Wesley Professional book is available online through Safari Books Online, along with more than 5,000 other technical books and videos from publishers such as Cisco Press, Exam Cram, IBM Press, O'Reilly, Prentice Hall, Que, and Sams.

**SAFARI BOOKS ONLINE** allows you to search for a specific answer, cut and paste code, download chapters, and stay current with emerging technologies.

## Activate your FREE Online Edition at
## www.informit.com/safarifree

> **STEP 1:** Enter the coupon code: KXPDKFH.

> **STEP 2:** New Safari users, complete the brief registration form.
> Safari subscribers, just log in.

If you have difficulty registering on Safari or accessing the online edition, please e-mail customer-service@safaribooksonline.com